nps tchoban voss

ALF M. PRASCH   PETER SIGL   SERGEI TCHOBAN   EKKEHARD VOSS

nps tchoban voss

VOM DETAIL ZUM STADTRAUM | FROM DETAIL TO URBAN SPACE   FALK JAEGER

BIRKHÄUSER   BASEL · BOSTON · BERLIN

INHALT | CONTENTS

Bauen im Dienst der Gesellschaft
Building for Society

Fragt man die Architekten von nps tchoban voss nach ihrem architektonischen Glaubensbekenntnis, so zucken sie zusammen. Keiner der aktuellen gängigen „-ismen" hilft ihnen beim Versuch einer Definition des eigenen Tuns weiter, allenfalls der altgediente Funktionalismus mit seiner Forderung nach der Funktionserfüllung als vornehmster Aufgabe der Architektur, sowie der etwas modischere Kontextualismus, der Architekten anhält, sich auf der Suche nach Entwurfsprämissen tunlichst in der Umgebung ihrer Bauprojekte umzusehen. Und vielleicht der römische Traktatschreiber Vitruv, der vor zweitausend Jahren die Dreieinigkeit utilitas, firmitas und venustas als konstituierende Grundlage allen Bauens entdeckte. Denn zunächst einmal muss der Bauherr zufrieden sein. Zufrieden ist er laut Vitruv, wenn die Funktion (utilitas) stimmt und wenn die Wirtschaftlichkeit gegeben ist, die wiederum voraussetzt, dass die Konstruktion (firmitas) stimmt, dass also solide gebaut wurde. Über den Kontext, den Standort, den Genius loci machen sich die Architekten darüber hinaus Gedanken, wenn es gilt, ein Gebäude zu strukturieren und zu gestalten, was wiederum die Wohlgestalt (venustas) einschließt.

Asking after the architectural principles followed at nps tchoban voss elucidates a shudder from the architects. None of the currently popular "-isms" is of much help in defining their activities, at best perhaps the trusted principle of functionalism, with its focus on the fulfilment of purpose as the primary task of architecture, and the somewhat more fashionable contextualism, exhorting architects wherever possible to refer to typological legacy in the search for premises that inform their architecture. Perhaps also the principles set down two thousand years ago by the Roman writer Vitruvius who in his treatise elaborated the trinity of utilitas, firmitas and venustas as the fundamental characteristics of all construction. After all, it is the client who must first be satisfied. Vitruvius tells us this is the case when the building fulfils its function (utilitas) and its realisation has been cost-effective, which in turn presupposes that the structure is sound (firmitas), solid and durable. In addition, architects consider the context, location and its genius loci when elaborating the form and proportion of a building, all of which contribute to its attractive appearance (venustas).

Büro Hamburg, Oberstraße, 1972
Hamburg Office, Oberstraße, 1972

Peter Neve, 1970

Alf M. Prasch, Peter Neve, Wolfgang Nietz,
Peter Sigl, 1972

Die in allen Epochen existente und heute besonders bei der populären und spektakulären internationalen Stararchitektur verbreitete Haltung, architektonisches Entwerfen mit der Gestaltfindung zu beginnen, also zunächst nach einer signifikanten, möglichst außergewöhnlichen Form zu suchen und dieser alles andere unterzuordnen, ist ihnen fremd. Raumbildung und sinnliche Wahrnehmung der das Ambiente formenden architektonischen Elemente sind ihnen von Anbeginn wichtiger gewesen als die als vordergründig empfundenen modischen Effekte. Das Streben nach Nutzwert, Solidität und Werthaltigkeit hat sicher seine Gründe auch im Werdegang des Büros, dessen Ursprünge in die frühen dreißiger Jahre zurückreichen.

1931 hatten sich in Hamburg Herbert Sprotte und Peter Neve zusammengetan und ein gemeinsames Architekturbüro gegründet, dessen Aktivitäten dann durch den Krieg unterbrochen wurden. Nach Kriegsende leiteten sie zunächst das Aufräumungsamt, das vom Hamburger Senat bereits 1934 eingerichtet worden war und mit Trümmerbeseitigung sowie Bomben- und Munitionsräumung bis 1953 beschäftigt war.

1948 lebte das Büro Sprotte & Neve wieder auf und man bezog Räume im Kaufmannshaus an den Großen Bleichen. 1956 erfolgte der Umzug in die Oberstraße in Harvestehude. Die Bauaufgaben reichten vom Wohnungsbau über Schul- und Kulturbauten sowie Bürohäuser, Parkhäuser und Messehallen bis zu Ingenieurbauwerken wie Brücken, deckten also fast das gesamte Spektrum des in der Wiederaufbauzeit und im Zuge des „Wirtschaftswunders" boomenden Bauwesens ab. Das Büro bearbeitete alle Leistungsphasen bis hin zu Bauüberwachung und Abrechnung.

1958 trat der Bauingenieur Peter Sigl in das Büro Neve und Partner ein, zehn Jahre später der Architekt Wolfgang Nietz, der das Wettbewerbsteam verstärkte. Beide wurden 1970 von Peter

The notion that architectural design begins with a search for form – a distinct and ideally remarkable form to which all else is subordinated – is a notion that has existed throughout the ages and although currently particularly widespread among popular international star architects is foreign to nps tchoban voss. Since their beginnings, the definition of space and the sensory perception of architectural elements that contribute to the atmosphere of a place have always been more important than superficially perceived fashionable effects. This pursuit of utility, solidity and value is also most certainly grounded in the development of the office, whose origins extend back to the early thirties.

In 1931 in Hamburg, Herbert Sprotte and Peter Neve got together and founded a joint architectural practice whose activities were interrupted shortly after by the war. After the end of the war the partners at first headed the Public Works Clearance Department, which had already been established in 1934 by the Hamburg Senate and until 1953 was responsible for rubble clearance and bomb and ammunition disposal.

In 1948, Sprotte & Neve was resurrected and moved into rooms in the Kaufmannshaus in Großen Bleichen. In 1956 they moved to the Oberstraße in Harvestehude. The office undertook a wide variety of projects ranging from housing, school and municipal buildings to offices, multi-storey car parks and trade fair halls as well as engineering structures such as bridges, thereby covering almost the entire spectrum of building activities in the period of reconstruction and the ensuing boom in the building sector that accompanied the "economic miracle" after the war. The office undertook all planning phases in-house from concept to site supervision and cost controlling.

In 1958 the structural engineer Peter Sigl joined the office Neve and Partners, ten years later the architect Wolfgang Nietz,

Peter Sigl, Alf M. Prasch,
Wolfgang Nietz, 1979

Wolfgang Nietz, 1972

Alf M. Prasch, 1972

Peter Sigl, 1972

Neve in die Partnerschaft aufgenommen (Herbert Sprotte war 1962 verstorben). Im Jahr 1971 stieß der Architekt Alf M. Prasch zur Mannschaft hinzu und wurde 1975 bei Neve und Partner als Juniorpartner aufgenommen. Der Generationenwechsel war 1978 vollzogen, als Seniorpartner Peter Neve sich in den Ruhestand verabschiedete.

Mitte der siebziger Jahre waren der Kontextualismus aus den Hochschulen gekommen, der nicht nur ein konzeptionelles, sondern auch ein formales Eingehen auf den Charakter und die Umgebung des Bauplatzes nahe legte. Das Sheraton Hotel in Abu Dhabi, 1979 entstanden, reflektiert diese Anschauung, indem es örtliche Bauformen zitiert. Es passt sich in Material und Farbgebung den regionalen Gepflogenheiten an und erzählt von den Piratenwachtürmen, die zur Beobachtung des Schiffsverkehrs entlang der Küste standen. Die Golfregion war in den Fokus des Büros geraten, als die Architekten Ende der siebziger Jahre auf die Rezession mit verstärkter Auslandsakquisition reagierten. Wolfgang Nietz verlegte seinen Arbeitsschwerpunkt an den Persischen Golf, um Bauten in Saudi Arabien und Abu Dhabi zu betreuen.

Ein ehemaliger Pferdestall im Hof der Hamburger Ulmenstraße 40 in der Nähe des Stadtparks wurde 1987 neues Domizil, wo das Büro ab 1989 als „Nietz - Prasch - Sigl Architekten BDA" firmierte. Die Architekten drückten dem Gebäude beim Umbau ihren Stempel auf, ohne dessen Charakter und dessen Charme aufzugeben. Fenster wurden neu eingefügt oder vergrößert und gläserne Trennwände eingebaut. Damit auf dem ehemaligen Heuboden reguläre Arbeitsplätze untergebracht werden konnten, wurde das Dach angehoben. Um eine Eingangshalle zu schaffen, wurden zwei Deckenfelder herausgenommen und die Halle durch eine Brücke überspannt, alles in einem rustikalen Stahlbau, der mit dem historischen Baugefüge gut zusammengeht. Die Archi-

who strengthened the competition team. Peter Neve promoted both to partners in 1970 (Herbert Sprotte had died in 1962). Shortly after, in 1971, Alf M. Prasch joined the team as an architect, becoming a junior partner of Neve and Partner in 1975. By 1978 the office had passed from one generation to the next following the retirement of the founder and senior partner Peter Neve.

In the mid-seventies, the principle of contextualism, which proposed both a conceptual as well as formal response to the character and surroundings of the site, had spread beyond the universities. The Sheraton Hotel in Abu Dhabi, realised in 1979, reflects this attitude in its reference to local building forms. It picks up the materiality and colour of regional customs, referring to the pirates' watchtowers that once stood along the coastline to spot approaching ships. The Gulf States became the focus of attention as the recession deepened towards the end of the seventies and architectural offices began looking abroad for commissions. Wolfgang Nietz shifted the centre of his activities to the Persian Gulf in order to run building projects in Saudi Arabia and Abu Dhabi.

In 1987, a former stable building in the courtyard of Ulmenstraße 40 in Hamburg, not far from the Stadtpark, became the office's new domicile, which from 1989 took the name "Nietz - Prasch - Sigl Architekten BDA". The architects' conversion gave the building a distinctive impression without sacrificing its character and charm. New windows were inserted or existing ones enlarged and glazed partitions were installed. The roof was raised in order to use the former hayloft for regular workplaces. To create an entrance hall, two ceiling panels were removed and a bridge inserted that crossed the hall, all in a rustic steelwork that harmonises with the historical structure. The architectural

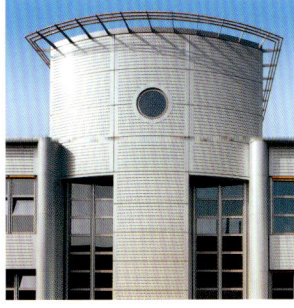

Sheraton Hotel, Abu Dhabi
Historischer Piratenwachturm, Abu Dhabi
Historic pirates' watchtower, Abu Dhabi

IKEA-Möbelmarkt, Hamburg
IKEA furniture store, Hamburg

Lufthansa-Turbinenwerkstatt, Hamburg
Lufthansa turbine construction works,
Hamburg

tektursprache und die Anmutung des Gebäudes sind bis heute Visitenkarte des Büros und haben sich als weitgehend zeitlos erwiesen. Weniger nachhaltig war das Raumangebot, weshalb man inzwischen auch das Vorderhaus mit Beschlag belegt hat.

In die Zeit der Wende ging es mit größeren Aufträgen, zum Beispiel für ein Möbelhaus IKEA an der A7 in Hamburg-Schnelsen, wo es gelang, für die weitläufigen Baulichkeiten, Freiflächen und Werbeanlagen des Einrichtungsmarkts ein integriertes Gestaltungskonzept zu entwickeln, das dem Bedürfnis des Bauherrn nach einer corporate identity entspricht und gleichzeitig die so häufig ignorierte ästhetische Komponente des Gewerbebaus im Auge behält. Auch die Lufthansa gehörte nun zur Klientel. Für die Turbinenwerkstatt der Flugzeugwerft am Flughafen Fuhlsbüttel bedienten sich die Architekten einer adäquaten Architektursprache, indem sie auf das Design des Flugzeugbaus mit seinen Aluminiumformteilen zurückgriffen.

Nach der Wiedervereinigung Deutschlands wurde das aufstrebende Berlin für die Hamburger Architekten nps interessant. Der Erfolg bei einem Wettbewerb für den Zentralen Omnibusbahnhof ZOB am Messedamm mit umgebender Bebauung gab Anlass, in der Hauptstadt ein Zweigbüro zu eröffnen. Eine zweite Niederlassung wurde 1992 in Dresden etabliert. Dort in der Leipziger Straße wurde ein historischer Gewerbebau als Architekturbüro adaptiert, eine Gießerei aus dem Jahr 1870, die mit dem Hamburger Büro erstaunliche Ähnlichkeiten aufweist. Auch hier sind die Obergeschossebenen an den Gebäudeenden quer durch die zentrale Halle mittels einer Brücke verbunden. Für die häufigen Besuche der Kollegen aus Hamburg steht eine Wohnung im Obergeschoss zur Verfügung. Größtes in Dresden bearbeitetes Projekt ist das 1994-96 entstandene World Trade Center, das mit seiner imposanten Erscheinung wie kaum ein zweites Bauwerk

language and the allure of the building remain an effective advertisement for the office today and have proven to be largely timeless. By contrast, the available space has proven more limiting and the office has since expanded into the building on the street as well.

Around the time of the reunification of East and West Germany, the office worked on larger commissions, for instance for a furniture retail store for IKEA on the A7 motorway near Hamburg-Schnelsen, for which an integrated design concept was developed for the extensive buildings, external areas and advertising hoardings that incorporated the client's need for corporate identity whilst addressing the often-neglected aesthetic aspects of commercial warehouse buildings. Their clients also included Lufthansa. For the design of the turbine construction works for the aircraft factory at Fuhlsbüttel Airport, the architects employed a fitting architectural language that draws on the construction of aircrafts and its moulded aluminium sections.

After the reunification of Germany, the Hamburg architects nps turned their attention towards the emerging boom city of Berlin. A successful competition entry for the ZOB, the central bus station on the Messedamm and the surrounding buildings, provided the impetus to open a branch office in Berlin. A further branch followed in Dresden in 1992. Here too the architects chose to convert a historical factory building in the Leipziger Strasse, a foundry built in 1870 bearing remarkable similarities to their Hamburg office. Here too the upper levels are connected at each end of the building by bridges that cross the central hall. A flat was fitted out in the upper floor to accommodate the regular visitors from Hamburg. Of the projects undertaken in Dresden, the World Trade Center, built from 1994-96, is the

Büro Hamburg, Ulmenstraße
Hamburg office, Ulmenstraße

Büro Berlin, Hackesche Höfe
Berlin office, Hackesche Höfe

Büro Dresden, Leipziger Straße
Dresden office, Leipziger Straße

in dieser Stadt den Aufschwung symbolisierte. Mit dem neuen Standort hatte das Büro Anteil am expansiven Baugeschehen nach der Wende in den neuen Bundesländern. Später wurden von dort aus auch Projekte im Rheinland betreut.

Anfang der neunziger Jahre war auch die Zeit, als Ekkehard Voss sowie Sergei Tchoban aus St. Petersburg mit nps in Kontakt kamen. Beide traten 1992 zunächst als Mitarbeiter in das Büro ein und bilden seit 1995 die dritte Partnergeneration, was sich im neuen Büronamen ausdrückte: „Nietz - Prasch - Sigl und Partner Architekten BDA", der sich 2003 nach dem Tod von Wolfgang Nietz im Jahr zuvor nochmals in „nps tchoban voss Architekten BDA" änderte.

Nach dem Umzug des Berliner Büros aus der Wundtstraße in die Hackeschen Höfe verlegte Sergei Tchoban seinen Standort nach Berlin und übernahm die Leitung der Berliner Dependance. Von hier aus wurde die steigende Zahl von Projekten in Berlin, aber auch das neue Aktionsfeld Russland bearbeitet.

Fragt man heute nach der Haltung des Büros, nach der gemeinsamen Überzeugung der vier so unterschiedlichen Partner, so ist dieser Blick zurück in die Anfänge des Büros aufschlussreich. Die sich überschneidenden Dienstzeiten der Partnergenerationen sorgten dafür, dass heftige Umbrüche ausblieben und Kontinuitäten gepflegt werden konnten. So glaubt man, den Pragmatismus der Wiederaufbauzeit nach dem Krieg noch zu spüren. Und die an der Moderne orientierte, den wechselnden Moden abholde architektonische Haltung ist nie wirklich in Gefahr geraten, selbst in Zeiten der Postmoderne nicht und auch nicht in den letzten Jahren, da vielfach mit Kreationen aus der Welt des Dekonstruktivismus, des Dynamismus oder der Blobarchitektur publizistische Erfolge erzielt wurden. Dennoch verstehen sie sich in der Entwicklung ihrer Architektur als in die Bedingungen

largest and its striking appearance symbolises the boom of the early nineties probably more than any other building in Dresden. The new location enabled the office to participate actively in the expanding building activities in the new states of Germany after the reunification. Later this office also ran building projects in the Rhine area.

The beginning of the nineties also marks the time when Ekkehard Voss and Sergei Tchoban from St. Petersburg came into contact with nps. Both joined the office as employees in 1992, becoming the first of a third generation of partners in 1995. This is reflected in the new office name: in 2003, one year after the death of Wolfgang Nietz, "Nietz - Prasch - Sigl und Partner Architekten BDA" once again changed name to "nps tchoban voss Architekten BDA".

After the move of the Berlin office from the Wundtstraße to the Hackesche Höfe, Sergei Tchoban relocated to Berlin and took over the Berlin branch. The office has since been responsible for an increasing number of projects in Berlin as well as for the new market in Russia.

This review of the history of the office and its origins is instructive when considering the question of a common attitude within the office, a common conviction that the four very different partners share. The overlapping periods of different generations of partners has avoided the occurrence of major upheavals and helped ensure an atmosphere of continuity. Traces of the pragmatism of the period of reconstruction after the war are, so to speak, still evident today. The central, primarily modernistic architectonic approach has remained averse to changing fashions, never really being threatened even during the period of post-modernism and even in recent years where creations ascribing to deconstructivism, dynamism or blob architecture

Sergei Tchoban, 1991   Ekkehard Voss, 1992

der Zeit eingebundene Architekten, die nicht individualistisch autonom wirken wollen, sondern aus dem Sehen, Erleben, Verstehen der Gegenwartsarchitektur heraus nach zeitgemäßen, werthaltigen Lösungen suchen. Die heute gebotenen technischen Möglichkeiten und Materialien werden begrüßt und möglichst sinnvoll eingesetzt. Als Pionier auf diesem Gebiet sieht man sich jedoch nicht. Den Ehrgeiz, die neuesten Konstruktionstechniken aus dem Flugzeugbau beim Häuserbauen zu erproben, überlässt man anderen. Auch gesteht man den neuen Techniken und Materialien nicht das Primat des architektonischen Ausdrucks zu. High-Tech, anschauliche Technik als gestalterische Motivik, ist kein Thema, man nutzt die technischen Errungenschaften, doch man demonstriert und thematisiert sie nicht.

Den ganzheitlichen Charakter der Arbeiten aus dem Büro nps tchoban voss bestimmt sicherlich auch die Arbeitsweise im Team. Das Engagement der Mitarbeiter ist gefragt, nicht nur bei der Ausarbeitung vorgegebener Konzepte. Ihnen fällt im „offenen System" des Büros eine wichtige Rolle als Ideen- und Impulsgeber zu.

So ist der Architektur von nps tchoban voss das Moment der bemühten individuellen Originalität oder gar der Provokation fremd. Die Bauten werfen sich nicht in die Brust, sie schmeicheln sich nicht ein, nehmen nicht für sich ein, sondern sie überzeugen. Sie suchen nicht die Konfrontation mit der vorgefundenen Situation, aber sie halten auch nichts von bedingungsloser Anpassung. Vielleicht ist das Wort von der „Angemessenheit" hier angebracht, mit der die Architektur sich artikuliert.

Es hat wohl auch etwas mit der Keimzelle des Büros in Hamburg zu tun, denn die Hansestadt scheint insgesamt immun zu sein gegen den Hype architektonischer Moden und Sensationen und stattdessen auf die sprichwörtliche hanseatische Seriosität und Solidität zu setzen. Kein Dekonstruktivist hat in Hamburg

have attracted considerable media attention. Nevertheless, in the ongoing development of their architecture, the architects do consider themselves as standing firmly in the context of the respective time, as architects whose work should not be autonomous or individualistic but is the product of perceiving, experiencing and understanding contemporary architecture and searching for relevant, up-to-date and worthwhile solutions. The technical possibilities and materials available today are welcomed and also employed as appropriately as possible. They do not, however, regard themselves as pioneers in this area. Ambitious endeavours such as the transfer of methods from aircraft construction to housing are left to others. Similarly, new technologies and materials are not elevated to the level of architectural expression. High-tech and vivid technology as a design motif is not a theme of their architecture; technical advances may be utilised but they are not demonstrated overtly or made the central theme.

The holistic character of the work undertaken by nps tchoban voss is without doubt a factor of their team-based working method. Members of staff are able to participate actively, not just in the elaboration of predetermined concepts. In the 'open system' of the office, their input is also valuable during the generation of concepts and initial ideas.

Accordingly, nps tchoban voss' architecture is not characterised by the moment of laboured originality or by a provocative stance. Their buildings are not self-important or overbearing, they neither ingratiate themselves nor overpower one, they are simply convincing. They do not seek confrontation with the existing situation, but they also do not subordinate themselves unconditionally. Perhaps the term "appropriate" best describes the manner in which their architecture is articulated.

Alte Oberpostdirektion, Hannover
Former Post Office Headquarters, Hanover

Berolinahaus, Berlin

Herrenhaus Wellingsbüttel, Hamburg
Wellingsbüttel Manor, Hamburg

Fuß fassen können, aber, und das ist erstaunlich, auch kein Rekonstrukteur und kein Retroarchitekt. Keines der im Krieg zerstörten Kulturdenkmale ist aus dem Nichts heraus als 1:1-Kopie wieder aufgebaut worden und die Hanseaten blicken kopfschüttelnd nach Dresden, Berlin, Potsdam und Braunschweig ob der dortigen Umtriebe um die Wiedergänger längst zu Staub gewordener Schlösser und Bürgerhäuser. Auch im Kleinen, bei der Sanierung, Ergänzung und Umnutzung von Baudenkmalen ist in Hamburg die Rekonstruktion kein angestrebter Weg, sondern man betreibt Denkmalpflege durch kreativen Umgang mit dem bauhistorischen Erbe.

Die Sanierungsprojekte von nps tchoban voss sind in diesem Sinn genuin entwerferisch gehandhabt worden. Wertvolles erhalten, in Szene setzen, doch Verlorenes nicht replizieren, sondern durch Neues ersetzen, Erweiterungen und Ergänzungen in moderner Formensprache hinzufügen und als zeitbezogene Zutat ausweisen, diese Prinzipien galten für das Team schon in den neunziger Jahren bei den historischen Geschäftsbauten am Hamburger Gänsemarkt und lagen der Umnutzung des Herrenhauses Wellingsbüttel ebenso zu Grunde wie dem Umbau der ehemaligen Oberpostdirektion Hannover, der Mälzerei in Berlin-Friedrichshain oder der Sanierung des Berolinahauses von Peter Behrens am Berliner Alexanderplatz.

Gerade das Berliner Büro hat sich in jüngerer Zeit mit Sanierungsprojekten hervorgetan. Sergei Tchoban hat trotz großer Engagements im Bereich des Neubaus bis hin zum Moskauer Federation Tower sein in St. Petersburg geprägtes Faible für die Bauhistorie nicht vergessen. Das Berliner Team begibt sich oft in das mühevolle Geschäft des Umgangs mit dem architektonischen Erbe. Besonders die kongeniale Ergänzung der Moderne wie beim Berolinahaus oder beim Projekt für das aus den fünfziger Jah-

This may also be a factor of the office's origins and nucleus in Hamburg. The Hanseatic city, so it seems, is generally immune to the hype and sensationalism of architectural fashion, preferring the proverbial Hanseatic integrity and solidity. As yet no single deconstructivist architect has been able to gain a foothold in Hamburg and, perhaps more remarkably, neither have retro-architects or advocates of reconstruction. None of the cultural monuments destroyed during the war have been rebuilt from the ground up as a 1:1 replica. The citizens of Hamburg can only shake their heads over the machinations in Dresden, Berlin, Potsdam and Braunschweig to resurrect the ghosts of long destroyed castles and town houses. Even at a small scale in the renovation, extension and conversion of monuments, reconstruction is pursued only rarely. Instead conservation is understood as a creative response to the historical built legacy.

The renovation projects undertaken by nps tchoban voss are in this respect more akin to regular design projects. Conserve what is valuable, show it off to its best effect, but do not replicate what is lost, instead replace with new, extend and complement in a modern architectural language, explicitly denoted as a contemporary ingredient – these principles were practised by the team in the nineties for the historical commercial buildings on Hamburg's Gänsemarkt and likewise governed the conversion of Wellingsbüttel Manor as well as the conversion of the former Post Office Headquarters in Hanover, the Old Maltings in Berlin-Friedrichshain or the renovation of the Berolinahaus by Peter Behrens on the Alexanderplatz in Berlin.

The Berlin office in particular has distinguished itself with a series of recent renovation projects. Despite his intensive activities in the field of new building, not least the Federation Tower in Moscow, Sergei Tchoban has not forgotten his fondness for

Synagoge Chabad Lubawitsch, Berlin
Lubavitch Chabad Synagogue, Berlin

Federation Tower, Moskau
Federation Tower, Moscow

ren stammende Zentrum am Zoo in Berlin ist ein Thema in der Hauptstadt. Auch wenn es gilt, einen neoklassizistischen Bau zu adaptieren, wenn dichte, räumliche Atmosphäre mit spirituellem Fluidum gefragt ist wie beim Jüdischen Bildungszentrum Chabad Lubawitsch und dessen Synagoge in Berlin, so gelingt auch dies mit dem modernen Formenrepertoire und mit der Auswahl von Materialien entsprechender Anmutung, warmbraunes Walnussholz, rotes Leder, Naturstein. Geht dieser Entwurf sicherlich auf ein ganz spezifisches Bedürfnis nach einem transzendent aufladbaren Ambiente ein, so gelingt es Tchoban auch in anderen Arbeiten, die emotionale Saite mitschwingen zu lassen.

Gerade Sergei Tchoban hat auf Grund seiner Herkunft und Ausbildung in St. Petersburg eine intensive Beziehung zur Historie der europäischen Stadt. Das vorgefundene Repertoire des gestalterischen Kontextes genügt ihm, daraus neue Funken zu schlagen. Wo die historische Stadt das Auge mit Farbe und Dekor zu beschäftigen weiß, versucht auch er, von der Nutzung vorgegebenen seriellen Rasterfassaden mehr Relief und Tektonik, Ausdruck und Tiefe zu geben. Wo die Nachbarschaft in erzählerischen Posen schwelgt, sucht er nach zeitgemäßen Möglichkeiten, plastisches und figürliches Dekor in die Epoche von Bits und Pixels zu transformieren. Es geht ihm um das Mitreden im Gespräch der Häuserfamilie, nicht um das vorlaute Auftrumpfen und Übertönen, um die Arbeit am Stadtkörper, nicht um einen singulären Objektfetischismus. Der historisch gewachsene Körper der vielbeschworenen „europäischen Stadt", der sich unter weitaus begrenzteren als den heutigen Mitteln und Möglichkeiten entwickelt hat, ist gegenüber dem Einzelhaus das höhere Gut.

In dieser Haltung trifft er sich wieder mit den Partnern, deren Entwürfe ebenso ohne Provokationspotenzial auskommen. Vielleicht lässt sich diese Haltung mit dem Konterpart verdeutlichen.

historical building substance, influenced by his background in St. Petersburg. The team in Berlin repeatedly takes up the painstaking challenge of working with the architectural heritage. A particular theme in the capital city is the sympathetic extension of modernist architecture such as the Berolinahaus or the project for the Zentrum am Zoo in Berlin, originally built in the fifties. And even when the task is to adapt a neo-classicistic building, where an intense spatial atmosphere with spiritual qualities is required such as for the Chabad Lubavitch Jewish Education Centre and its synagogue in Berlin, this is achieved through the use of a repertoire of modern forms and the choice of suitably rich materials: warm brown walnut, red leather and natural stone. Although the requirements of this particular project – a space invested with a transcendental atmosphere – were very specific, Tchoban has been able to strike an emotional chord with similar means in other work too.

Sergei Tchoban, due to his origins and education in St. Petersburg, has an especially intense relationship to the history of the European city. The existent repertoire of the immediate built context is usually sufficient to set the sparks flying. Where in the past the urban environment engaged the eye with colour and decoration, Tchoban too attempts to enrich the prescribed grids of serial façades through greater modulation, tectonic expression and depth. Where neighbourhoods revel in expressive figurative poses, he searches for contemporary means with which to transform such sculptural decoration into the age of bits and pixels. His aim is to join in the dialogue of a row of houses, not to impertinently show off or drown out, his focus is the urban ensemble rather than the fetishism of a singular object. The historical organic texture of the much-vaunted "European City", which developed out of far more modest means

Hauptverwaltung Imtech, Hamburg
Imtech Headquarters, Hamburg

Mövenpick Hotel, Düsseldorf

Oval Office, Hamburg

Es gibt derzeit – auch in Hamburg – eine Tendenz, dem Investorenklientel für Büro- und Geschäftsbauten architektonische Fanale zu liefern, selbstverliebte Objekte, die hier oder ebenso gut an ganz anderem Ort stehen könnten, deren wichtigste Eigenschaft das marktgängige Alleinstellungsmerkmal ist. Oft werden sie zusätzlich mit einem so klingenden wie kulturlosen Namen „gelabelt", denn es geht einzig um das Marketing, um den – oft nur kurzfristig interessanten – wirtschaftlichen Erfolg einer Investition. Häufig werden die Investitionsobjekte bereits vor der Fertigstellung veräußert und dem Architekten kommt der Bauherr abhanden. Ein Investitionsobjekt muss also als Marke funktionieren, als möglichst spektakulärer „Leuchtturm" im Stadtgefüge. Selten nur stellt sich die Überzeugung ein, dass dessen stadtgestalterischer Anspruch als Landmarke durch Nutzung und Bedeutung auch gerechtfertigt ist.

Die Architekten von nps tchoban voss treibt solcher Geltungsdrang nicht um. Ihre Leidenschaft richtet sich auf die genuin architektonischen Tugenden, das Erschaffen von Raum und die Sinnlichkeit des Materials, den Spannungsbogen von der Gestaltung des Stadtraumes über das Objekt bis zur Sorgfalt im Detail.

Man merkt ihren Bauten an, dass sie sich vor dem Entwerfen auf dem künftigen Bauplatz gründlich umsehen. Dass eines ihrer wichtigsten Ziele ist, die jeweilige städtebauliche Situation zu verbessern, zu vervollständigen, oft zu heilen. Wo andere Architekten darauf Wert legen, jeweils ihre unverwechselbare „Handschrift" zu hinterlassen, kommt es ihnen darauf an, der Einmaligkeit des Ortes und der Eigenart der Nutzung gerecht zu werden. Imtech in Hamburg oder das Mövenpick Hotel in Düsseldorf sind Beispiele für ihre Vorgehensweise, die Maßstäbe, Richtungsvorgaben und Typologien aufzunehmen und in ihren

and possibilities than those available today, is of greater worth than the individual building.

In this respect he concords with his partners whose designs likewise eschew any recourse to provocative means. This can perhaps best be illustrated by examining their counterparts. A current tendency that can be observed almost everywhere – in Hamburg too – is the design of buildings for investors that have a beacon-like effect, self-indulgent objects that could just as easily stand elsewhere and whose most important characteristic is their unique selling proposition in marketing terms. Very often such buildings are "labelled" with an attractive sounding but arbitrary name, its sole purpose to help market the building, to promote the often only short-term interest in the economic success of an investment. In many cases, the investment object is sold before completion; and gone is the architect's client. An investment object must function as a brand, a spectacular "lighthouse" in the urban environment. Only rarely do the "landmark qualities" that the design seeks to express prove themselves over time through use and the importance accorded to the building itself.

The architects at nps tchoban voss are not driven by such a desire for attention. Their passion is directed towards genuine architectural virtues, the creation of space, the sensuous qualities of materials, the arc of tension from the design of the urban space to the object itself and its precise elaboration in detail.

In their buildings one can see that they have carefully scrutinised the site before beginning with the design, that one of their most important aims is to improve the respective urban situation, to complete it, often to heal it. Where other architects aim to leave their own unmistakable "signature", nps tchoban voss seek to do justice to the uniqueness of a place and

Cubix-Kino, Berlin
Cubix Cinema, Berlin

Hauptverwaltung SAGA/GWG, Hamburg
SAGA/GWG Headquarters, Hamburg

Bauten zu interpretieren, weiterzuführen und teilweise zur Kulmination zu bringen. Wenn manche ihrer Häuser oberflächlich den Eindruck erwecken, schon immer an diesem Ort gestanden zu haben, so ist dies Ergebnis einer solchen Einfühlungsarbeit. Der zweite Blick zeigt dann allerdings, dass die Entwürfe auf dieser Stufe der gedanklichen Durchdringung keineswegs stehen geblieben sind, sondern ihre vielfältigen Qualitäten einem ganzheitlichen komplexen Denken verdanken. Wenn dann zum Beispiel eine bestimmte (durchaus nicht willkürlich gewählte) Motivik durchgespielt wird, wie beispielsweise beim Javaturm und beim Oval Office in Hamburg, bei Imtech Hamburg oder beim Cubix-Kino Berlin, kommt es trotzdem zu Bauwerken, denen es an Markanz und Zeichenhaftigkeit nicht mangelt, die Merkzeichen in der Stadt bilden, ohne unangemessen zu wirken. Und diese Art der Signifikanz, das lässt sich vorhersagen, wird nicht in ein paar Jahren schon langweilig und unmodern sein.

Was aber auch in der Annäherung an die Bauten gilt, aus der Binnensicht, aus der Perspektive von Bewohnern und Benutzern. Die Hauptverwaltung der SAGA/GWG in Hamburg oder das Cubix-Kino in Berlin sind beispielhafte Bauten aus dem Werk von nps tchoban voss, die den ganzheitlichen Ansatz deutlich machen. Die Aufmerksamkeit der Entwerfer gilt dem funktionalen Organisationsprinzip und dem schlüssigen konstruktiven Gefüge. Sie gilt aber auch uneingeschränkt der handwerklich soliden Ausführung und der bewussten Materialwahl im Hinblick auf die optischen und haptischen Eigenschaften des Hauses als der „dritten Haut" des Menschen. Und sie gilt der sensuellen Erfahrung des Raumes und seiner Oberflächen, der eine mit allen Sinnen erfahrbare Umwelt bildet, ein Ambiente, das rationales Erkenntnisfeld und emotionales, atmosphärisch wirksames Erlebnisfeld gleichermaßen ist. „Es gibt eigentümliche Erscheinun-

the specifics of its use. Imtech Headquarters in Hamburg or the Mövenpick Hotel in Düsseldorf are examples of their approach in which they pick up on the scale, directionality and typologies of the existing situation and interpret and develop these further in their buildings, often adding a final piece to complete the situation. If some of their buildings at first glance convey the impression that they have always stood on this spot, then this is the result of such sensitive consideration. On closer inspection it becomes evident that the designs have gone beyond this level of reflection alone and that their manifold qualities are the product of a holistic and complex process of deliberation. When, for example, a particular motif or theme is chosen (and in no way arbitrarily) and followed through, as can be seen in the Java Tower, Oval Office or Imtech in Hamburg or the Cubix Cinema in Berlin, buildings come about that are striking and distinctive, that form landmarks in the city yet never seem inappropriate. This kind of significance, one can safely predict, will not become tired and dated in a few years time.

This is equally important in how one gets to know a building, from an insider point of view, from the perspective of the inhabitants and users. The headquarters of the SAGA/GWG in Hamburg or the Cubix Cinema in Berlin are exemplary buildings in nps tchoban voss' oeuvre in that they demonstrate the architects' holistic approach. The designers pay careful attention to the functional and organisational principle and a sound structural system. However, no less attention is given to the workmanship and the deliberate choice of materials with regard to their optical and haptic qualities as the "third skin" of its inhabitants. Likewise, they carefully design the sensory experience of the space and its surfaces, which together form an environment that is felt with all the senses, an ambience that

Überseequartier, Hamburg

gen, wahrhafte Schöpfungen des Menschen, die Anteil haben am Gesicht und am Tastsinn – oder aber am Gehör – zugleich aber auch am Verstand, an der Zahl und am Wort", lässt Paul Valéry Sokrates in „Eupalinos oder der Architekt" das Wesen der Architektur bestimmen. Diese oft widerstreitenden Aspekte miteinander in Beziehung zu setzen, ist das Bestreben der Architekten. Das bedingt, sie ganzheitlich im Blickfeld zu behalten und die Aufmerksamkeit nicht zu Gunsten spektakulärer Effekte auf einzelne Parameter zu konzentrieren, wie es bei mediengängiger Modearchitektur Methode ist.

Hinzu kommt das unablässige Streben nach handwerklicher Perfektion und Solidität der Bauausführung. Wo andere ruppige Details sympathisch finden, wo wieder andere Oberflächeneffekte mit wenig dauerhaften Materialien erkaufen oder die Gesetze der Bauphysik leichtfertig ignorieren, sind für nps tchoban voss die „anerkannten Regeln der Bautechnik" Gesetz, dessen Gültigkeit und Berechtigung nicht infrage gestellt werden. Der Stadtraum einerseits und das Detail andererseits werden somit im Werk der Architekten zu Schwerpunkten. Doch die beiden Aspekte sind jene, die für den eigentlichen Architekturbenutzer wichtiger als die Gestalt des Einzelgebäudes sind, der Stadtraum als Handlungsfeld, als Ort der Identifikation des Individuums mit dem Gemeinwesen, und das Detail als jener Punkt, an dem der Nutzer mit der Architektur optisch und haptisch am direktesten in Kontakt kommt. Dahinter steht die Überzeugung, dass sich das Leben im Medienzeitalter auch mittelfristig nicht in Kabeln und an Bildschirmen abspielen wird, sondern dass der Mensch auch in einer telematischen Gesellschaft von seiner Natur her auf eine Umwelt angewiesen ist, die alle Sinne anspricht. Dass nach wie vor Orte benötigt werden, die der Identifikation und dem Zusammenleben dienen und dass es sich lohnt, diese Orte

is at once recognised rationally as well as experienced emotionally in terms of its atmosphere. "There are strange apparitions, genuine creations of mankind, that appeal in part to the face and sense of touch – or sense of hearing – and in part to the intellect, to the number and word," Paul Valéry has Socrates say in "Eupalinos, or the Architect" in his description of the nature of architecture. This requires one to consider all these aspects holistically and not to concentrate on individual parameters in favour of spectacular effects as is common for more media-oriented architectural fashions.

To this one can add an unremitting desire to achieve perfect workmanship and a sound, solid construction. Some architects enjoy the directness of rough and ready details, others achieve specific superficial effects at the cost of using low-durability materials or ignoring the material's essential physical characteristics; for nps tchoban voss, the "established state of the art" is a rulebook which is not to be idly compromised or called into question. Two focal areas crystallise in the work of the architects: on the one hand the urban space and on the other the detail. Both of these areas are also those that are most important for the user of a building, more so than an individual building's form. The urban space is a place of negotiation, a place in which individual identity meets society; the detail is the point at which the users comes into contact with the architecture most directly, both visually as well as haptically. Behind both of these lies the conviction that even in the age of information and media, life will, at least in the medium term, not take place on screen and in cables, but that people in our telematic society are naturally dependent on an environment that appeals to all the senses; that places will continue to be needed that promote identification and support cohabitation; and that it is worthwhile to design

Messezentrum Expo-Gate, St. Petersburg
Expo-Gate Trade Fair, St. Petersburg

Newskij-Rathaus, St. Petersburg
Newskij City Hall, St. Petersburg

des sinnlichen Raumempfindens qualitätvoll zu gestalten und die Häuser nicht zu rasch wechselnden billboards verkommen zu lassen. „Orte sind es, die die Stadt prägen, die Geschichte, Erinnerung und Identität geben" (O. M. Ungers).

Die Orte, die Quartiere, die größeren städtebaulichen Zusammenhänge gehören zu den neuen Herausforderungen, denen sich das Büro derzeit und in naher Zukunft stellt. Entwürfe wie die Neuordnung des Bahngeländes in Hamburg-Altona gehören schon in die visionäre Kategorie des Städtebaus, während der erfolgreiche Entwurf für das Hamburger Überseequartier eine nun in die Konkretisierung eintretende Vision darstellt.

Bedeutende Projekte sind auch für St. Petersburg in Arbeit, unter anderen das Messegelände und, sicherlich von besonderem Renommee, das Rathaus.

So kommen ständig neue Aufgaben auf die Architekten zu, die Architektur verändert sich, auch die Methoden, die Instrumente, die Arbeitsweisen. Doch nps tchoban voss bleiben sich treu. Sie bleiben empfänglich für das Neue, aber ihr Credo bleibt dasselbe, die Herangehensweise und die Grundhaltung, die letztlich eine ethische ist, da sie auf der Verantwortung gründet, die der Architekt vor der Gesellschaft hat. Denn der Architekt arbeitet treuhänderisch, er gestaltet keine selbstreferenziellen Kunstwerke, sondern er baut mit dem Geld anderer für andere an einer Umwelt, die unser aller Lebensraum ist. Eine Erkenntnis, die längst nicht alle am gegenwärtigen Architekturbetrieb Beteiligten gewonnen haben.

such places of sensory experience with a degree of quality so that buildings do not simply degenerate into rapidly changing billboards. "It is places that characterise the city, that engender a sense of history, memory and identity." (O. M. Ungers)

Designs for localities, entire quarters and larger urban ensembles feature among the new challenges that the office is tackling now and in the near future. While designs such as the reorganisation of the railway site in Hamburg-Altona belong to the visionary category of urban design, the successful design for the Überseequartier, also in Hamburg, is a vision that is steadily becoming ever more concrete.

Important projects are also being developed for St. Petersburg, including the trade fair grounds and a project of particular prestige, the new city hall.

And so, the architects are continually presented with new tasks, architecture undergoes transformations, as do the methods, instruments and ways of working. Nevertheless nps tchoban voss remain true to their roots. While they remain open for the new, their credo, their approach and basic attitude, remains the same, as it is ultimately an ethical stance that is founded on a sense of responsibility that the architect has for society. After all, the architect works on our behalf, he does not design self-referential works of art but designs with the money of others, for others, in an environment which serves as a habitat for us all – an awareness that not all those involved in current architectural production appear to have understood.

Fragen an die Architekten

Alf M. Prasch, Peter Sigl, Sergei Tchoban und Ekkehard Voss im Gespräch mit Falk Jaeger

Von welchen Lehrern sind Sie in Ihrer Ausbildung geprägt worden?

SIGL Das liegt ja bei mir ganz weit zurück. Ich habe an der Bauschule Hamburg eine Bauingenieurausbildung absolviert. Die Namen der Lehrer kennt man heute nicht mehr. Dort waren es die konstruktiven und bauwirtschaftlichen Aspekte, die mich interessiert haben. Und in der Folge ist das ja auch der Schwerpunkt meiner Tätigkeit im Büro geworden.

PRASCH Ich habe an der TU Berlin studiert. Da waren es vor allem Professor Willi Kreuer, bei dem ich auch am Lehrstuhl gearbeitet habe und Professor Bernhard Hermkes, der das Fach Baukonstruktion in hervorragender Weise vertrat, dem hing man an den Lippen. Ich habe auch eine Arbeit bei Ungers gemacht, aber der hat mich nicht so beeindruckt.

TCHOBAN Bei mir war es in St. Petersburg Professor Sergei Speranskij, vor allem mit seinem städtebaulichen Ansatz mit Blick auf das Ensemble. Ansonsten ist es die Stadt Petersburg, die mich wie ein Lehrer geschult hat, mit ihren Stadträumen, die man erlebt, und den Gebäuden, die vor Augen stehen. Bis heute stelle ich mir die Frage, weshalb dieses oder jenes Gebäude so interessant wirkt, ohne spektakulär sein zu müssen. Als Architekt wird man von der Stadt, in der man aufwächst, sehr intensiv geprägt. Das beeinflusst später unbewusst viele Entscheidungen.

VOSS Ich habe in Aachen studiert und habe den wesentlichen Teil der Reifejahre im Studium mit Wolfgang Döring verbracht, der stark von Egon Eiermann geprägt war und jeden rausgeworfen hat, der keine klaren Konzepte auf die Beine stellen konnte.

Seine Architektur war der klassischen Moderne verpflichtet. Ich merke es noch heute, wenn ich bestimmte städtebauliche Situationen vorfinde, dass ich zu Konzepten neige, die mit klaren Formen und einfachen Elementen Innen- und Außenräume verbinden. Das kommt von Döring her.

Zudem liegt Aachen im Dreiländereck und so hatten wir die Grands Projets im Frankreich der achtziger Jahre einerseits und das spannende Holland andererseits im Blick. Eine weitere Facette brachte Manfred Speidel, Hochschullehrer an der RWTH Aachen, ins Spiel, der Architekten wie Nouvel, Alsop oder Fuksas zu Vorträgen einlud, die damals noch nicht bekannt waren und die die Hochschule begeistert haben.

Welcher Architekturströmung, welchem Stil würden Sie sich zurechnen?

TCHOBAN Für mich ist es langweilig, ein Kleid zu suchen, das auf alle Fälle passt. Bauen im Stadtkontext und Bauen eines isolierten Objektes sind zwei verschiedene Vorgänge. Auch Städte teilen sich für mich in Städte der Räume und Städte der Objekte. In diesen zwei Situationen gehe ich unterschiedlich vor. Was mich im städtischen Zusammenhang nicht mehr interessiert, ist das minimalistische Bauen. Architektur, die nicht altern kann, ohne Details, die im Laufe der Zeit nur stärker hervortreten und durch Verwitterung noch interessanter wirken, ist nach meiner Meinung nicht nachhaltig. Im Stadtkontext spielt für mich das Detail eine enorme Rolle, nicht das minimalistische, sondern das Relief, das Dekor, eine aufwändige Gestaltung der Oberfläche mit unterschiedlich tiefen Ebenen. Wenn Architektur keinen Aufwand zeigt, hat sie für mich keinen Gehalt. Wenn die Architektur jedoch nicht den Raum umgrenzt, sondern als

Falk Jaeger (Mitte) im Gespräch mit Ekkehard Voss, Sergei Tchoban, Alf M. Prasch und Peter Sigl (von links nach rechts).
Falk Jaeger (centre) in discussion with Ekkehard Voss, Sergei Tchoban, Alf M. Prasch and Peter Sigl (from left to right).

einzelnes Objekt im Stadtraum steht, ein Hochhaus etwa, das ohne Kontext wie eine Skulptur wirkt, gelten andere Kriterien. Dann kann es sich auch um autonome plastische Formen handeln, kann das Dekorative an der Oberfläche, zu Gunsten der minimalistischeren Fassadenhaltung zurücktreten.

VOSS Mich interessiert es nicht, eine formale Sprache zu entwickeln. Als ich hier 1992 ins Büro kam, wurde die individuelle Antwort aus dem Kontext heraus gesucht. Heute haben wir noch immer keine einheitliche Gestaltungs-Handschrift, das finde ich gut, denn wir können uns so auch sehr unterschiedlichen Bauaufgaben stellen.

PRASCH Ich vertrete keine dogmatische Grundhaltung, sondern bei mir steht der Genius loci im Vordergrund. Das drückt sich in der Formensprache und in der Materialwahl aus und wird wie bei meinen Partnern ergänzt durch eine individuelle Interpretation des Orts. Deshalb sind unsere Entwürfe auch so unterschiedlich. Zum Beispiel bei dem Sheraton Hotel in Abu Dhabi habe ich untersucht, was dort typisch ist. Außer Barastis, den traditionellen Lehmhütten mit Palmzweigdächern gab es dort nur die Wachtürme der Piraten, und das wurde dann zum Gestaltungselement für diesen Entwurf. So ergeben sich die Lösungen meist aus dem Standort.

Aber um auf die Unterschiede zu sprechen zu kommen: Wenn Sie so ein Dekor wie Sergei Tchoban zeichnen müssten, da würde Ihnen doch der Griffel abbrechen?

PRASCH Das ist richtig, da bin ich einfacher gestrickt und in der Formensprache zurückhaltender. Ich bewundere aber auch die Selbstverständlichkeit, mit der Sergei solche Dinge vertritt, die ich nicht bringen könnte. Dennoch kommen aus unseren Büros, was die Baukörpersprache betrifft, ähnliche Ergebnisse.

TCHOBAN Heute ist der Bau als Skulptur technisch möglich geworden, eine dreidimensional entworfene, objekthafte Form, die nach allen Seiten gleich interessant wirkt, wo ein städtischer Kontext das erlaubt. Das würde nicht nur mich, sondern auch – so denke ich – jeden von uns reizen.

VOSS Es kommt darauf an, ob man den räumlichen Kontext erst einmal heilen muss. Und das Gebäude muss Emotionen auslösen. Sonst hast du nur eine funktionierende Hülle gebaut und eine Dienstleistung erbracht. Ich würde den Bauherrn am liebsten an die Hand nehmen und sagen: Hier musst du dich auf etwas einlassen, nicht nur wirtschaftlichen Mehrwert generieren, denn das Entscheidende ist, was gebaut wird, das steht dann 50 Jahre.

TCHOBAN Das ist doch dann der Mehrwert, und diesen künstlerischen Mehrwert musst du im Bauprozess immer wieder verteidigen.

Nun kann man ja vordergründig eine städtebauliche Situation heilen oder man betreibt fraktalen Städtebau, stellt sich quer und verhält sich widerborstig. Das ist doch auch eine Möglichkeit, Emotionen auszulösen. Schließen Sie die aus?

VOSS Es ist nicht so, dass Gebäude immer auf Konsens orientiert sind. Ich habe jedoch eine große Verantwortung, wenn ich entscheide, will ich mich einfügen, oder will ich durch Freistellen, Alleinstellen im Betrachter etwas auslösen und für meinen Bau eine andere Bedeutung schaffen, als wenn er im Blockrand unterginge.

TCHOBAN Ich finde, das ist sehr davon abhängig, wie gehaltvoll die Umgebung ist. Wenn die städtebauliche Situation sehr wertvoll ist, wird es nichts zu streiten geben und ich würde sie mit meinem Bau ergänzen. Wenn die Situation sehr heterogen ist und Ensemble-Qualitäten nicht eindeutig erkennbar sind, halte ich eine Verstärkung der Dissonanz für möglich. Aber nur wenn die Heterogenität zur Qualität erklärt wird, ist diese Haltung nicht egoistisch.

Ist es so, dass ein Architekt es immer nur mit gegnerischen Kräften zu tun hat?

SIGL Würde ich schon sagen, hundertprozentig!

PRASCH In der vielfältigsten Art, vom untersten Brandschützer bis zum Stadtplanungschef und zum Bauherrn.

VOSS Vielleicht braucht man auch diesen Impuls als Motivation.

Herr Sigl, Sie sind der Verwaltungschef des Büros, machen die Verträge und regeln die Finanzen; stehen Sie manchmal im Gegensatz zu den entwerfenden Partnern?

SIGL Gegensatz möchte ich das nicht nennen. Ich bringe mich schon ein, wenn ich anderer Auffassung bin.

VOSS Wohltuendes Korrektiv könnte man sagen. Warum machst du die Dinge nicht einfacher, fragt er oft und provoziert damit klarere Lösungen mit wenigen, aber guten Details.

Wie ist die Arbeit im Büro organisiert?

PRASCH Wir arbeiten kollegial eng zusammen, wir, Peter, Ekkehard und ich, sitzen ja zu dritt in einem Raum.

Aber jeder hat seine Bauherren. Dadurch ergibt sich, wer welches Projekt bearbeitet. Je nach Projekt machen wir dann Workshops am Wochenende, um die Lösungswege zu erkunden und die Richtung festzulegen. Im Workshop bringen auch die jungen Leute ihre Ideen mit ein.

Wie setzen Sie Ihre Vorstellungen in der Praxis durch, übernehmen Sie nach Möglichkeit bei jedem Projekt auch die Bauleitung?

PRASCH Es geht noch weiter, wir versuchen auch die Ausführungsplanung in unserer Hand zu halten, aber mit diesbezüglich spezialisierten Büros mithalten zu können, ist für uns oft Harakiri. Wir wollen aber bis zum Schluss mitreden, wenn eingespart werden muss. Die Bauleitung gehört auch dazu, weil im Verlauf der Realisierung viele Entscheidungen getroffen werden. Etwa 80 Prozent der Projekte behalten wir auf diese Weise unter Kontrolle.

TCHOBAN Das hängt vom eigenen Wunsch ab, denn manchmal ist das finanziell kaum zu leisten. Wenn man sich vorstellen kann, in der Ausführungsplanung deutliche Einbußen hinzunehmen, dann gelingt das fast durchgehend, denn man wird oft angefragt, alle Leistungsphasen zu übernehmen. Diese Politik des Strebens nach der durchgehenden Qualität war ein Grund, weshalb ich mich damals für den Eintritt in das Büro entschieden habe.

Ein krasses Beispiel: Wir haben auch schon eine Fassade auf unsere Kosten herunternehmen und ersetzen lassen, die nicht mit uns abgestimmt war. Dem Bauherrn war das egal, er wollte nur Geld sparen.

SIGL Es gelingt uns aber meist, die Fäden in der Hand zu behalten, auch wenn wir nicht mit der Ausführungsplanung betraut werden, weil wir immer die künstlerische Oberleitung übertragen bekommen.

Aber Kosten- und Terminsicherheit sind heute Faktoren, die die Investoren dazu bewegen, andere Wege zu gehen. Wir können in der Ausführungsphase nicht in die Haftung eintreten, denn die Versicherungen für Architekten werden immer teurer.

VOSS Schade ist, dass den Architekturbüros mitunter die technische Kompetenz abgesprochen wird. Wir sind ein Büro, das die Planungen auch umsetzt. Hier wird ein gut gestaltetes Detail auch technisch richtig gelöst.

PRASCH Wir hatten aber auch zwei Fälle, bei denen der Bauherr uns unbedingt im Team halten wollte, obwohl der Generalunternehmer gesagt hat, er mache das mit seinem Architekten

100.000 Euro billiger. Die Bauherren, die uns wertschätzen, gibt es auch; es sind meist jene, die man schon lange Jahre kennt.

In welchem Wirkungskreis betreiben Sie Ihre Aktivitäten?

PRASCH Wir streben durchaus die Überregionalität an, erst bundesweit, dann auch in andere Kulturkreise.

VOSS Die Plattform ist dabei größer geworden. Wir sind keine Architekten, die ländliches Bauen betreiben, wir arbeiten überwiegend für den urbanen Kontext.

TCHOBAN Es ist wichtig, dass man nicht auf einen bestimmten Ort festgelegt wird, sonst wird man erpressbar. Es ist viel schöner, an unterschiedlichen Orten zu arbeiten, es macht dich freier und bringt mehr Erfahrung. In Osteuropa wird zum Beispiel mehr die Masterplan-Erfahrung aus Hamburg und Berlin gefragt, während die Erfahrungen im Hochhausbau aus Moskau inzwischen wieder in Deutschland gefragt sind.

Empfinden Sie die Größe des Büros als ideal und wäre es bei entsprechender Auftragslage noch ohne Weiteres zu vergrößern?

PRASCH Für Arbeiten in anderen Ländern suchen wir Partnerbüros. Wir haben zum Beispiel eines in Abu Dhabi.

SIGL Die Bürogröße hier in Hamburg mit derzeit ca. 55 Mitarbeitern bei bisher drei, seit Beginn 2008 zwei verantwortlichen Partnern hat den Vorteil, dass wir auf Aufgaben, die spontan an uns herangetragen werden, schnell reagieren können. Wir können dann rasch Teams zusammenstellen.

VOSS Auf der anderen Seite ist das Büro nicht so unübersichtlich, dass wir nicht Herr der Vorgänge wären. Die Entwürfe müssen etwas mit uns zu tun haben und die Bauherren müssen uns noch persönlich kennen.

TCHOBAN Die Größe des Berliner Büros mit ca. 55 Mitarbeitern, von dessen Basis aus ich allein als Partner wirke, ist schon grenzwertig. Da wird schon mal ein Projekt ohne mich absolviert, was ich mir absolut nicht wünsche. Im Entwurfsprozess darf es nicht zum anonymen Verfahren kommen. Jeder Entwurf muss die Handschrift des Verfassers tragen. Sonst verliert der Architektenberuf für mich den ursprünglichen Sinn.

An Interview with the Architects

Alf M. Prasch, Peter Sigl, Sergei Tchoban and Ekkehard Voss in discussion with Falk Jaeger

Which teachers influenced you most during your education?

SIGL In my case that was a long time ago. I studied civil engineering at the Bauschule Hamburg and the names of the teachers are no longer well known today. During my studies I was particularly interested in aspects of construction and the economics of building, and that has therefore also become the focus of my activities in the office.

PRASCH I studied at the Berlin University of Technology. I particularly remember Professor Willi Kreuer, in whose department I worked for a while, and Professor Bernhard Hermkes who lead the excellent building construction course – we savoured every word of his. I also did a project with Ungers, but I was not so impressed by him.

TCHOBAN I my case it was Professor Sergei Speranskij in St. Petersburg, particularly his approach to urban design, which paid special attention to the ensemble. Apart from him, the city of St. Petersburg schooled me much like a teacher, especially the experience of its urban spaces and the buildings one can see. Even today I ask myself why one or the other building looks so interesting without needing to be spectacular. As an architect one is particularly influenced by the city in which one grows up. That subconsciously influences many decisions one makes later.

VOSS I studied in Aachen and spent a large part of the formative years of my studies with Wolfgang Döring, who was heavily influenced by Egon Eiermann and threw out anyone who couldn't put together a clear concept. His architecture

was one of high modernism. Sometimes even today, when I discover certain urban constellations, I notice that I tend to develop concepts that employ clear forms and simple elements to connect indoor and outdoor spaces. That comes from Döring.

Aachen also lies in a region where three countries meet, so on the one side we had the *Grand Projets* in France and on the other the exciting developments in Holland. Manfred Speidel, who taught at RWTH Aachen University, added a further facet to our course by inviting architects such as Nouvel, Alsop or Fuksas, who at the time were still relatively unknown, to lecture at the school. Their contributions were met with much enthusiasm.

Which architectural school or style would you ascribe yourselves to?

TCHOBAN For me it is tedious to develop a style that can be applied in all situations. Building in the context of the city and the building of an isolated object are two different things. Cities too can be divided into cities of spaces and cities of objects. I take different approaches for each of these two situations. What no longer interests me in the urban context is minimal architecture. Architecture that cannot age, without details, that over time become ever more stark, only becoming more interesting as they weather, is in my view not sustainable. In the urban context I find that detail has an enormous contribution: not minimalism but surface detail, decoration, elaborately designed surfaces with different degrees of depth. If architecture does not show the effort that has gone into making it, it is lacking content. Different criteria apply for a work of architecture that does not en-

Alf M. Prasch

Peter Sigl

Sergei Tchoban

Ekkehard Voss

close space but is a freestanding isolated object in the urban environment, for example a skyscraper that appears like a sculpture dislocated from context. In such cases an autonomous sculptural form can be appropriate and the decorative surface treatment can recede in favour of a more minimalistic approach to the façade.

VOSS I too am not interested in developing a formal language. When I joined the office in 1992, individual solutions were derived from the context. Today we still do not have a uniform design language or common signature. I think that's good too, as it enables us to take on very different architectural tasks.

PRASCH I have no particular dogmatic stance – for me the genius loci is most important. This is expressed in the formal language, in the choice of materials, and my colleagues then complement and extend this through their individual interpretations of the place. This is why our designs are so different. For example, for the Sheraton Hotel in Abu Dhabi I examined what was typical there. Except for the barastis, the traditional earth huts with palm frond roofs, there were only the watchtowers used by the pirates – and this became the design element for the project. As such, solutions are usually provided by the location.

To pick up on the differences between your approaches: I can imagine that if you had to draw a decoration of the kind Sergei employs, you'd be snapping your pencil?

PRASCH Yes, you're quite right, I take a simpler approach and prefer more reduced forms. But I also admire how naturally Sergei is able to present things that I would not be able to produce myself. Nevertheless, the architecture we create in our offices does produce similar results, certainly with regard to the language of body and mass.

TCHOBAN Today, it is now technically possible to create buildings as sculptures, as three-dimensionally designed object-like forms that appear equally interesting from all sides where the urban context makes this possible. I'm sure this would appeal to all of us, not just myself.

VOSS It depends on whether one first has to repair the spatial context. And the building has to evoke an emotional response. Otherwise all you have done is to erect a functional shell and provide a service. Ideally I would like to take the client by the hand and say: "Listen, you really have to be prepared to make the most of this. It's not just about economic profit and added value. After all, what will be built will stand there for 50 years."

TCHOBAN Yes, that *is* the added value. And we find ourselves having to defend this added design value again and again during the building process.

One approach is primarily to seek to repair urban constellations, another is to adopt a fractal understanding of the urban realm, to contradict and to adopt a contrary position. Is that not also a means of stirring up emotions? Do you categorically exclude such an approach?

VOSS I would not say that buildings always have to follow the prevailing consensus. However, I have to be aware of my responsibility when I decide whether to insert my building into its context or whether to provoke a response from the viewer by setting it apart, thereby investing it with a different importance to that which it would have if it blended seamlessly with its neighbours.

TCHOBAN I find that it depends very much on the character of the context. When the surrounding urban situation is particularly valuable, there is no reason to contradict and my building would augment what is already there. If the surroundings are particularly disparate and an ensemble character is not readily apparent, then, certainly, a possible approach would be to strengthen the dissonance. But only if it helps to explain the heterogeneity as a quality of the place, such an approach would not be egotistical.

Is it true that an architect is always up against opposing forces?

SIGL I would say so, definitely!

PRASCH In a whole variety of ways, from the junior fire protection officer to the head of the planning authority and the client too.

VOSS Perhaps one needs these as motivational impulses.

Mr Sigl, you are the administrator in the office, you negotiate the contracts and take care of the finances; does this sometimes put you in a position of opposition to your designing partners?

SIGL I would not call it opposition. I speak my mind when I am of a different opinion.

VOSS A useful corrective one could say. Often he will ask why we don't take a simpler approach and provokes us into finding clearer solutions with perhaps fewer but better details.

How do you organise the work in the office?

PRASCH As colleagues we work closely with one another. Three of us, Peter, Ekkehard and myself, all sit in the same room. But each of us has his own clients and this usually determines who works on which project. Depending on the project, we will have a weekend workshop to examine possible approaches to the solution and the direction we want to follow. The workshops also offer our younger colleagues the chance to bring in their own ideas.

How do you follow your ideas through in practice; do you try as far as possible to supervise every project on site?

PRASCH We go further, we also try to undertake the working drawing programme in-house, but we would be committing hara-kiri if we always tried to compete with the offices that have specialised in this area. One way or the other, we always want to have a say right up to the end, especially when cost-cutting measures are necessary. Site supervision is also part of our remit as many decisions are made during the construction itself. In this way we retain control of about 80% of the projects we design.

TCHOBAN That depends on our own aspirations, as it is sometimes simply not financially viable. When one is willing to accept significant losses during the working drawing programme, then it almost always works out as we are often asked to take over the entire planning process. This drive for consistent quality throughout the entire process was one reason why I joined the office in the first place.

By way of example, if a little extreme: we have in the past had an entire façade that had not been agreed with us taken down and replaced entirely at our own cost. For the client it wasn't important – he only wanted to save money.

SIGL In most cases we can usually maintain control, even if we do not undertake the working drawings, as we are always entrusted with the overall design supervision.

But security with regard to costs and deadlines are factors that do cause investors to look elsewhere. In such cases we cannot assume liability for the working planning phase as professional indemnity insurance is becoming ever more expensive for architects.

VOSS It is a pity that architectural offices are sometimes no longer regarded as technically competent. We are, after all, an office that implements our plans. Our details are not only well designed, they are also technically correct.

PRASCH We have had two cases where the client has steadfastly kept us in the team although the main contractor had quoted 100,000 Euro less if he worked with his own architect. There are therefore clients who value our input at every stage – they are usually those who we have known for many years.

How far does the sphere of your activities reach?

PRASCH We do seek to cast our net beyond our own region, primarily nationally, but also in other cultural environments.

VOSS In the process the platform has become larger. We are not architects who work at a rural scale; our work is predominantly in an urban context.

TCHOBAN It is important that one does not become dependent on a particular place, or else one becomes susceptible to manipulation. It is also much nicer to work in different places; it makes you freer and widens your horizon. For example, in Eastern Europe there is a demand for master planning experience from Hamburg and Berlin, whereas the experience with skyscraper building in Moscow is now in demand in Germany.

Do you think the size of the office is ideal as it is or would you expand further providing you had sufficient commissions?

PRASCH For projects in other countries we typically work with partner offices. For example, we have a partner in Abu Dhabi.

SIGL The size of the office here in Hamburg with 55 members of staff run previously by three, since 2008 now two responsible partners, has the advantage that we are able to react quickly to cater for commissions that arise spontaneously. We can rapidly put together appropriate teams.

VOSS And on the other hand, the office is not so large that we are not able to oversee all that goes on. The designs have to have something to do with us and the clients must know us personally.

TCHOBAN The size of the office in Berlin with 55 members of staff, where I work from as the sole partner, is at its limit. There have been projects that have been completed without my input, which is absolutely not what I want. The design process should not become an anonymous process. Each design must bear some indication of its author. If this is not the case, the job of the architect has in my view lost its original purpose.

BAUTEN | BUILDINGS

CUBIX-KINO
CUBIX CINEMA
BERLIN

Der Ort am Alexanderplatz in Berlin-Mitte trägt die Erinnerungen an die zwanziger Jahre und deren Dynamik und Modernität. Das Multiplex-Kino reflektiert als Unterhaltungszentrum dieses Stadtgefühl und knüpft mit seinen Bauformen an die Architektur der klassischen Moderne an, wie sie auch gegenüber an den Peter-Behrens-Bauten anzutreffen ist. Der polierte Naturstein der Fassade, ein schwarz schimmernder Nero Impala, wurde mit feinem, aber offenen Fugennetz bewusst als Hülle eingesetzt und gibt dem Haus die Gestalt eines präzise geschnittenen, stereometrischen Körpers. Die Fassade bildet funktionale Einheiten ab, zeigt die beiden zweigeschossigen Restaurants im Erdgeschoss, dazwischen die Eingangshalle, darüber zwei Galeriegeschosse sowie ganz oben das zweigeschossige Foyer des großen Saals.

The cinema's location on the Alexanderplatz in Berlin-Mitte recalls the dynamism and modernity of the twenties. The multiplex cinema reflects this urban feeling through its function as a centre for entertainment as well as through its form, which relates to modernist architecture of the kind that can be seen opposite it in the buildings by Peter Behrens. The polished stone cladding of the façade, made of panels of shimmering black Nero Impala with thin open joins, is deliberately expressed as an enveloping skin, lending the building a precise clear-cut stereometric form. The façade reflects the functional areas within, clearly displaying both of the two-storey restaurants on the ground floor, between them the entrance hall, over them two levels of galleries and at the top the two-storey foyer of the large auditorium.

Die Fenstererker zitieren Berliner Architektur der
Moderne der zwanziger Jahre.

The projecting bay windows refer to Berlin's modernist
architecture from the twenties.

Die Panoramafenster holen das Großstadtleben in Cinema-scope-Format ins Haus und konfrontieren es mit den virtuellen Realitäten auf den Leinwänden. Die dem Stadtgetriebe zugewandten Foyerbereiche des kompakt organisierten Baus mit den inszenierten Treppen und dem intensiven, auf Weiß, Rot und Schwarz reduzierten Farbkonzept der Bauhausästhetik bieten dem Kinobesucher auf fünf Geschossen ein eindrückliches Architekturerlebnis. Am Außenbau wie auch in den Foyers im Inneren ist es gelungen, der Filmwerbung mit all den Plakaten, Werbeeinrichtungen, Monitoren und Hinweisschildern einen definierten Ort zu geben und sie auf diese Weise architekturverträglich zu bändigen.

The panorama windows draw in the vibrancy of big city life in cinemascope format, juxtaposing it with the virtual reality of the big screens. The foyer area of the compact building faces outwards towards the bustle of the city and with its theatrical staircases and sparse, Bauhaus-inspired palette of white, red and black offers cinema visitors an impressive architectural spectacle on all five storeys. On the exterior of the building as well as in the foyer inside, the film advertising with its posters, billboards, monitors and signage have been given defined places so that they do not overpower the architecture of the building.

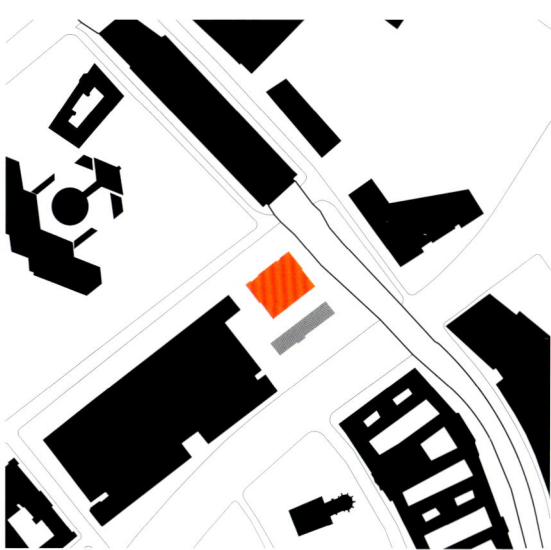

Das gestalterische Gesamtkonzept sorgt für eine homogene Architektursprache innen und außen.

The overall design concept creates a consistent architectural language inside and outside.

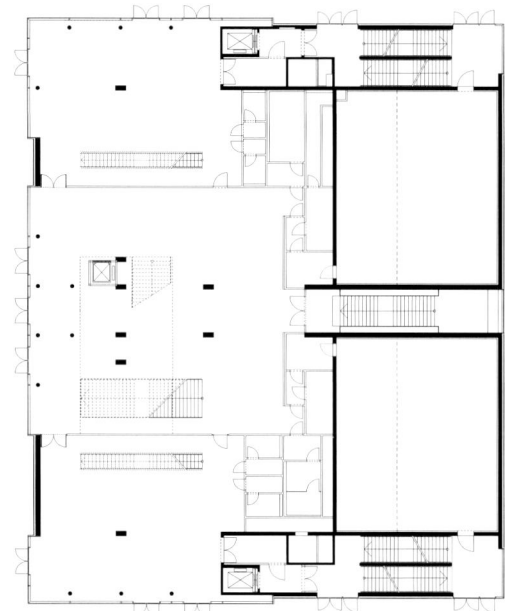

Grundriss Erdgeschoss | Ground floor plan

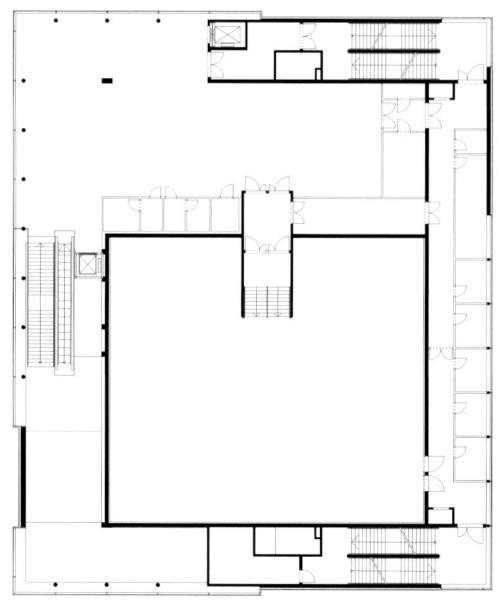

Grundriss 2. Obergeschoss | Second floor plan

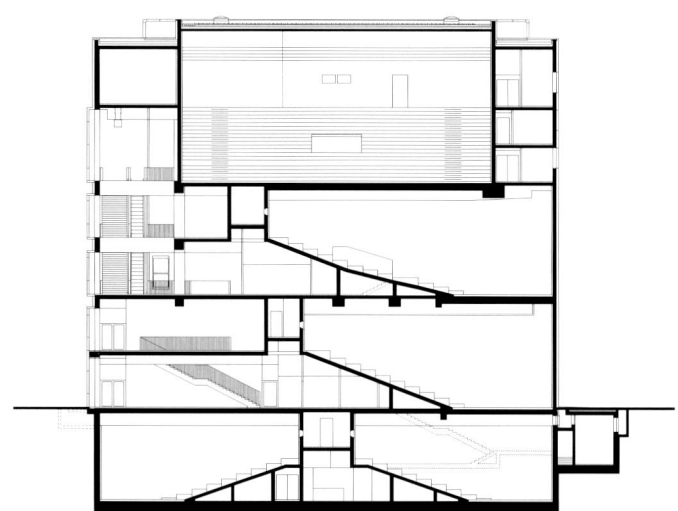

Querschnitt | Cross section

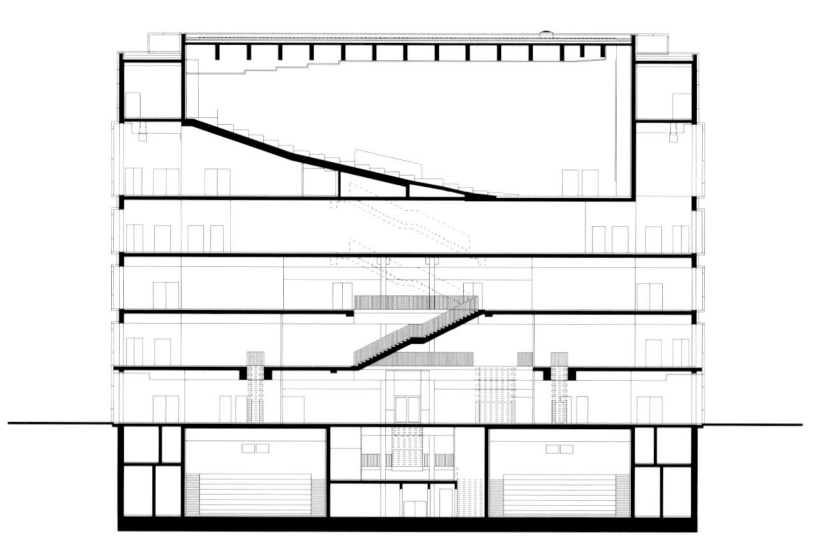

Längsschnitt | Longitudinal section

0   10m

In den Kinosälen herrscht Kintopp-Atmosphäre in
klassischem Purpur.

The auditoria with their crimson furnishings evoke
the atmosphere of classic cinemas.

MENSA UND BIBLIOTHEK
HOCHSCHULE ZITTAU/GÖRLITZ
UNIVERSITY REFECTORY AND LIBRARY
ZITTAU

Der Systembau aus DDR-Zeit wurde durch gezielte räumliche Eingriffe zu einem attraktiven Servicekomplex mit Mensa, Caféteria, Studentenwerk, Studentenclub und Bibliothek umgebaut. In dem bis auf die Tragstruktur entkernten Gebäude wurde ein Atrium geschaffen, das nun die natürliche Belichtung und Belüftung der angrenzenden Räume ermöglicht. Die audiovisuellen Arbeitsplätze sind auf den ruhigen Innenhof hin orientiert.

Die Fassade bekommt durch das dreiseitig durchlaufende Fensterband mit vorgehängten Sonnenschutzlamellen im Obergeschoss ein zeitgemäßes, charakteristisches Gesicht.

A prefabricated building dating from GDR times was upgraded through a series of carefully planned spatial interventions to create an attractive service complex with refectory, cafeteria, student union, student club and library. Except for the load-bearing structure, all partitioning walls were removed and a courtyard created in the centre to provide natural illumination and ventilation for the spaces around it. The audiovisual workspaces face onto the peaceful interior courtyard.

On three sides of the building, a continuous band of windows with louvres as sunshades lends the façade a characteristic contemporary appearance.

Die neue Außenfassade zeigt ein aktualisiertes Design (oben). Der neu eingefügte Innenhof (unten).

The new external façade (top) lends the building a contemporary design and clads the new interior courtyard (bottom).

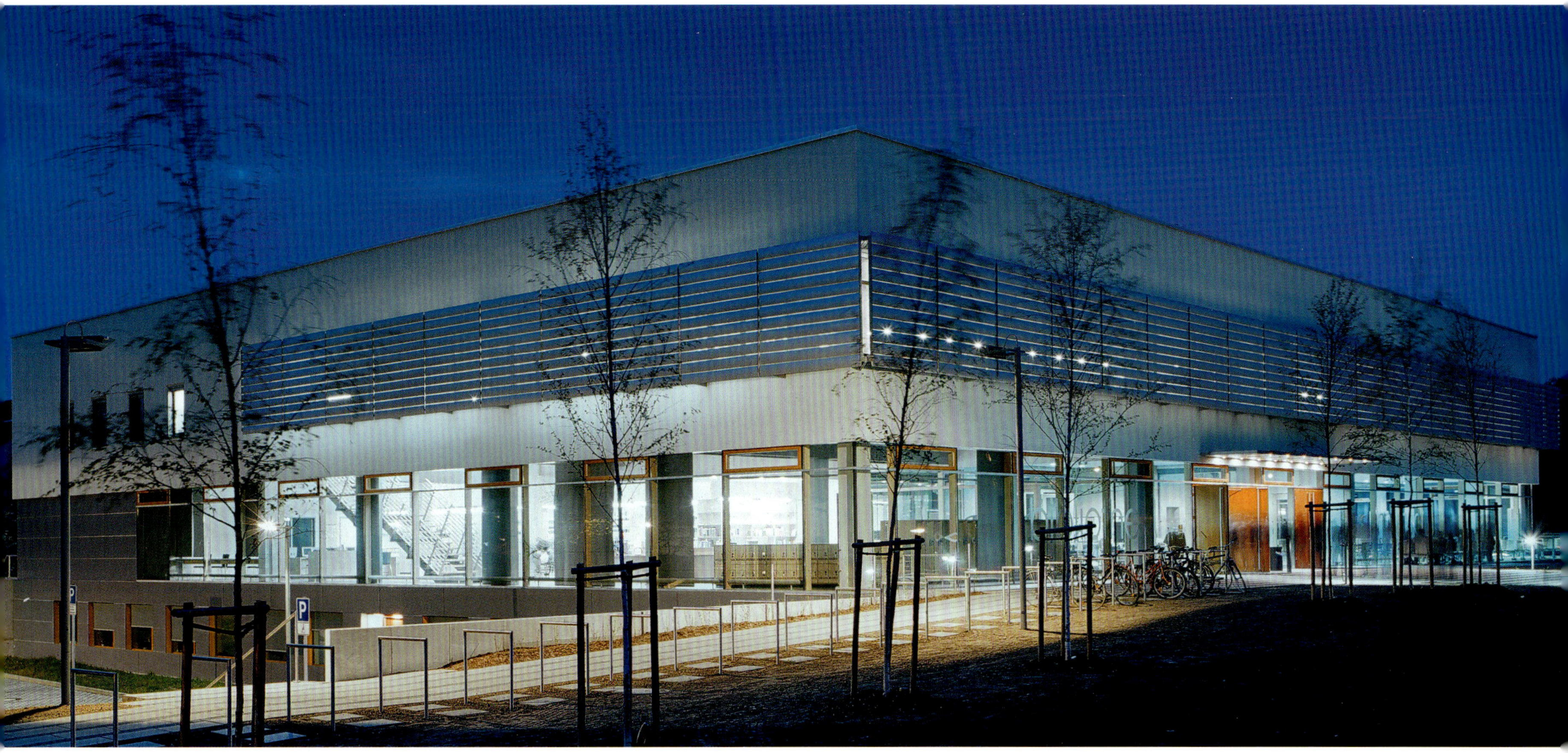

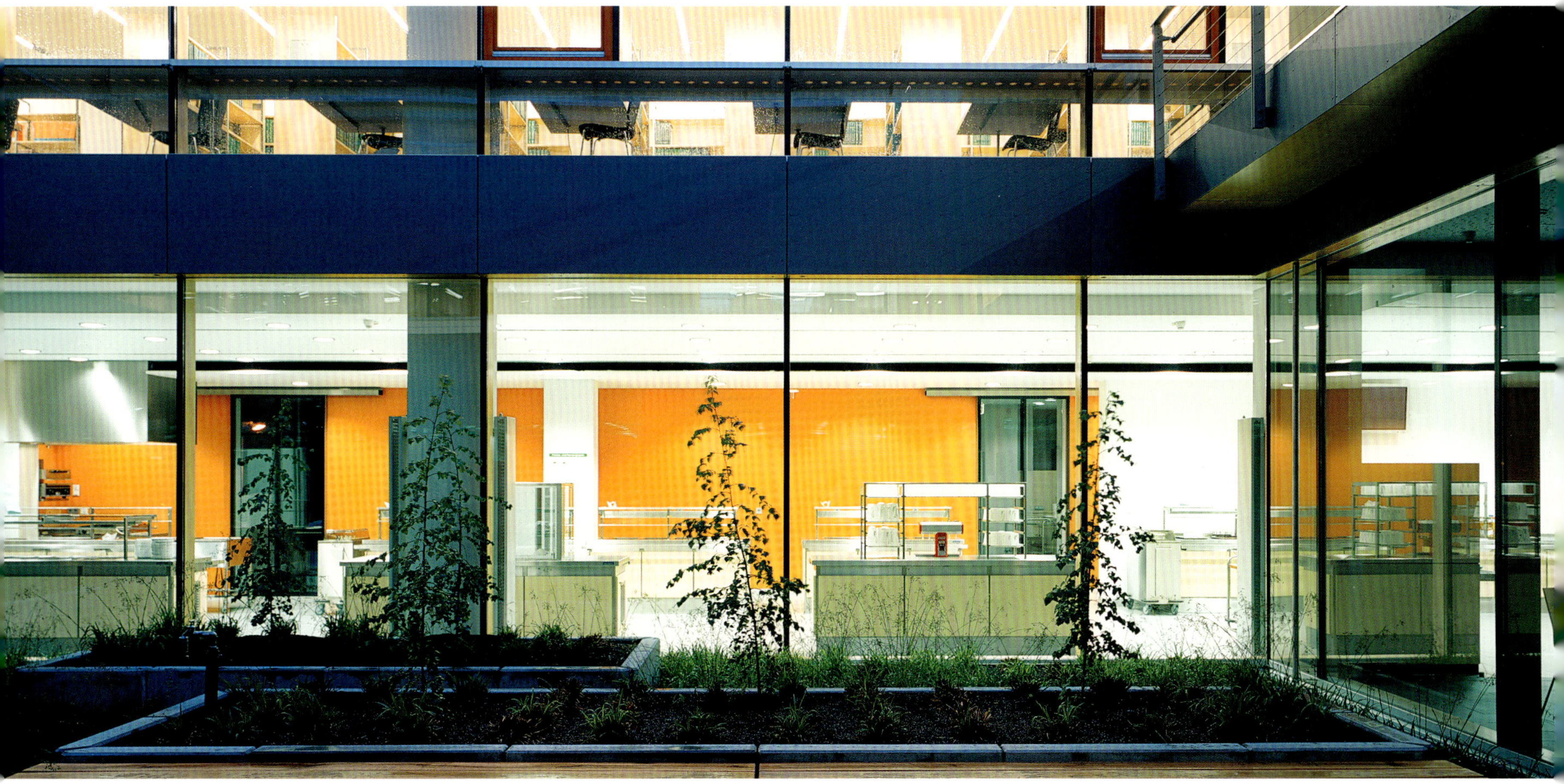

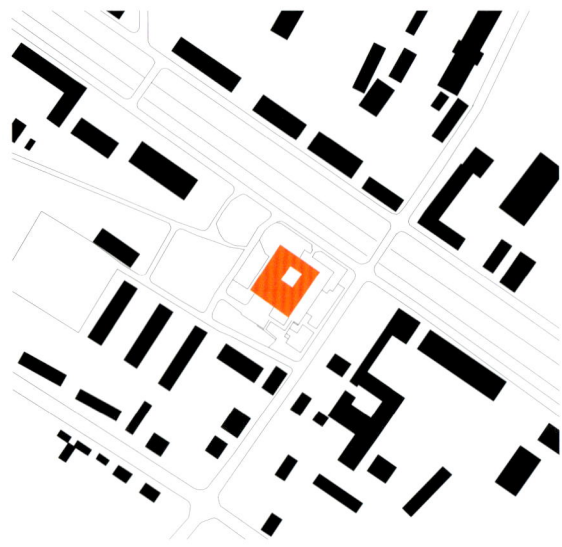

Der Erker im Innenhof beherbergt die audiovisuellen Arbeitsplätze.
The projecting bay in the courtyard contains the audiovisual workplaces.

Treppenhaus, Bibliothek, audiovisuelle Arbeitsplätze und Speisesaal des Gebäudes mit gemischter Nutzung. In den Räumen der Bibliothek und der Mensa ist der Charakter des Betonskelettbaus noch erlebbar.

Stair, library, audiovisual workspaces and refectory in the multi-functional building. In the library and the refectory, the character of the concrete frame building is still noticeable.

WORLD TRADE CENTER
DRESDEN

"Elbflorenz", der Name der geschätzten Schokoladenfabrik, die hier bis zur Wende die beliebten gleichnamigen Pralinen produzierte, klingt noch im Namen des Vier-Sterne-Hotels mit 280 Betten nach, das zum Komplex des World Trade Center Dresden gehört. Das umfangreiche Projekt war eine der ersten größeren Entwicklungsmaßnahmen in der Dresdner Innenstadt nach der Wiedervereinigung. Auch das Boulevardtheater „Komödie", die Stadtbibliothek und eine Shoppingmall ergänzen die zentrale Büronutzung des World Trade Center, eines von weltweit 318 WTC, die sich durch standardisierte Leistungsmerkmale des Büroangebots und der Serviceeinrichtungen wie Kongressräume oder Dolmetscherdienst auszeichnen. Der Theatersaal mit seinen 660 Plätzen kann multifunktional als Konferenzraum oder als Ballsaal mit Gastronomiebestuhlung genutzt werden.

Das Ensemble aus sieben Einzelgebäuden ist durch eine großzügige Passage zusammengefasst. Der Stuttgarter Ingenieur Jörg Schlaich hatte die filigrane Glastonne über der Passage und den raumschließenden membranartigen Glasvorhang entwickelt. Mit einer großen Geste des dramatisch spitz zulaufenden Baukörpers entlang der Ammonstraße öffnet sich die Passage gegen die Freiberger Straße und komplimentiert die Passanten in das Haus.

"Elbflorenz", the name of the respected chocolate factory that produced the much-loved chocolates of the same name until the end of the GDR, is echoed in the name of the 4-star hotel with 280 beds that belongs to the complex of the World Trade Center in Dresden. The comprehensive project is one of the first larger projects that was undertaken in inner city Dresden after the reunification. The popular theatre venue "Komödie", the city library and a shopping mall augment the primary office function of the World Trade Center, one of 318 WTCs worldwide which offer a standardised set of office facilities and services including congress spaces, interpreting services and so on. The theatre auditorium that seats 660 is a multifunctional space that can be used as a conference space or as a ballroom with dining tables and full catering.

The ensemble consists of seven individual buildings arranged around a spacious arcade. The filigree glass barrel roof and membrane-like glass curtain walling at either end was developed by the Stuttgart engineer Jörg Schlaich. In a sweeping gesture at the end of the dramatically tapering building along the Ammonstraße, the arcade opens onto the Freiberger Straße, ushering passers-by into the arcade.

Die Passage mit dem Charakter einer überdeckten Straße bildet einen geschützten Innenraum zum Flanieren.

The arcade has a character similar to a covered street and forms an enclosed urban promenade for strolling and meeting.

Ein Büroturm akzentuiert weithin sichtbar das Ensemble des World Trade Center. Der Westflügel öffnet sich mit dynamischem Schwung und diese Geste lädt Passanten zum Eintritt in die Passage.

An office tower announces the presence of the World Trade Center ensemble far and wide. The dynamic sweep of the west wing opens out onto the street, inviting passers-by to enter the building.

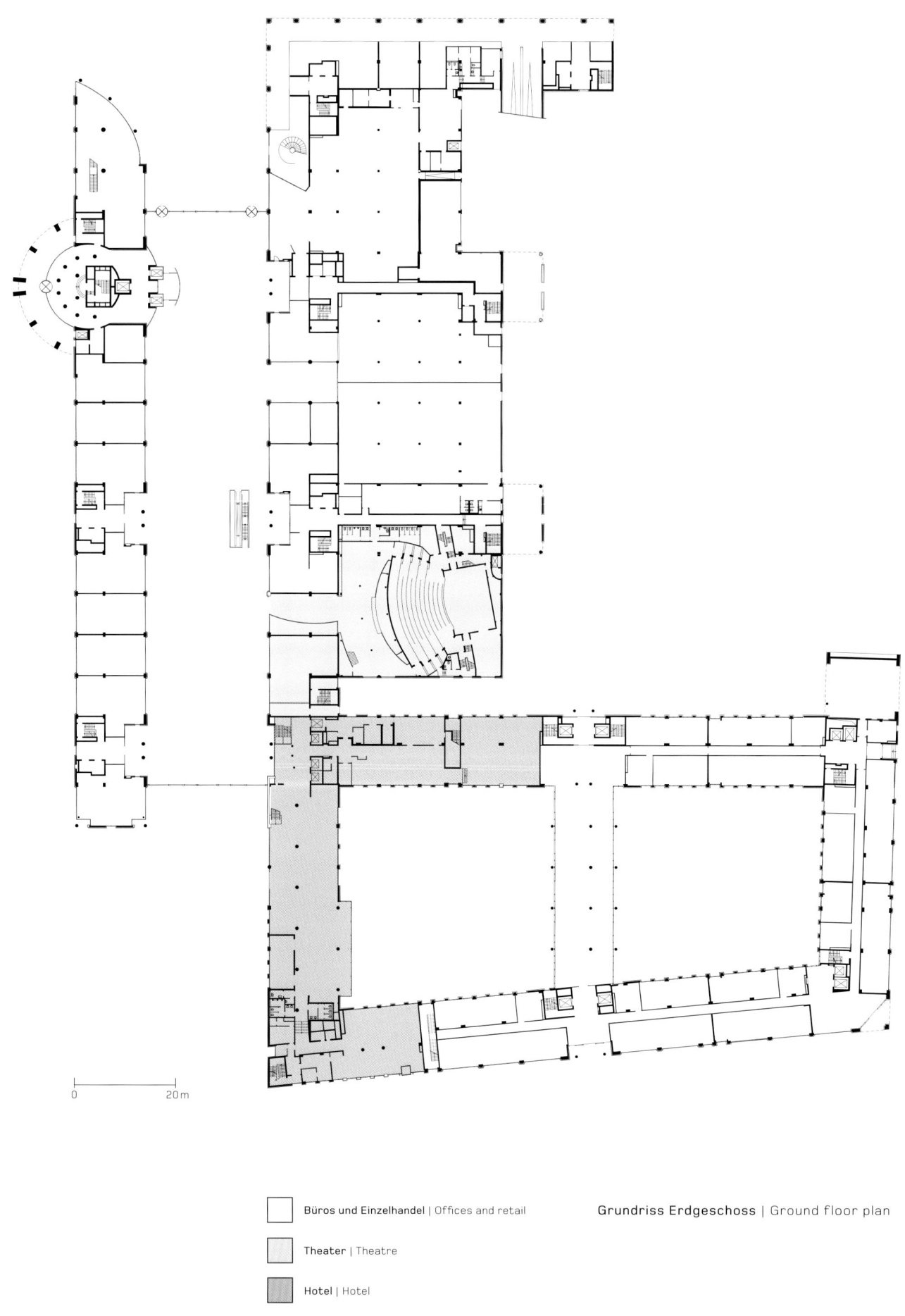

0   20m

Büros und Einzelhandel | Offices and retail

Theater | Theatre

Hotel | Hotel

Grundriss Erdgeschoss | Ground floor plan

Den markanten städtebaulichen Akzent setzt das World Trade Center jedoch durch den gläsernen Turm, der sich mit 16 Geschossen über dem Ensemble erhebt und allein 10.000 Quadratmeter Bürofläche bietet. Zwar war der Turm schlanker geplant, doch höher durfte er aus Rücksicht auf die historische Silhouette der Stadt nicht werden. Die übrigen Trakte des Ensembles sind nach gängigem Dresdner Command mit Sandsteinplatten verkleidet. Die zweigeschossige Geschäftszone und das Kragdach über einem gläsernem Staffelgeschoss vertreiben jedoch nostalgische Anwandlungen und weisen das World Trade Center als modernes Stück Stadtkultur aus. Noch nicht gelungen ist es von Seiten der Stadt, das städtebauliche Umfeld zu ergänzen, wie es der Planung des WTC-Areals zu Grunde liegt.

The World Trade Center's most prominent urban feature is, however, the glazed tower, which with its 16 storeys stands high above the ensemble, providing 10,000 square metres of office space alone. The tower was originally intended to be more slender but it was not allowed to be any higher so as not to impact on Dresden's historic silhouette. The remaining wings of the ensemble are clad, in typical Dresden manner, with sandstone panels. The two-storey business zone and the cantilevering roof over the stepped-back glazed upper storeys, however, dispel any nostalgic inclinations and identify the World Trade Center as a piece of modern urban architecture. As yet, the city of Dresden has not been able to develop the surrounding area as originally envisaged in the master plan for the WTC complex.

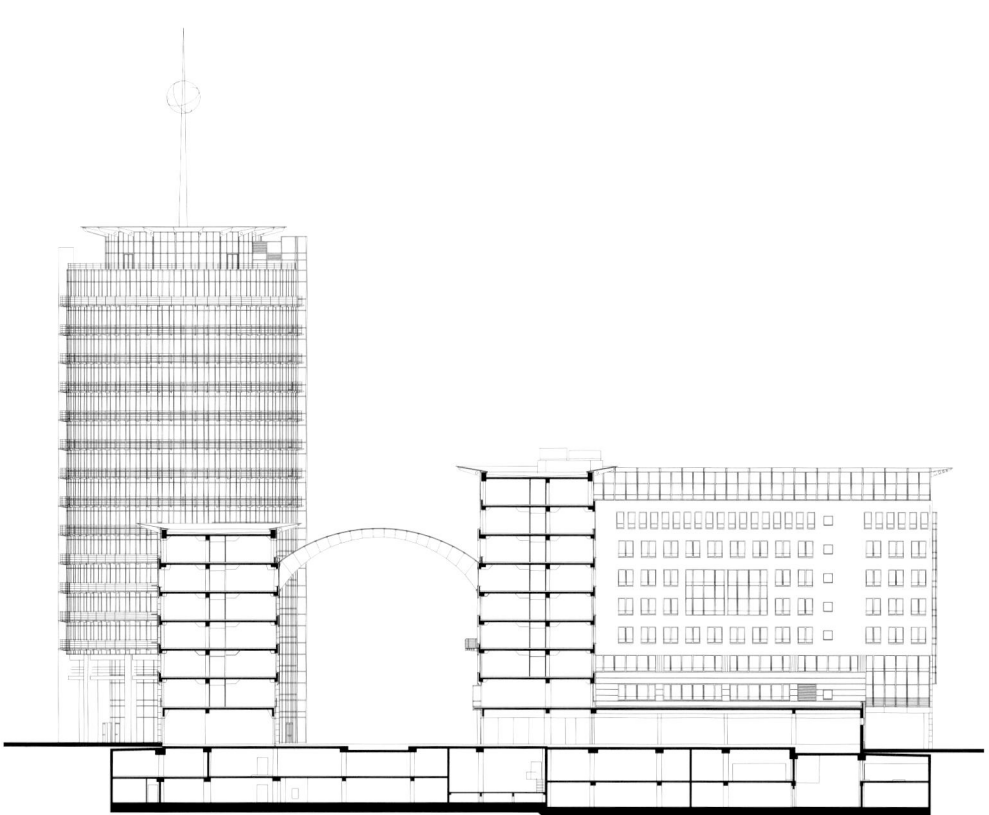

Schnitt | Section

Hoteltrakt, Hoteleingang und Saal des Boulevard-
theaters. Vielfältige Nutzungen sind im World Trade
Center vereint.

Hotel wing, hotel entrance and the auditorium in the
"Komödie" theatre. The World Trade Center unites a
variety of different uses.

ALTE OBERPOSTDIREKTION
FORMER POST OFFICE HEADQUARTERS
HAMBURG

Der stattliche Neorenaissancebau, die größte der von Generalpostmeister Heinrich von Stephan im ganzen Reich initiierten Oberpostdirektionen, entstand 1883-87 am Stephansplatz nach einem Entwurf des Berliner Architekten Julius Raschdorff und wurde um die Jahrhundertwende entlang des Gorch-Fock-Walls nach Westen erweitert. Bei der Sanierung des Erweiterungsbaus für ein Bankhaus ging es darum, die historische Substanz des Baudenkmals mit der prächtigen bauplastisch geschmückten Fassade und originalen stuckierten Räumen und Treppenanlagen im Inneren zu sichern und zum Teil zu rekonstruieren, um sie wieder zu repräsentativer Wirkung kommen zu lassen. Gleichzeitig waren die Innenräume im Interesse einer zeitgemäßen Nutzung neu zu gliedern. Neue Bauteile wie die gläsernen Eingangsbereiche, Trennwände und Deckenspiegel wurden in moderner Architektursprache eingefügt und verbinden sich mit den historischen Partien zu einem attraktiven Gestaltungskonzept.

The impressive neo-renaissance building, the largest of the post office headquarters to be founded under Postmaster General Heinrich von Stephan in the entire German Empire, was built from 1883-87 on the Stephansplatz according to a design by the Berlin architect Julius Raschdorff. Around the turn of the century the building was extended to the west along the Gorch-Fock-Wall. The renovation of the extension for use by a bank focussed on the restoration and partial reconstruction of the historical building substance with its magnificent modulated façade and original stucco ceilings in the rooms and staircases, restoring it to its original prestigious appearance. At the same time the interior spaces were restructured to fulfil contemporary usage requirements. New elements such as glazed entrance lobbies, partitions and ceiling panels were inserted, introducing a modern architectural vocabulary that together with the historical building substance results in an attractive design concept.

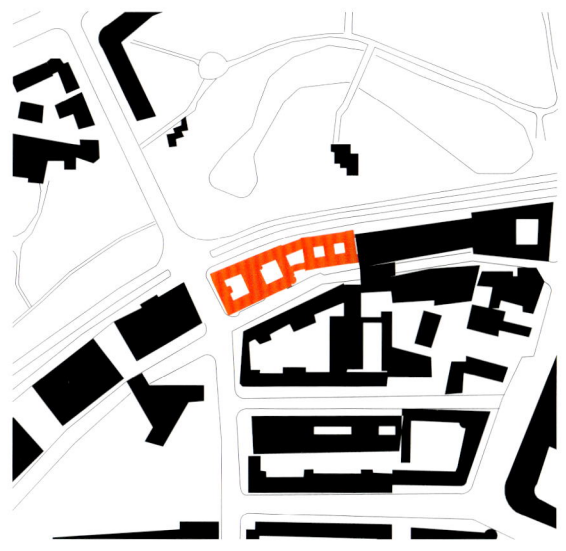

Das Treppenhaus wurde nach historischem Vorbild rekonstruiert. In den Fluren erinnern die schmuckvollen gussei-
sernen Säulen an die Geschichte des Hauses während
in die Büros das Design der Gegenwart eingezogen ist.

The staircase has been reconstructed according to
historical details. In the hallways, only the ornamental
cast-iron columns recall the history of the building,
while in the offices an entirely contemporary interior
design has been implemented.

DOMAQUARÉE
BERLIN

Nach dem Abriss des Palasthotels aus DDR-Zeiten bestand die Aufgabe darin, das Stadtgefüge dieses historischen Viertels an der Spree zurückzugewinnen und die ehemaligen Blockränder und Straßenzüge wieder zu besetzen. Nach einem Masterplan der Architekten Martin + Pächter aus dem Jahr 1994 entstand ein Ensemble aus vier Einzelbauten, einem Hotel, zwei Bürogebäuden und einem Wohnhaus, die durch glasgedeckte Passagen miteinander verbunden sind. Eine Passage größter Offenheit lädt die Passanten ein, ohne Schwellenangst den Weg ins Blockinnere zwischen dem Radisson SAS-Hotel und dem Bürogebäude zu nehmen. Zwei Baumreihen und Wasserspiele signalisieren den urbanen Charakter der überdachten Heiligegeistgasse und leiten über zum rückwärtigen Heiligegeistkirchplatz.

Die kraftvoll reliefierten, durch Licht- und Schattenspiel belebten Natursteinfassaden erinnern in einer modernen Sprache an die historische Großstadtarchitektur. Die beiden zurückgeneigten Dachgeschosse sind dagegen mit einer dünnen Folienhaut überzogen.

After the demolition of the Palasthotel built during the GDR, the task was to restore the urban form of the historic quarter on the banks of the Spree and to re-establish the former line of the perimeter block and the streets. According to a master plan drawn up in 1994 by the architects Martin + Pächter, an ensemble was built that consists of four individual buildings – a hotel, two office buildings and an apartment building – connected with one another by covered glazed passageways. The largest and most open passageway between the Radisson SAS Hotel and the office building invites pedestrians to pass through to the interior of the block from the street. Two rows of trees and fountains help signify the urban character of the covered Heiligegeistgasse which leads on to the Heiligegeistkirchplatz at the rear.

The strongly modulated stone façade, enlivened by the play of light and shadow, echoes the urban presence of the historical buildings in a modern architectural language. By contrast, the two upper stories slope away from view and are encased in a thin foil skin.

Appartementhaus und Hotel bilden ein Gegenüber zum Berliner Dom. Die Querpassage ist auf die Domkuppel ausgerichtet.

The apartment house and hotel stand opposite the Berliner Dom. The axis of the smaller passageway is aligned with the dome of the cathedral.

Hotel und Bürohaus warten mit halböffentlichen Hallen auf, die zu den attraktivsten Lichthöfen im neuen Berlin zählen. Die Trapezform des Grundstück zeichnet sich in allen Grundrissen der Anlage bis hin zu den Hotelzimmern ab. Im Atrium des Hotels Radisson SAS, gleichzeitig Hotelfoyer und Café, steht das weltweit höchste Meerwasseraquarium, ein Zylinder aus Acrylglas, in dessen Innerem ein zweigeschossiger Aufzug zur Erschließung der Dachgeschosse, aber auch zur Beobachtung der Fische auf und ab fährt. Gläserne Panorama-Aufzüge, Balkons und die Erschließungsbrücken zwischen dem Aufzug im "AquaDom" und den Dachgeschossen ermöglichen das Erleben des spektakulären Raums aus verschiedenen Blickwinkeln. Die beiden voll verglasten Dachgeschosse mit grandioser Aussicht sind prädestiniert für dem Publikum offene Nutzungen wie Fitness und Gastronomie.

Das Wohnhaus, an der ruhigen Spreeseite gelegen, bietet 75 sehr unterschiedliche, großzügig geschnittene Mietwohnungen gehobenen Standards. Die Erschließungsflure liegen an zweigeschossigen Wintergärten und sind natürlich belichtet.

The hotel and office building each have a semi-public entrance atrium, which are among the finest to be found in Berlin. The trapezoidal form of the site is apparent in the floor plans of all the buildings, right down to the hotel rooms. In the centre of the atrium of the Radisson SAS Hotel, which serves simultaneously as foyer and café, stands the world's tallest seawater aquarium, an acrylic glass cylinder with a two-storey lift that travels up and down through its centre, providing access to the uppermost floors and affording a view of the fish around it. Glazed panorama lifts, balconies and access bridges between the lift in the "AquaDom" and the top storey allow the spectacular space to be experienced from numerous different viewpoints. The two fully glazed storeys at roof level offer a magnificent view and are predestined for publicly accessible functions such as fitness and restaurants.

The apartment block is located on the quieter side towards the Spree and contains 75 very differently proportioned, spacious luxury flats available for rent. The access hallways are arranged around two-storey conservatories and naturally lit.

Ansicht | Elevation

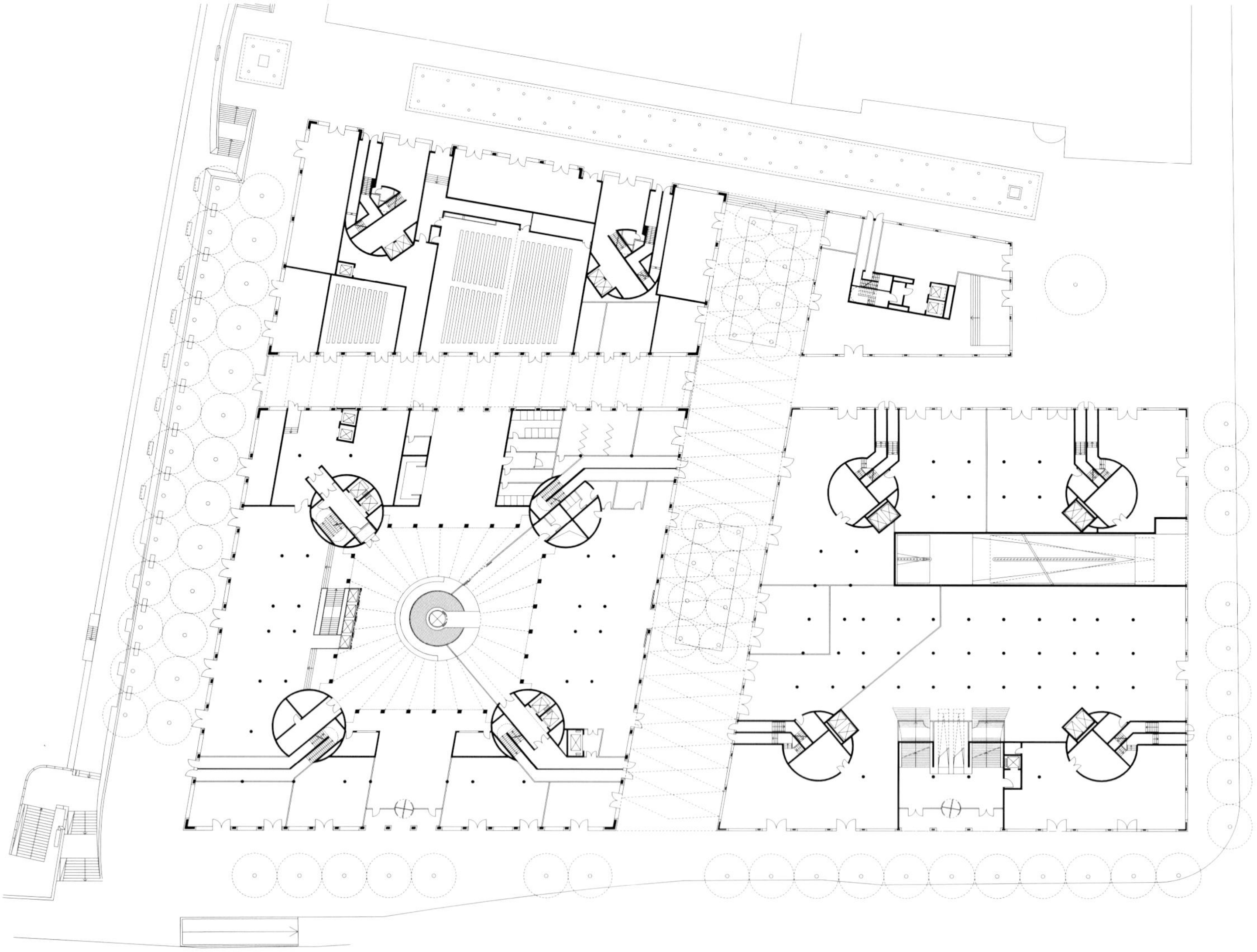

Grundriss Erdgeschoss | Ground floor plan

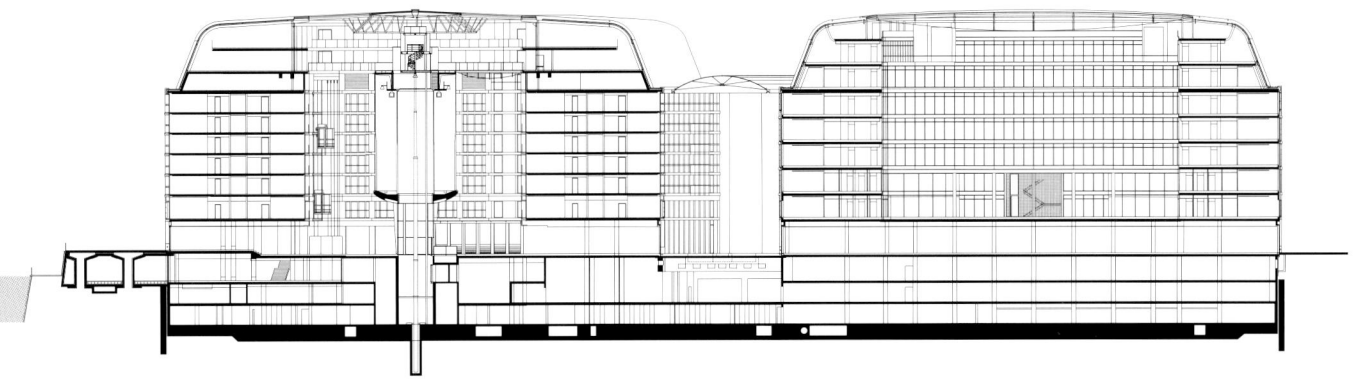

Längsschnitt | Longitudinal section

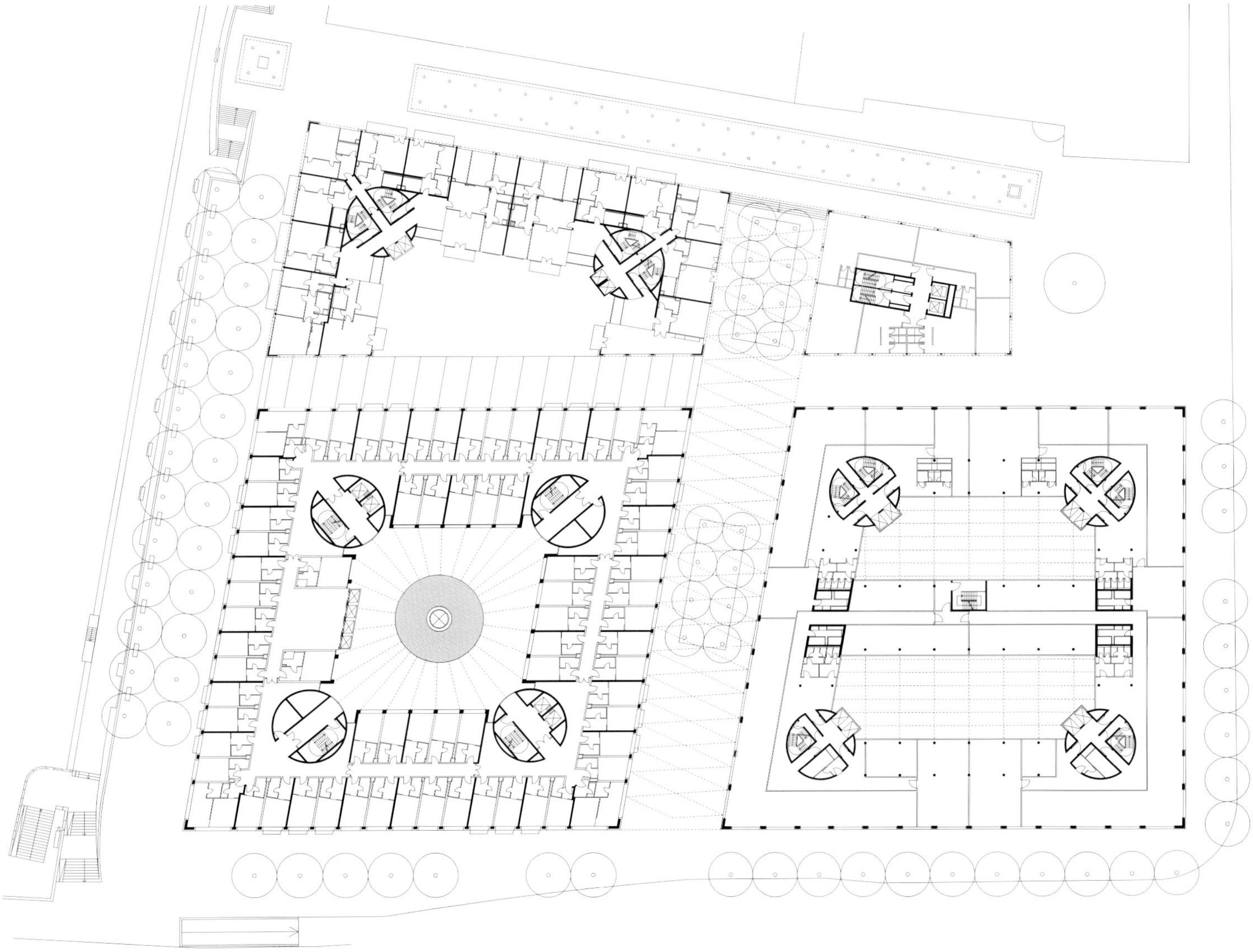

Grundriss Regelgeschoss | Typical floor plan

0   20m

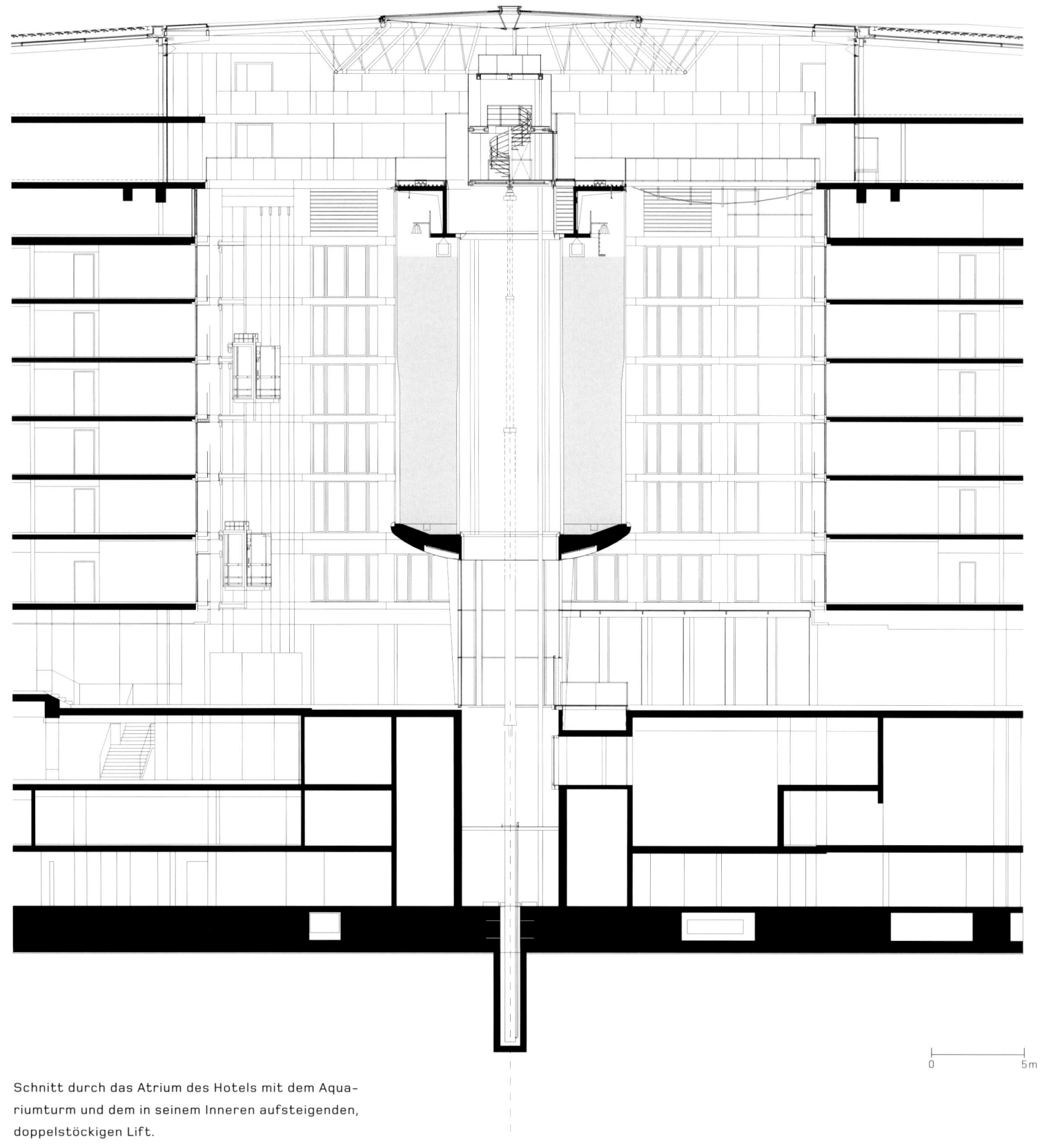

Schnitt durch das Atrium des Hotels mit dem Aqua-
riumturm und dem in seinem Inneren aufsteigenden,
doppelstöckigen Lift.

Section through the hotel atrium with the cylindrical
aquarium tower and the two-storey lift that ascends
through its centre.

Die Außen- und Innenfassaden des Hotels sind von
einer kraftvollen Tektonik geprägt.

The external and internal façades of the hotel share
a pronounced tectonic modulation.

Das Aquarium ist von Bar und Café im Foyer und von den innen liegenden Hotelzimmern aus zu erleben. Der Wellnessbereich liegt im Untergeschoss an der Spreeseite (Bild rechts unten).

The aquarium can be seen from the bar and café in the foyer and from the inward-facing hotel rooms. The wellness area is located in the basement on the Spree side (bottom right).

Der östliche Bauteil des Quartiers wird von Büroetagen eingenommen. Links Fassade, Eingangshalle mit Rolltreppen ins Atrium und Wasserlauf, rechts daneben eine Wasserwand im Atrium des ersten Obergeschosses.

Rechts oben Bürolandschaft mit „Denkerzellen" und „Nomaden-Arbeitsplätzen" sowie eine informelle Kommunikationseinheit im Musterbüro (rechts unten).

The eastern section of the quarter contains offices. Top left, a detail of the façade, bottom left the entrance hall with escalators and water cascade, near left a water wall in the atrium on the first floor.

On the right a typical office with "thinking cells" and "touch-down" workstations, bottom right an informal staff area in the show office.

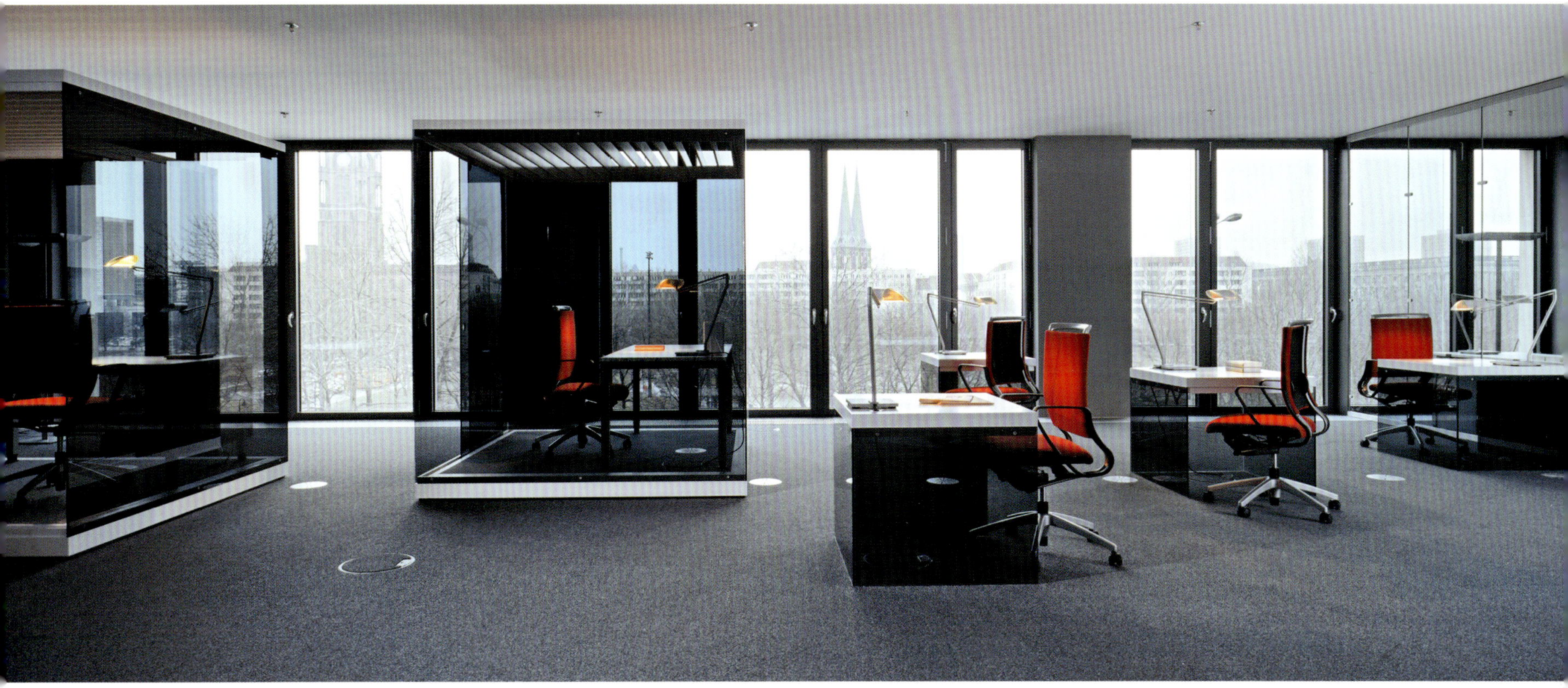

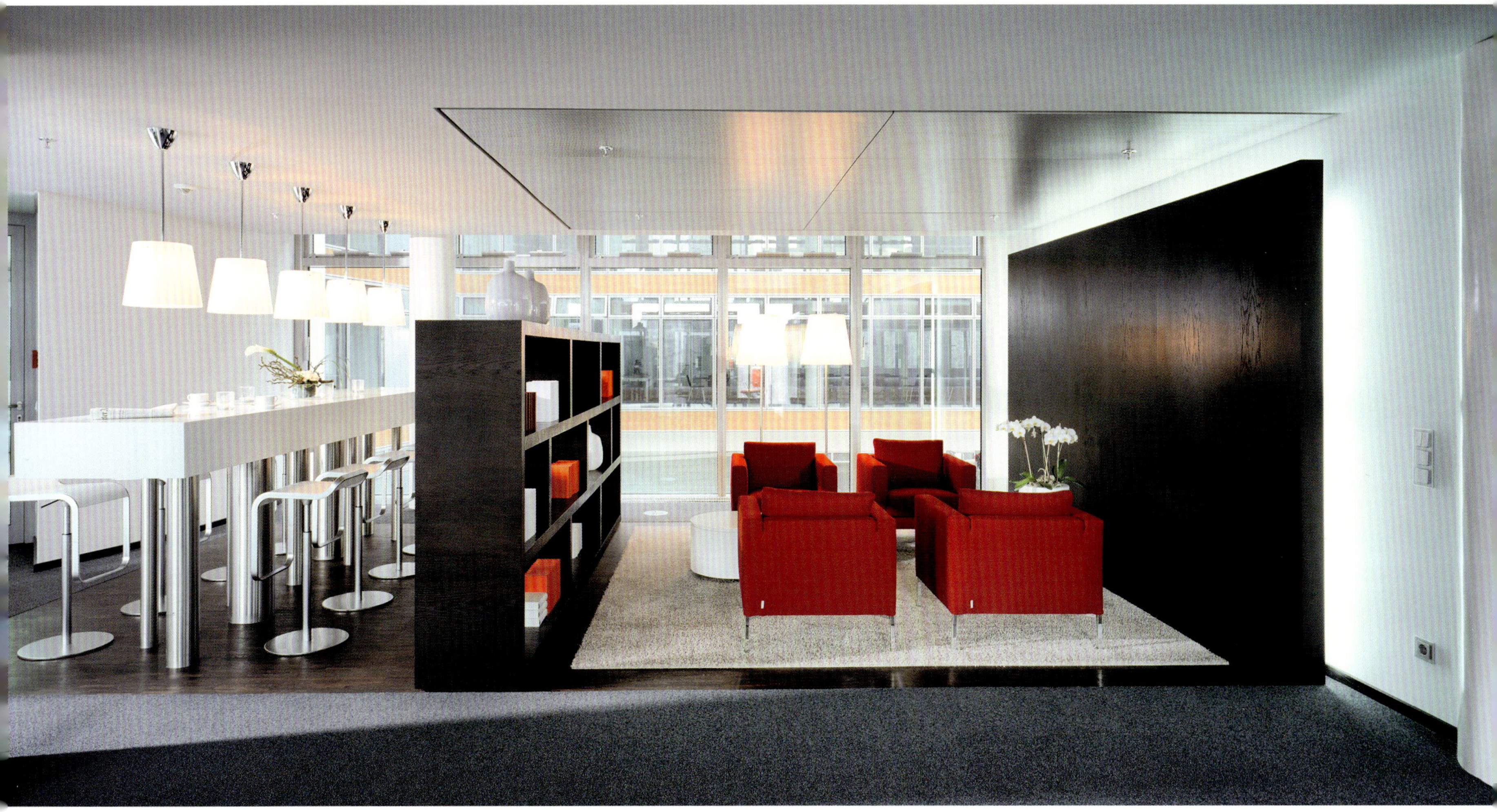

Im nördlichen Gebäude des Ensembles sind großzügige Appartements untergebracht. Auch dessen Naturstein-fassade zeigt ein kräftiges Relief. In der Eingangshalle befindet sich ein Empfang. Die Wohnungen sind geprägt von fließenden Räumen und bodentiefen Fensterfronten mit bester Aussicht auf die geschichtsträchtige Umgebung.

The building at the north of the ensemble contains spacious apartments. Here too the stone façade exhibits a vigorous surface texture. The entrance hall has its own reception desk. The open plan apartments have floor-to-ceiling windows affording an excellent view of the historical surroundings.

INTERCITY HOTEL
HAMBURG

Das InterCity Hotel am Glockengießerwall gegenüber der Hamburger Kunsthalle ist städtebaulich als Komplettierung des Straßenblocks konzipiert. Der Eckbaukörper übernimmt die Traufhöhen der Nachbarschaft oder stellt sie wieder her. Mit der zweigeschossigen Sockelzone zeigt das Haus großstädtischen Charakter. Die Natursteinfassade mit ihrer fein reliefierten Tektonik ist die Antwort auf die historistische Kunsthalle aus dem 19. Jahrhundert. Als Besonderheit weist das Haus eine dezentrale Lüftung mit Klimamodulen in jedem einzelnen Raum auf, die individuell konditionierte Frischluft in die Zimmer bringen und gleichzeitig den Lärm der Hauptverkehrsstraße abhalten. Dieses System erlaubte es auch, trotz enger Bebauungsplanvorgaben großzügige Raumhöhen zu realisieren.

The InterCity Hotel on the Glockengießerwall opposite the Kunsthalle art gallery in Hamburg completes the corner of an urban block. The building picks up and reinforces the eaves lines of the neighbouring buildings. With its two-storey arcade at ground level it firmly asserts its urban character. The finely modulated tectonics of the natural stone façade responds to that of the historical Kunsthalle from the 19th century. Unusually, the building utilises a decentralised ventilation system with air-conditioning units in each room that provide individually conditioned fresh air and reduce traffic noise from outside. This system made it possible to achieve generous ceiling heights despite the tight constraints of the urban development plan.

Schräg gegenüber dem Hamburger Hauptbahnhof
empfängt das InterCity Hotel seine Gäste mit einem
Arkadenrestaurant und einer zweigeschossigen Halle.
Der Frühstücksraum hat Blickbeziehung zu den einfah-
renden Zügen.

The InterCity Hotel across from the central railway
station in Hamburg greets its guests with an arcaded
restaurant and two-storey entrance hall. From the
breakfast room guests have a direct view of the
arriving trains.

GRUNDSCHULE HEIDHORST
HEIDHORST PRIMARY SCHOOL
HAMBURG

Wie unterteilt man eine Schule in überschaubare Einheiten ohne den Gesamtzusammenhang zu zerstören? Wie vermeidet man lange Flure, wie gewinnt man trotz serieller Nutzungseinheiten räumliche Vielfalt?

Die Grundschule im Heidhorst in Hamburg-Bergedorf ist in sechs „Klassenhäuser" und einen Kopfbau gegliedert, wobei die Zwischenhöfe durch einen Luftbalken überbrückt sind, um die Großform zu erhalten. Das gemeinsame Rückgrat zur Erschließung weitet sich mehrmals zu Galerien und Wintergärten und bietet beim Durchschreiten ein abwechslungsreiches Raumerlebnis aus offenen und geschlossenen, hellen und dunklen Zonen. Der westliche Zwischenhof ist multifunktional als Haupteingang einerseits und lichte Aula andererseits ausgebildet. Rotbunte Ziegelwände auch im Inneren, hellbraune Holzfenster sowie Holz- und Natursteinböden bestimmen die Palette natürlicher Materialien und prägen die fast wohnlich zu nennende Atmosphäre.

How does one divide a school into distinct elements without destroying its overall coherence? How does one avoid long corridors, and how does one ensure spatial variety despite the serial nature of the functional units?

The primary school in the Heidhorst area in Hamburg-Bergedorf is divided into six "classroom buildings" and a further entrance building with courtyards in between that are bound together by a brick beam that delineates the perimeter of the overall form. The backbone of the central access route widens and narrows repeatedly, forming galleries and conservatories and creating a succession of spaces that alternate between open and closed and light and dark zones. The multipurpose courtyard to the west serves both as the main entrance as well as an open assembly hall. Reddish brick walls, used also in the interiors, light brown timber windows as well as wood and stone floors dominate the palette of natural materials and create what one could almost call a homely atmosphere.

Grundriss Erdgeschoss | Ground floor plan

Wie durch Bilderrahmen blickt man aus den Schulräumen in die Landschaft. In einem der Zwischenräume der Schultrakte liegt die Aula (Bild links Mitte), gegenüber die Eingangshalle (Bild rechts unten).

From the classrooms one looks out over the landscape as if through a picture frame. One of the intermediary spaces serves as the assembly hall (centre left), opposite it the entrance (bottom right).

ALTE MÄLZEREI
OLD MALTINGS
BERLIN

Büroräume mit dem besonderen Fluidum der Berliner Fabrikarchitektur des 19. Jahrhunderts sind auf sieben Geschossen in der ehemaligen Mälzerei der Löwenbrauerei in der Friedenstraße untergebracht. Die mit allerlei neoromanischem Dekor einer Kaiserpfalz ausgeschmückten Fassaden erfuhren eine Sanierung und eine behutsame Vergrößerung der Fensteröffnungen, um die Belichtungsverhältnisse der verhältnismäßig tiefen Grundrisse zu verbessern. Im Inneren entfaltet sich der Charme der historischen Bausubstanz durch die weitgehend freigelegten Ziegelwände. Der weitere Ausbau der Büroetagen wurde durch den Eigentümer vorgenommen.

Mit dem Umbau ist es gelungen, das günstig gelegene Gebäude optimal für Bürozwecke zu nutzen und gleichzeitig das charakteristische Baudenkmal mit Industriepatina am Rand des historischen Brauereiensembles in Berlin-Friedrichshain als stadtbildprägendes Kulturdenkmal zu erhalten.

The seven floors of the former maltings of the Löwen Brewery in the Friedenstraße have been converted to provide office spaces suffused with the atmosphere of 19th century Berlin industrial architecture. The façades, richly decorated with neo-Romanesque ornamentation as if an imperial palace, were restored and the window openings enlarged sensitively to allow more light into the comparatively deep spaces within. Inside, the charm of the historical building substance is communicated through the exposed brick walls. The fitting out and furnishing of the office floors was undertaken by the owner.

The conversion successfully adapts the maltings for office purposes while maintaining the industrial patina and characteristic of the listed building, which is located in an advantageous position on the edge of the historic brewery complex, a local landmark and cultural monument in Berlin-Friedrichshain.

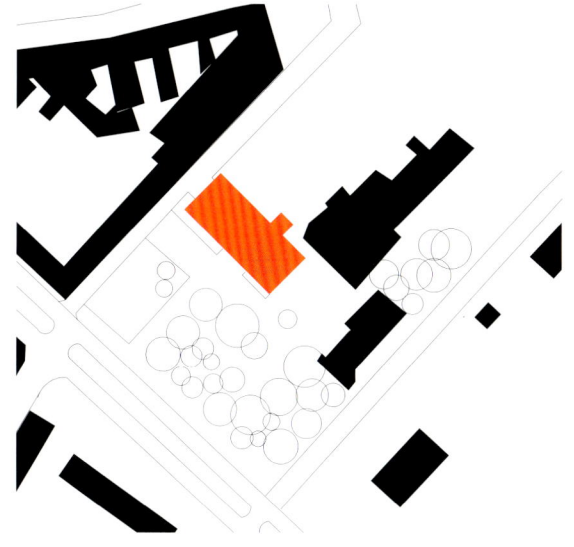

Die Eingangshalle stimmt auf den Charakter des Hauses
ein, das Geschichte atmet und Moderne präsentiert.
Die historische Hülle, von hundertzwanzig Jahren inten-
sivem Gebrauch gezeichnet, steht im reizvollen Kontrast
zur Perfektion der modernen Einbauten.

The entrance hall already hints at the character of
the house, visibly modern yet suffused with history.
The historic exterior, its surface marked by 120 years
of intensive use, contrasts strikingly with clean lines
of the modern insertions.

Die historischen Fassaden wurden rekonstruiert und behutsam mit zusätzlichen Fensteröffnungen versehen. Auch im Inneren konnten Partien aus der Ursprungszeit erhalten werden und als dekorative Elemente in die neue Innenraumgestaltung integriert werden.

The historic façades were reconstructed and additional openings sensitively added. In the interior too it was possible to retain sections of the original substance as decorative elements in the new design.

GALERIE ARNDT
ARNDT GALLERY
BERLIN

Der kleine Galeriebau steht in einem der Hackeschen Höfe, einem touristischen Brennpunkt in Berlin-Mitte. Eine weitergehende formale Reduktion des Entwurfs ist kaum denkbar, denn der Baukörper des Einraums besteht aus einem Betonrahmen, der die beiden Giebelwände und die Deckplatte bildet, und den beiden Längswänden aus Glas. In der Vorderfront gibt es lediglich eine Glastür; Nebenräume sind nicht vorgesehen, die sparsame Haustechnik ist im Boden verborgen. Ein Archetypus als gebautes Manifest also, der ausschließlich für Ausstellungszwecke gedacht ist.

The small gallery stands in one of the courtyards of the Hackesche Höfe, a tourist attraction in Berlin-Mitte. It would be hard to imagine a more formal reduction of the design; the building consists of a concrete frame that forms the ceiling panel and two end walls, and two long side walls that are glazed entirely. In the front face there is a glass door, nothing more. There are no other ancillary spaces and the minimal technical installations are concealed in the floor. It is the archetype of a built manifesto, a space conceived exclusively to exhibit.

GESCHÄFTSHAUS KURFÜRSTENDAMM
SHOPS AND OFFICES KURFÜRSTENDAMM
BERLIN

Die Architektur des Kurfürstendamms in Berlin-Charlottenburg, soweit sie den Krieg überdauert hat, ist geprägt vom wilhelminischen Pomp der historistischen Fassaden und ist reichhaltig mit Erkern, Dachgauben und opulenten Ecktürmen ausgestattet. Der Neubau an der Ecke zur Knesebeckstraße reflektiert diesen Typus des Wohn- und Geschäftshauses mit erkerartigen Vorsprüngen, mit einer gerundeten Gebäudeecke und mit zwei ellipsenförmigen Turmgeschossen als markanter Eckbetonung. Statt der gründerzeitlichen Putzfassaden kam ein heller Sandstein mit scharrierter Oberfläche und ähnlicher Farbwirkung zum Einsatz. Der Bau enthält sich jedoch historisierender Bauzier und korrespondiert stattdessen durch seine Fassade mit sorgfältig detaillierter, moderner Vertikalgliederung mit den Nachbarbauten aus den fünfziger Jahren.

Of the architecture on the Kurfürstendamm in Berlin-Charlottenburg that survived the Second World War, most is characterised by Wilhelminian pomp: historical façades rich with bay windows, roof dormers and opulent corner turrets. The new building on the corner of the Knesebeckstrasse reflects this type of residential and commercial building with bay-like projections, a rounded corner to the building and a two-storey elliptical turret marking the corner. However, instead of a rendered façade like the buildings from the turn of the century, the building is faced with a light bush-hammered sandstone of a similar basic colour. The building eschews historicist decorations, corresponding instead through its carefully detailed, modern vertical delineation with the neighbouring buildings from the fifties.

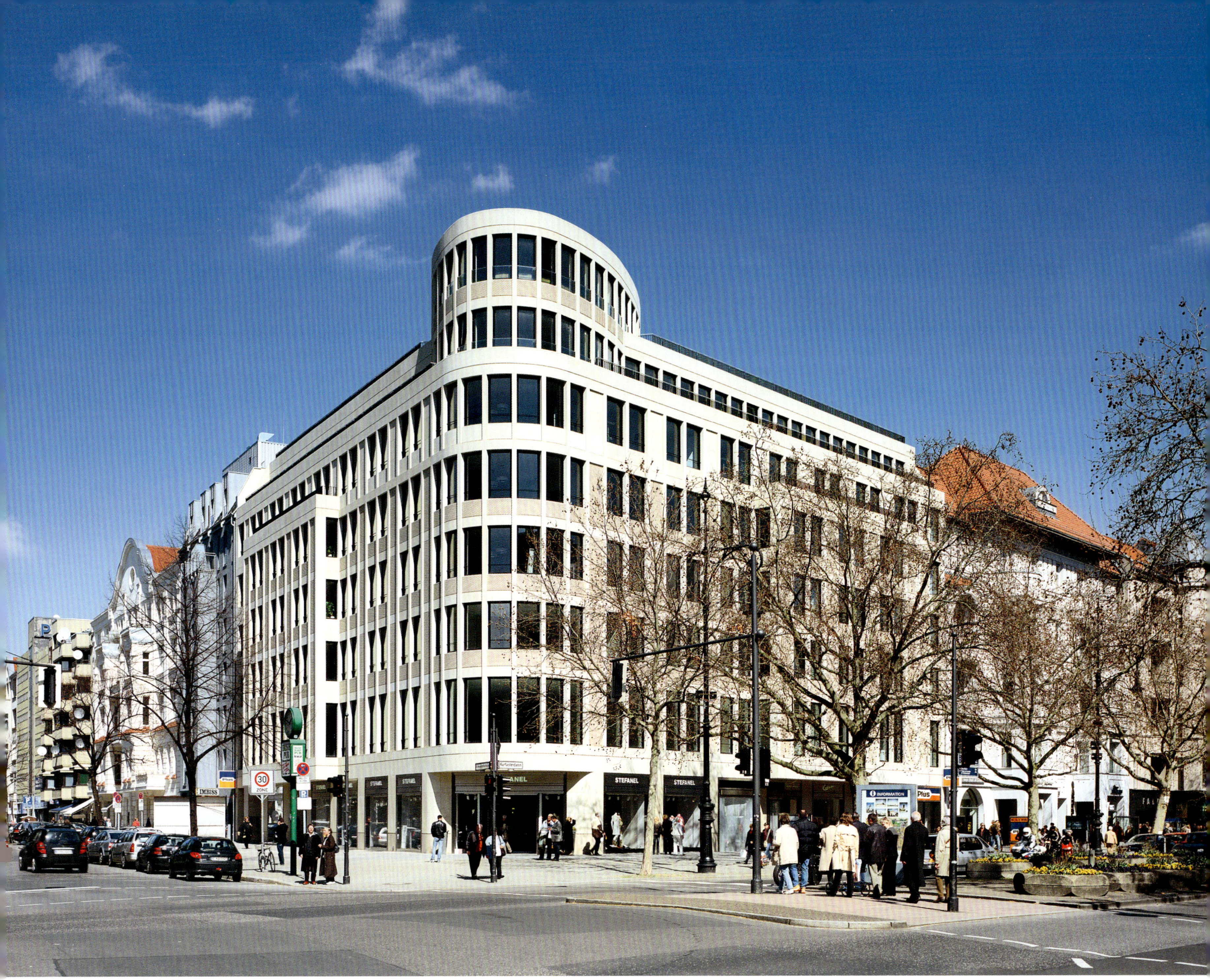
STEFANEL
IMBISS
30
ZONE
INFORMATION
Plus

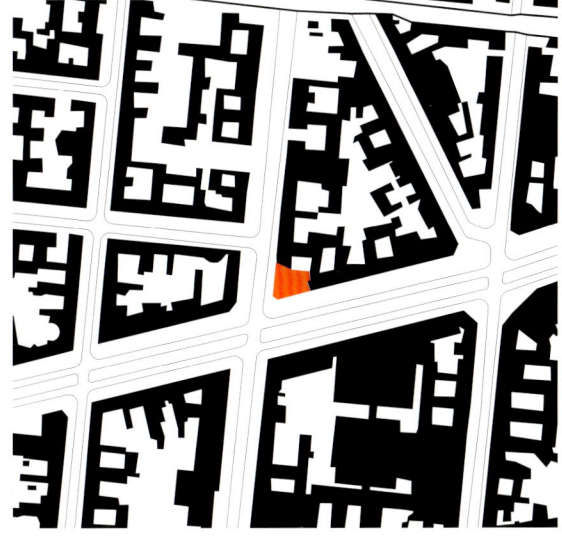

Durch die Relieftiefe und die sorgfältige Detaillierung der Natursteinfassade schafft der Neubau eine Korrespondenz zu den historistischen Nachbargebäuden und gliedert sich ein in die Häuserfamilie am Kurfürstendamm.

Through its strong surface texture and careful detailing of the stone façade the new building corresponds to its historic neighbours, assuming position alongside the other buildings on the Kurfürstendamm.

KRONPRINZENKARREE
BERLIN

Am Rand der historischen Innenstadt, wo einst die Alte Panke und die Akzisenmauer die Stadt abschlossen, reiht sich das Gebäude in die Häuserfamilie der Friedrich-Wilhelm-Stadt ein. Seine massive Fassade besteht aus durchgefärbten Betonsteinen mit ausgeprägtem Relief, die an die Natursteinfassaden der Nachbarschaft erinnern. Mit einem haushohen Wintergarten, der sich vor die konkav geschwungene Südfassade des Bürohauses legt, wurden die Probleme gelöst, die sich durch den unmittelbar vor dem Grundstück verlaufenden Bahnviadukt ergeben. Der attraktive gläserne Vorbau ist Schall- und Klimaschutzhülle zugleich. Im Innenhof entstand als Bindeglied zwischen dem Bürohaus und der Brandwand des Nachbargebäudes ein dreigeschossiges Lofthaus. Dessen bis auf Treppen, Bad und Küche nach Nutzerwunsch unterteilbare Wohnungen und Ateliers haben Freiflächenbezug zum Hof oder zur Dachterrasse. Sie lassen sich durch raumhohe Faltschiebefenster großflächig öffnen. Als Sicht- und Lichtschutz können beweglich montierte, golden eloxierte Lochblechelemente vor die Fenster geschoben werden, die mit individuellen Pixelmustern gelocht sind.

Situated on the edge of the historic inner city, where once the Alte Panke, a canalised creek, and the excise wall marked the boundary of city, the building completes a row of houses in the Friedrich-Wilhelm quarter. Its monolithic façade is made of pigmented concrete blocks with a pronounced surface relief reminiscent of the stone façades in the neighbourhood. A winter garden wraps around the concave arcing front of the south façade and extends the entire height of the building, a response to the problem of the railway viaduct directly in front of the site. The attractive glazed addition serves both as a thermal insulation buffer and as noise insulation. In the interior courtyard a three-storey loft building connects the office building with the firewall of the building behind. With the exception of the kitchen, bathroom and stairs, the apartments and ateliers within can be divided as required by the inhabitants and have outdoor access to the courtyard or the roof terrace. Entire sections of the wall can be opened by retracting the full-height folding and sliding windows. For privacy and shading, mobile sliding panels made of gold anodised metal sheeting, each with their own perforation pattern, can be shifted in front of the windows.

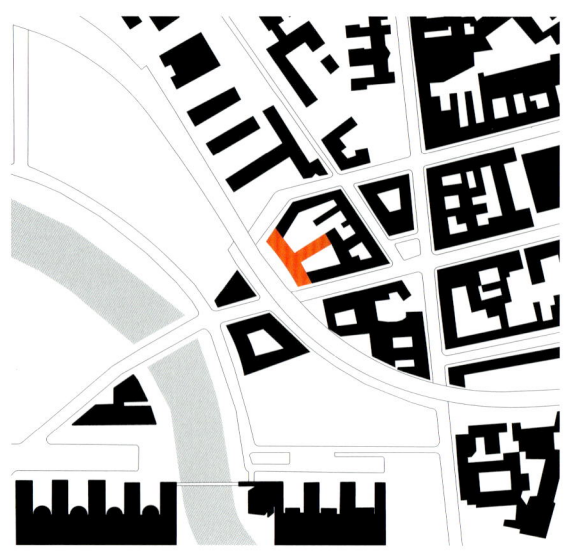

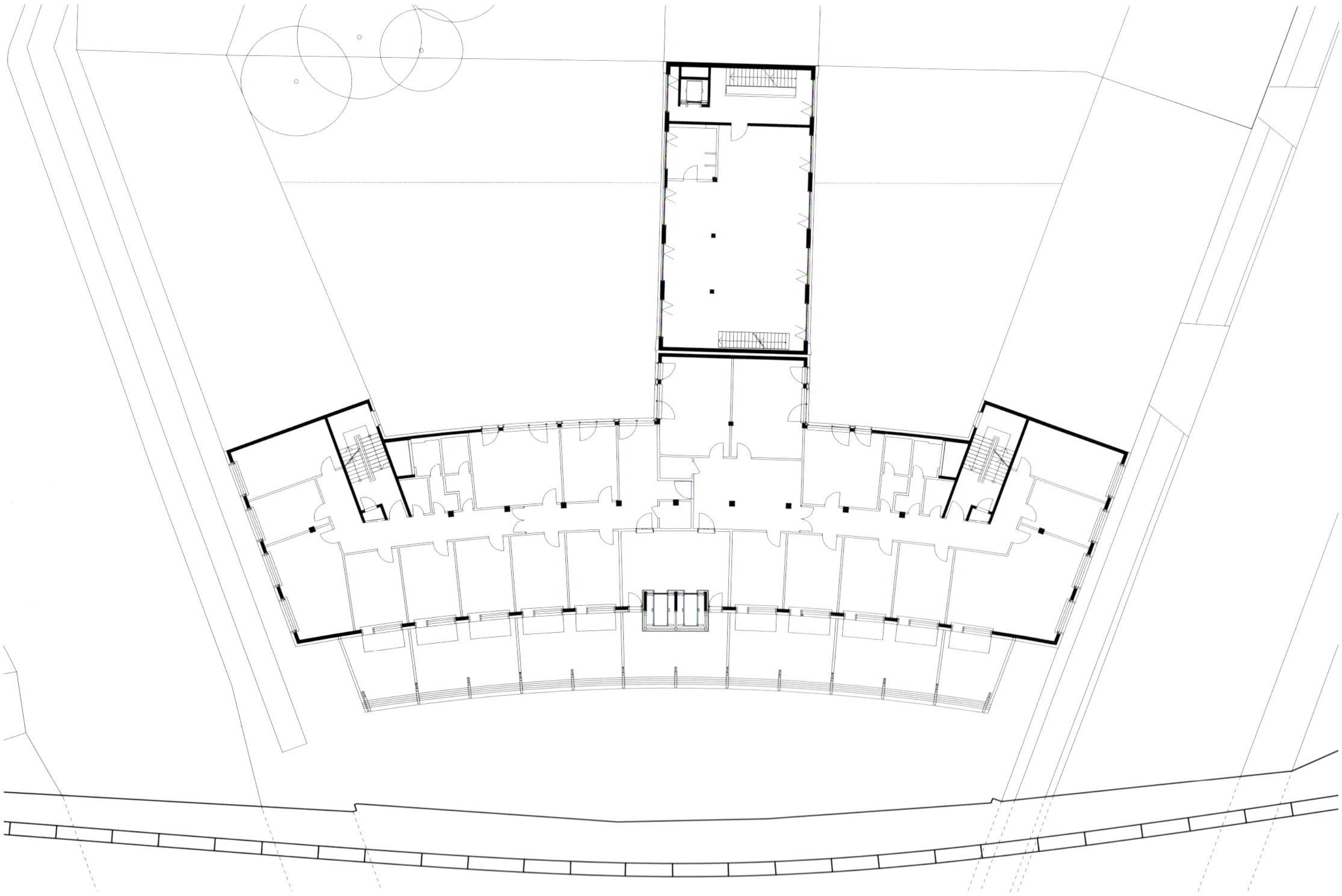

Grundriss Regelgeschoss | Typical floor plan

0   10m

Der gebäudehohe Wintergarten des Hauses unmittelbar am Bahnviadukt ist gleichzeitig Klimapuffer und Schallschutz.

The full-height winter garden behind the façade of the building facing the railway viaduct serves both as thermal and noise insulation.

Das Lofthaus im Hinterhof schließt an die Nachbarbebauung an und bietet großzügig geschnittene, frei unterglieder- und nutzbare Etagen. Die golden eloxierten Pixelfassaden wandeln ihr Gesicht durch das Verschieben der Sonnenblenden.

The loft building in the courtyard abuts the neighbouring building and contains spacious apartments that can be divided and used as required. The appearance of the gold anodised pixelated façade changes constantly as the mobile sun screens are shifted back and forth.

OVAL OFFICE
HAMBURG

Eine eigenständige Form war gefragt für das Verwaltungs-gebäude, das einen Plattenbau aus dem Jahr 1970 ersetzen sollte, eine Form, mit der der Bau unter all den anderen Solitären der Bürostadt City Nord Bestand haben konnte. So sind die fünf parallelen, geraden Bürotrakte mit einer ovalen Großform umschrieben. Die Form entsteht durch die äußeren Dachkanten, wobei die Höfe durch einen Luftbalken überbrückt sind, der das Oval vervollständigt. Das siebengeschossige Haus lässt sich in verschiedenen Einheiten vermieten. Die Vorfahrt bedient zwei Haupteingänge, wobei die eine Lobby mit dem Mitarbeiterrestaurant in Verbindung steht. Für einen weiteren Hauptmieter steht im Erdgeschoss eine zweite Lobby zur Verfügung.

Während die inneren Trakte der kammartigen Gebäude-struktur für Zellenbüros vorgesehen sind, eignen sich die außen liegenden, sichelförmigen Grundrisse als Gruppenbü-ros. Ein veritables „Oval Office" gibt es im Dachgeschoss, dessen zentraler Besprechungsraum den ovalen Kern des Hauses abbildet.

For the administrative building that was to replace a pre-fabricated block from 1970, a distinctive form was required that would distinguish the building from all the other solitary buildings in the Bürostadt City Nord business park. The result is a building with five parallel office wings circumscribed by a large oval. Its perimeter is defined by the outer edge of the roof which becomes a beam where it crosses the court-yards so that the oval is uninterrupted. The seven-storey building can be let in different units. Access is via two main entrances, with one of the lobbies providing access to the staff canteen. A second lobby is provided as an entrance for a second tenant.

While the inner wings of the comb-like footprint of the building provide small-scale spaces for office cells, the crescent-shaped plans of the offices at each end are ide-ally suited for use as larger group offices. A veritable "Oval Office" exists on the top floor, its central conference room representing the oval core of the building.

Zu Arne Jacobsens linearem HEW-Gebäude im Hintergrund bildet der schwungvolle Bürobau auf ovalem
Grundriss einen reizvollen skulpturalen Gegensatz.

The curves of the new building with its oval plan provide
an attractive sculptural contrast to the linear HEW
Building by Arne Jacobsen behind it.

Das zweigeschossige Foyer ist Empfang, Treffpunkt
und Verteilerhalle.

The two-storey foyer serves as reception, meeting place
and circulation hub.

Gartenkünstlerisch gestaltete Innenhöfe werden vom Ringbalken und dessen Stützen räumlich gefasst und bieten einen angenehmen Anblick für die Büronutzer.

The landscaped courtyard gardens are bound spatially by a perimeter beam and its supporting columns and are looked on to from the offices.

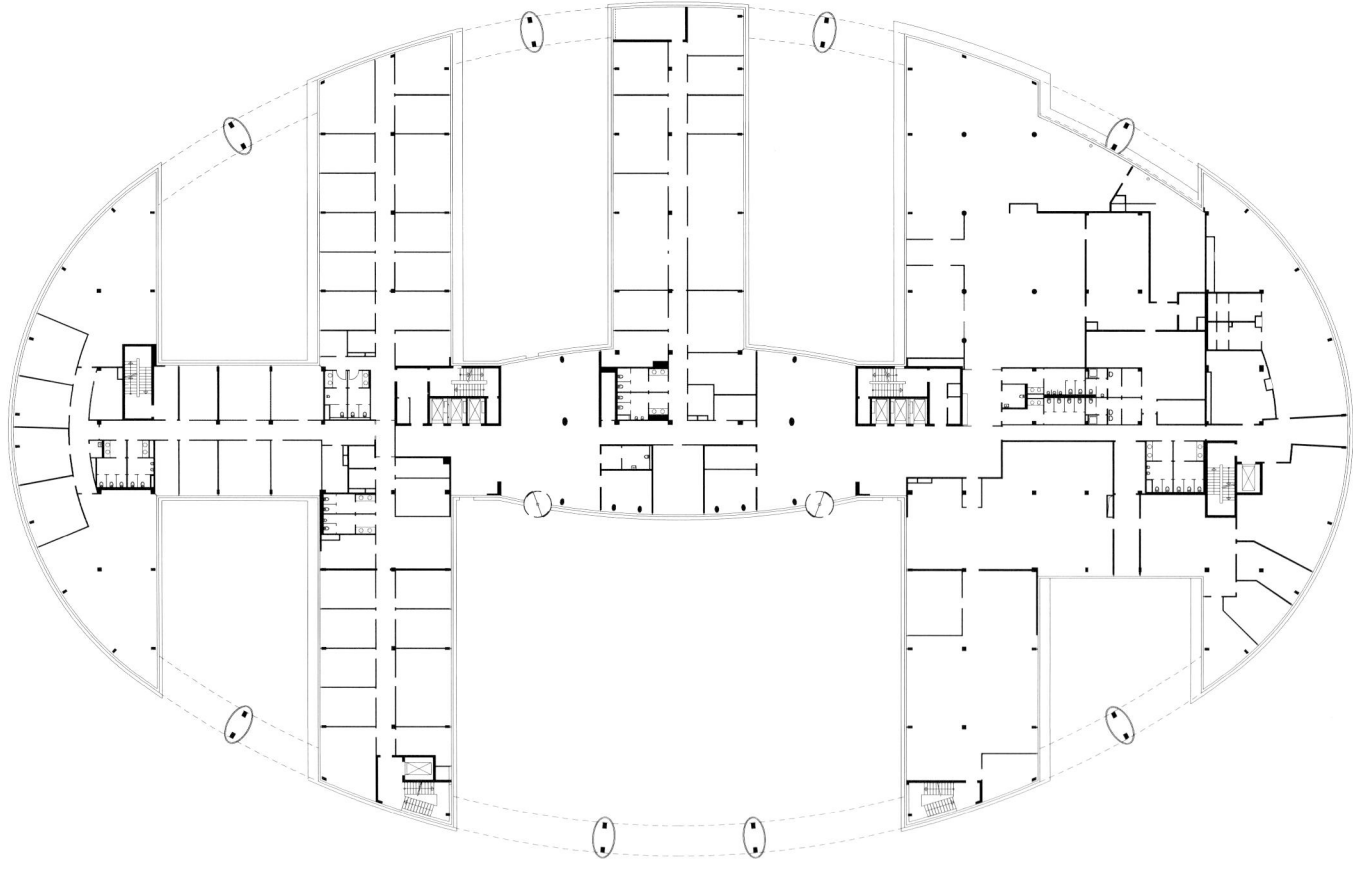

Grundriss Erdgeschoss | Ground floor plan

0   20m

Casino und Büroräume sind optimal mit natürlichem
Licht versorgt, die innen liegenden Flure und Treppen–
häuser durch effektvolle Beleuchtung akzentuiert.

The cafeteria and office spaces enjoy natural light,
the corridors and staircases within are accentuated
by dramatic artificial lighting.

GRAFENBERGER HÖFE
DÜSSELDORF

Grundanliegen des städtebaulichen Entwurfs ist die Vermittlung zwischen den in Typologie und Charakter sehr verschiedenen Bebauungsformen im Quartier. Das Projekt wurde in drei Baukörper gegliedert, um die Durchlässigkeit und die Bezüge zur rückwärtigen Parkanlage der Graf-Recke-Stiftung zu sichern. Zwei der Kuben sind U-förmig angelegt und bilden Höfe. In Reaktion auf die Nachbarhäuser steigt die Bauhöhe von Ost nach West von fünf auf sieben Geschosse an.

Gestalterisches Charakteristikum im Hinblick auf Identitäts- und Imagebildung im Interesse der beiden Mieter ist die Form der mit geneigten Wänden und Pultdächern versehenen Baukörper und deren Fassadenausbildung. An drei Seiten sind die Kuben mit einer kraftvoll rostrot gefärbten Metallfassade bekleidet. Lediglich die Südgiebel an der Walter-Eucken-Straße stehen senkrecht und sind durchgängig verglast. Es entsteht ein Effekt, als ob die plastischen Kuben an der Straßenfront abgeschnitten worden wären. Im Inneren führt die unkonventionelle Baukörperform an verschiedenen Stellen zu interessanten Räumen unterschiedlicher Höhe.

Die Bauformen haben skulpturalen Charakter und binden das Ensemble zu einer gestalterischen Einheit zusammen. Sie bringen eine starke Plastizität und eine große Dynamik mit sich, die dem Wunsch der Mieter nach individueller Repräsentanz entgegenkommen.

The basic intention of the urban design proposal is to mediate between neighbouring buildings with very different typologies and characters. The project is divided into three main elements for greater permeability and to provide a connection to the Graf Recke Foundation car park to the rear. Two of the cuboid forms are U-shaped, each enclosing a small courtyard. The height of the buildings responds to the surroundings, rising from east to west from five to seven storeys.

The characteristic formal qualities of the buildings, chosen with a view to communicating a strong identity and image for the two tenants, are the inclined walls and slanting roofs of the buildings and the elaboration of the façades. On three sides, the volumes are faced with metal cladding panels of an intense rust-red colour. Only the south gables facing the Walter-Eucken-Straße stand upright and are glazed from top to bottom. It appears as if the sculptural volumes have been sliced through where they meet the road. The unconventional forms of the building lead to interesting spaces of differing shape and height in the interior.

The forms of the buildings have a sculptural character lending the entire ensemble a formal unity. The expressive dynamism and plasticity that they embody reflects the desire of the tenants for a unique and representative public face.

Eine unverwechselbare Baugruppe mit skulpturalem Charakter und räumlicher Spannung präsentiert sich an der Walter-Eucken-Straße. Während die Giebelseiten wie durch einen nachträglich verglasten senkrechten Schnitt entstanden wirken, definieren die schrägen, geschlosseneren Seitenwände die eigentliche Kubatur.

A distinctive series of buildings with sculptural forms and dynamic spaces stand in a row along the Walter-Eucken-Straße. Their front façades appear as if the buildings have been sliced through and then glazed, while the slanted more opaque lateral façades define the building volume.

BUCHHAUS HABEL
HABEL BOOKSTORE
KREFELD

Die neue Fassade für das Geschäftshaus in der Krefelder Innenstadt sollte für die in den Obergeschossen untergebrachte Buchhandlung werben und den Mangel an Erdgeschossschaufenstern ausgleichen. So stellt sie also Bücher aus, als überdimensionales Bücherregal. 185 Verlage haben dazu über 2000 Titel beigesteuert; zusätzlich wurden auf drei Meter vergrößerte Buchrücken auf die inneren Scheiben der Doppelfassade gedruckt.

Die Bücher wurden nicht nach Sachgebieten, sondern als künstlerisches Arrangement nach den Regeln der Farbenlehre geordnet. Das 1000 Quadratmeter große „Buchregal hinter Glas" ist abends effektvoll hinterleuchtet und wirkt in der geschäftigen City als attraktiver Anziehungspunkt.

The new façade for the shopping centre and bookstore in the centre of Krefeld was to advertise the presence of the bookshop in the upper storeys and compensate for the fact that it has no shop windows on the ground floor. Accordingly it displays books in the form of an over-sized bookshelf. 185 publishers provided 2000 books for this purpose and the enlarged spines of books, each almost three metres high, are printed onto the inner pane of the dual-skin façade.

The books are not arranged according to subject but as an artistic arrangement according to the chromatic scale. The 1000-square-metre-large "bookshelf behind glass" is dramatically illuminated at night, becoming a visual attraction in the busy inner city.

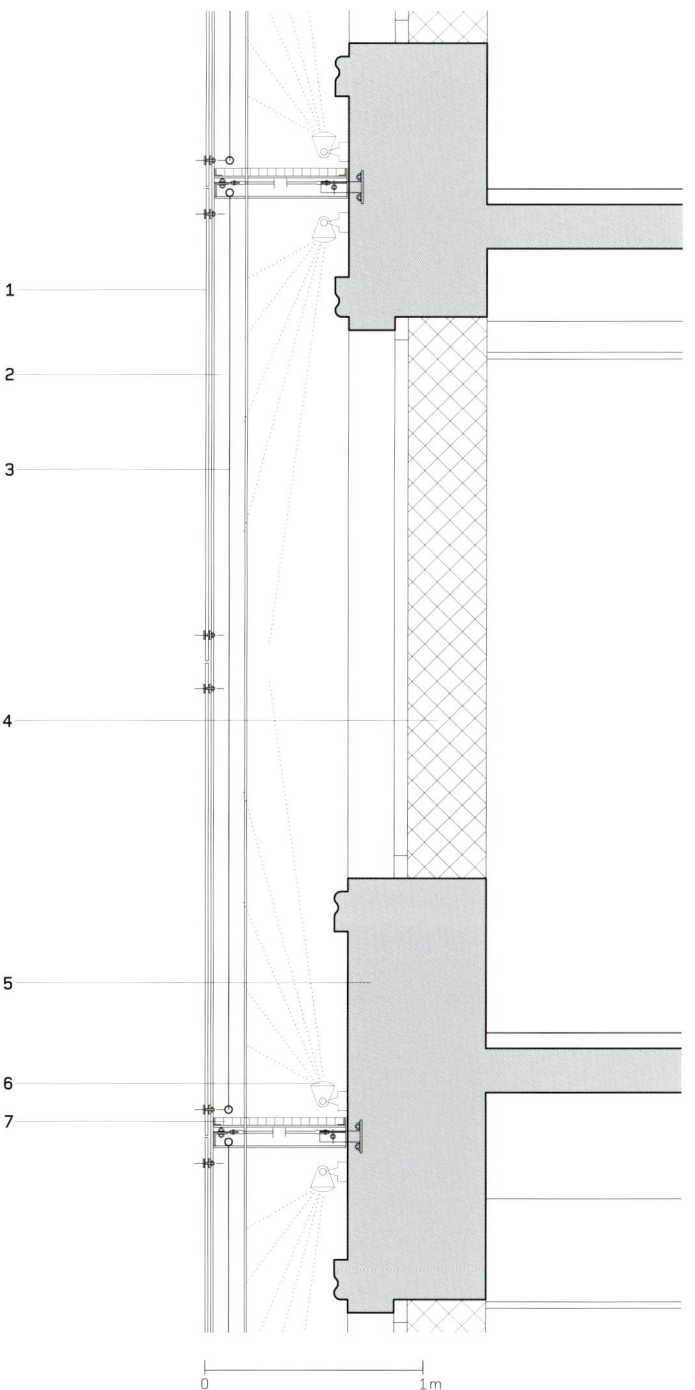

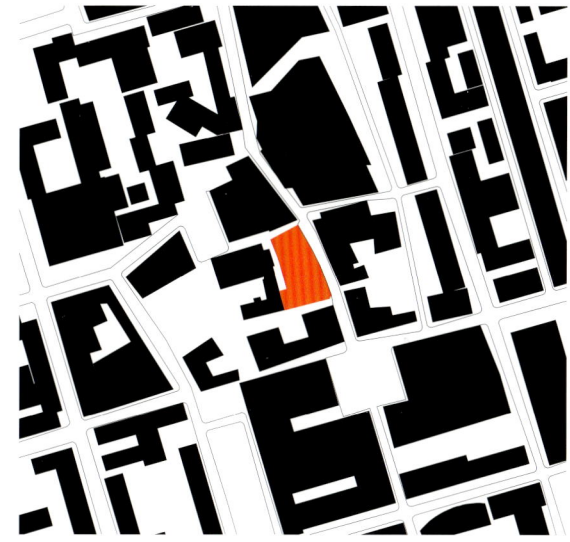

1

2

3

4

5

6

7

0   1 m

Nichts als Bücher zeigt die Fassade hinter ihrer Verglasung und bringt die Zweckbestimmung des Hauses zum Ausdruck. Der Schnitt macht deutlich, wie aus der Lochfassade eine gläserne Schauwand wurde.

1 Fassade aus Verbundsicherheitsglas
2 Unterkonstruktion aus Stahlprofilen
3 Mit Buchmotiven bedruckte Transparenzfolie
4 Vermauerte Bestandsfenster
5 Bestandsfassade
6 Flächige Fassadenbeleuchtung
7 Laufbühne des Wartungsgangs

Books and more books is all that can be seen behind the glazing of the new façade, highlighting the purpose of the building. The section shows clearly how a standard elevation punctuated with windows has been transformed into a glazed cabinet.

1 Laminated glass façade
2 Supporting structure, steel sections
3 Transparent foil printed with images of book spines
4 Bricked-up existing window openings
5 Existing façade
6 Backlighting
7 Maintenance gangway

HAUPTVERWALTUNG SAGA/GWG
SAGA/GWG HEADQUARTERS
HAMBURG

Der Gebäuderiegel nutzt die günstige Grundstückslage in Hamburg-Barmbek mit Längsseite nach Süden entlang des Osterbekkanals konsequent aus und entwickelt zum Kanal hin seine Schaufassade. Ein zweiter Flügel ist an der Rückseite rechtwinklig angefügt. Beide Gebäudeteile sind durch ein repräsentatives, voll verglastes Atrium miteinander verbunden, das sich bis unter das Dach erstreckt und die Orientierung erleichtert.

Der Ostgiebel des sechsgeschossigen Hauses für die Hamburger Wohnungsbaugesellschaft SAGA/GWG begrenzt den Hof des Museums für Arbeit und gibt gewissermaßen den maßstäblichen Vergleich für die dort im Freien aufgestellte riesige Tunnelbohrmaschine „TRUDE" (Abkürzung für „tief runter unter die Elbe"). Durch Zusammenfassung jeweils zweier Geschosse in der Fassadengliederung wird der Maßstab im Vergleich zu der zum Teil niedrigeren Nachbarbebauung relativiert.

Neben den auf einfache Prinzipien reduzierten Formen und Grundrissorganisationen kommen wenige formale Kunstgriffe zu besonderer Wirkung, etwa die geschwungenen Wände aus Jura, die die rückwärtigen Eingänge begleiten, oder die farbig verglasten, auf den Ebenen des Atriums wechselseitig angeordneten Besprechungsboxen.

The elongated building makes the most of the site orienting its long side to face south parallel to the Osterbek canal in Hamburg-Barmbek, and making the canal-ward side its representative façade. A second wing is attached at a right angle at the rear. Both parts of the building are connected by an impressive fully-glazed five-storey atrium that is open to the roof level and aids orientation.

The east gable of the six-storey house provides closure for the courtyard of the Museum of Work and in the process offers a scale for "TRUDE", the huge tunnel borehead that was used to bore the tunnel under the Elbe. By visually combining two storeys in the design of the façade, the scale is reduced in relation to the smaller neighbouring buildings.

Aside from the straightforward principle of simple forms and floor plans, a few formal tricks are used to maximum effect, for example the undulating walls of jura stone that line the entrance to the rear or the multi-coloured glazed conference boxes that project into the atrium, alternating from one side to the other.

Sowohl bei den Fassaden, als auch im Inneren ist Jura in unterschiedlichen Oberflächenbearbeitungen eingesetzt worden. Allerorten im Haus sind kontrastierende Materialien wie Sichtbeton und Ahornholz, Glas und Stahl sowie der Juramarmor präzise gefügt gegeneinander gesetzt und steigern sich gegenseitig in ihrer puristischen Materialwirkung. Lediglich in den Teeküchen ist die ansonsten diszipliniert-seriöse Gestaltung der Arbeitswelt durch fröhliche Farbakzente – wandfüllende, großformatige Fotodarstellungen von Früchten – aufgelockert und signalisiert Pause und Entspannung.

For the façades as well as the interior, jura stone is employed with different surface treatments. Throughout the building contrasting materials such as fair-faced concrete and maple wood, glass and steel or jura marble are carefully and precisely combined and contrasted to respectively heighten the purist material qualities of the other. Only in the kitchen areas does the sober and disciplined design of the work areas give way to more colourful highlights – entire walls covered with large-format photos of fruit – signalling spaces for rest and relaxation.

Neben dem Museum für Arbeit mit der gewaltigen Tunnelbohrmaschine „TRUDE" (rechts im Bild) präsentiert das Gebäude seine Hauptansicht nach Süden gegen den Osterbekkanal.

Situated next to the Museum of Work and "TRUDE", the huge tunnel borehead (in the photo on the right), the main façade of the headquarters faces south towards the Osterbek canal.

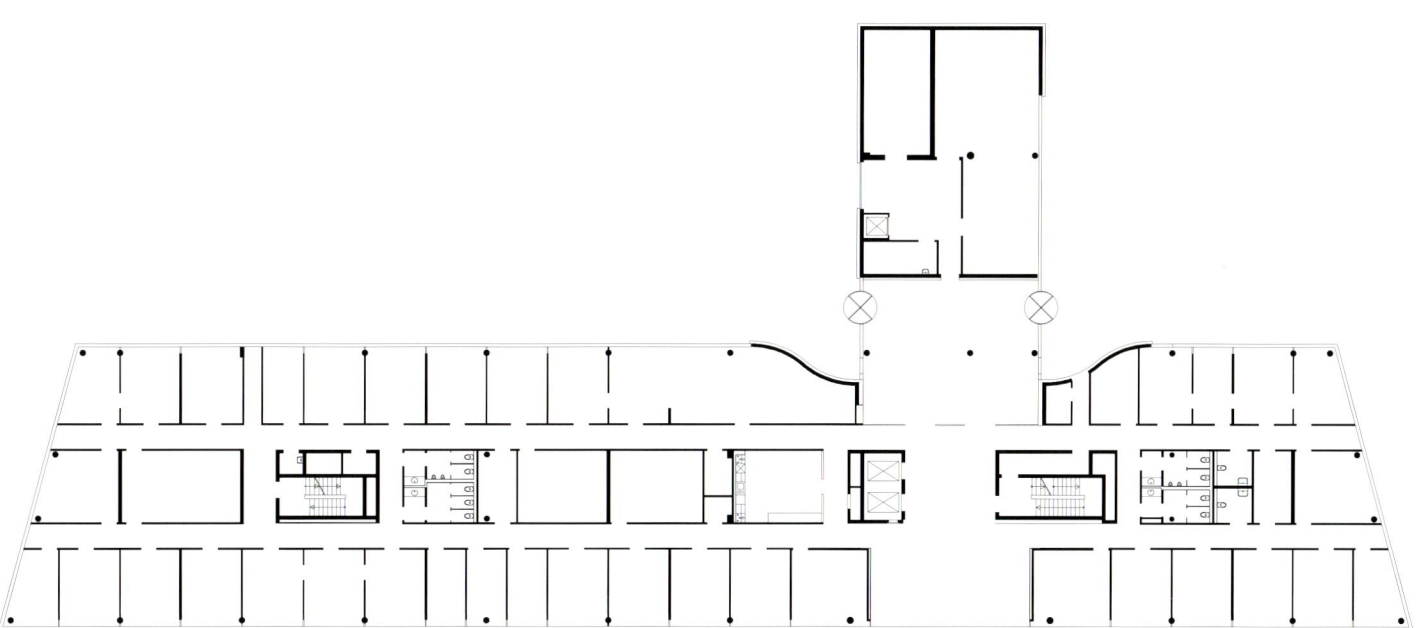

Grundriss Erdgeschoss | Ground floor plan

0   10m

Die Natursteinfassade fasst jeweils zwei Geschosse zusammen und ändert so den Maßstab des Gebäudes. Die Besprechungsräume im fünfgeschossigen Foyer scheinen zu schweben und sind durch farbiges Licht akzentuiert.

The stone façade visually combines two storeys, changing the perceived scale of the building. The meeting rooms, accentuated with coloured lighting, are suspended like boxes in the five-storey foyer.

Eine ruhige, disziplinierte Gestaltung bestimmt den Charakter der hellen Innenräume. Die Oberflächen der Flure und Treppenhäuser zeigen ein ebenso sorgfältig gestaltetes Gefüge und leben vom kontrastreichen Nebeneinander von Naturstein, Glas, lebhaft gemaserten Hölzern und Sichtbeton.

A sober and disciplined design defines the character of the light interiors. The surfaces of corridors and stairs are accorded equal care and attention and are enlivened by the contrast of materials such as stone, glass, woods with a distinct grain and fair-faced concrete.

WOHNGEBÄUDE POSSMOORWEG
POSSMOORWEG FLATS
HAMBURG

Die heterogene Bebauung der Umgebung in Hamburg-Winterhude – Wohnblocks am Poßmoorweg links und Blockrandbebauung gegenüber, flache Werkshallen rechts nebenan, ein Werftgelände nach Süden – lieferte wenig Ansatzpunkte für den Entwurf des genossenschaftlichen Wohnungsbaus. Um die Hauptorientierung nach Südosten zum Goldbekkanal hin und zur Sonnenseite Südwesten auszunutzen, wurde die Baumasse in zwei Körper geteilt. Ein lang gestreckter Riegel öffnet sich mit seinen Wohnbereichen und Balkons nach Südwesten, während der schmalere Kopfbau nach Südosten blickt. Die übrigen Fassaden sind nach dem Prinzip von Schale und Füllung mit geschlossener Lochfassade ausgeführt. Während die offenen Seiten als mit dunkel beschichtetem Aluminiumblech bekleidete Skelette erscheinen, die mit Glas und rot gefärbten HPL-Paneelen gefüllt sind, zeigt sich die „Schale" der Lochfassaden in einem goldbraunen Holzton. Ein gläsernes Treppenhaus verknüpft die beiden Bauteile miteinander. Von Maisonettes mit Vorgarten bis zur Sechszimmerwohnung im zurückgesetzten Staffelgeschoss reicht das vielfältige Angebot an unterschiedlichen Appartements.

The disparate nature of the urban surroundings in Hamburg-Winterhude – housing blocks on the Poßmoorweg to the left, a perimeter block opposite, low workshop buildings to the right, a wharf to the south – provided little in the way of pointers for the design of the cooperative housing project. To best exploit the principal orientation to the southeast and the Goldbek canal as well as the sunny side on the southwest, the building was divided into two volumes. The living areas and balconies of an elongated block open to the southwest while the shorter building at one end faces southeast. Following the principle of 'shell' and 'filling', all other façades are plain surfaces punctuated by windows. The open sides are expressed as a dark aluminium-clad framework with glazing and red HPL infill panels, while the "shell" is clad with golden wood veneer panels. A glazed staircase connects both parts of the building. The block contains a variety of different apartment types that range from maisonettes with a front garden to six-room apartments in the stepped-back top storey.

Um die Baukörper zu differenzieren sind die Fassaden –
abhängig von Lage und Funktion – jeweils mit unterschiedlichen Materialien und Farbgebungen verkleidet.

To differentiate the volumes, the façades of the buildings are clad in different materials and colours, varying
also with orientation and function.

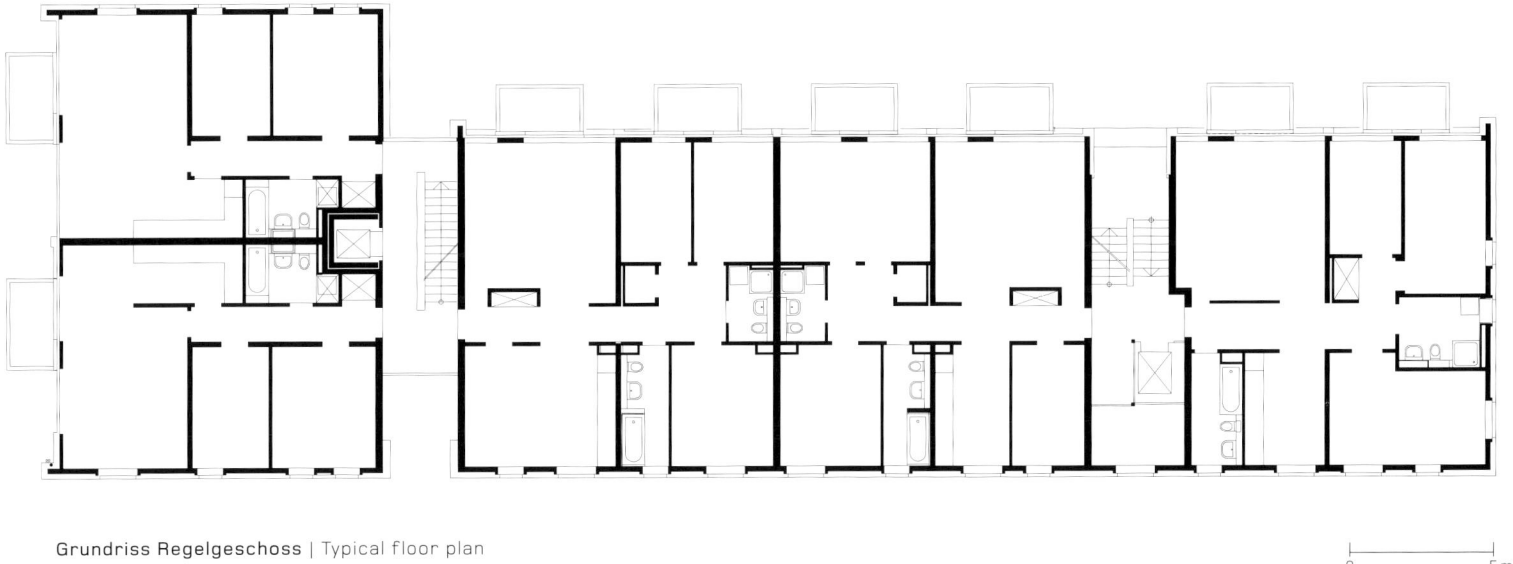

Grundriss Regelgeschoss | Typical floor plan

0   5 m

HAUPTVERWALTUNG IMTECH
IMTECH HEADQUARTERS
HAMBURG

Das gestalterische Durcheinander in der Nachbarschaft in Hamburg-Wandsbek mit Einfamilienhäusern, Bahndamm, Gewerbe- und Bürobauten verlangte nach einer kraftvollen, beruhigenden architektonischen Aussage. An der spitzwinkligen Kreuzung Pappelallee/Hammer Straße, eine exponierte, für ein städtebauliches Merkzeichen prädestinierte Stelle, war ein deutlicher Kopf auszubilden. Entlang der Hammer Straße sollte sich das Gebäude stärker artikulieren, während es an der Rückseite zur S-Bahn hin seine ungegliederte Langseite entwickeln konnte. So entstanden zwei Baukörper mit inneren Rundläufen, die durch den Längsriegel verbunden sind und auch real geteilt werden können.

Sein charakteristisches, unverwechselbares Bild entwickelt der Bau durch die ausgeprägten Bandfassaden mit den abgerundeten Ecken. Sie bestehen aus dunklen Fensterbändern und verklinkerten Brüstungen, gerahmt von erhabenen Gesimsbändern aus Aluminium, in denen die Sonnenschutzlamellen verborgen sind. Mit dieser Gliederung erinnern die Baukörper an Frank Lloyd Wrights Johnson Wax Building von 1939 oder an Erich Mendelsohns Warenhäuser aus den späten zwanziger Jahren.

The diverse types and forms of buildings in the neighbourhood in Hamburg-Wandsbek including detached family houses, a railway embankment and industrial and office buildings, required a strong but calm architectural presence. The head of the building was to be located in the acute angle of the junction between the Pappelallee and Hammer Straße, a prominent position well-suited for an urban landmark. Along the Hammer Straße the form of the building was to be more strongly articulated while to the rear in the direction of the railway embankment it was allowed to present a long façade. As a result a building consisting of two volumes each with their own internal circulation was created, which are connected by a long building at the rear but can also be used independently.

Its characteristic and unmistakable appearance results from the pronounced banding of the façade and the rounded corners. Dark bands of windows alternate with strips of brick parapet delineated by prominent aluminium cornices that conceal the slatted blinds. The pattern of the façade is reminiscent of Frank Lloyd Wright's Johnson Wax Building from 1939 or Erich Mendelsohn's warehouses from the late twenties.

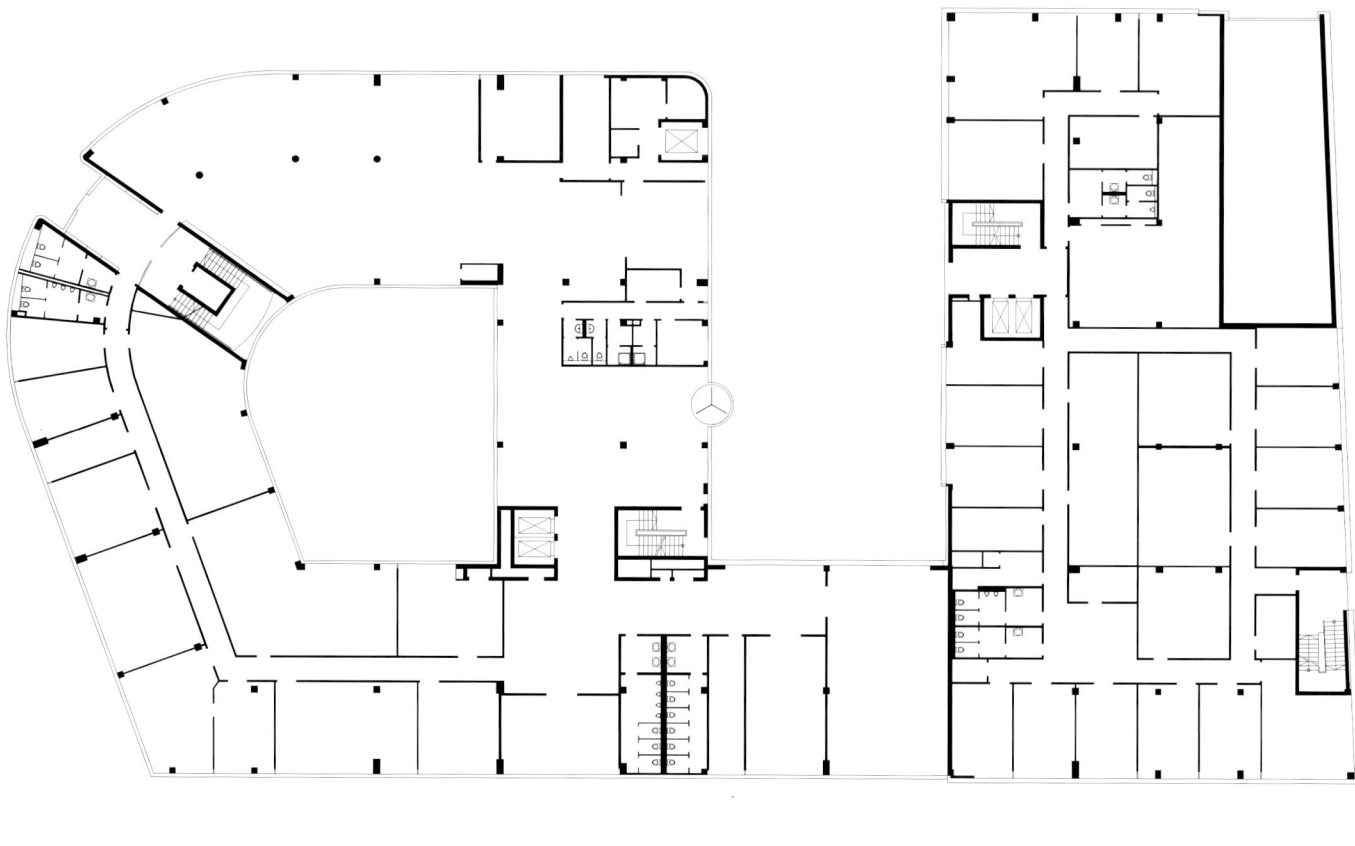

Grundriss Erdgeschoss | Ground floor plan

0   10m

Mit schwebenden Kuben, Glasbändern und Lichtleisten
setzt sich die Formensprache der klassischen Moderne
im Inneren fort.

Floating rectangular forms, glazed bands and strips
of light continue the formal language of modernism in
the interior.

Die Haupteingänge mit Vorfahrt befinden sich im Bauwich zwischen den beiden Baukörpern. Der zweigeschossige Bauteil, der sich an der Hammer Straße unter das Gebäude schiebt und sich durch eine Metallfassade als Sonderbau für Labornutzung auszeichnet, wurde im Bauverlauf für Büros umgewidmet, da sich die Mietsituation geändert hat. Im Übrigen sind die 4,50 Meter hohen Erdgeschosse durch ein Archiv mit 14 Regalkilometern, durch eine Kantine und Schulungsräume adäquat genutzt. In den Obergeschossen mit einem Kleinraster von 1,35 Metern, das zu den Achsmaßen 5,40 und 8,10 Meter führt, sind je nach Mieterwunsch Zellen-, Gruppen-, Kombi- und Großraumbüros eingerichtet. Das Untergeschoss bietet 175 Stellplätze.

The main entrances and approach are located in the divide between the two parts of the building. The two-storey element inserted into the corner of the building on the Hammer Straße is clad in metal to denote its original intended use as a laboratory, although a change in the planned tenancy during construction caused it to be repurposed for use as offices. The remainder of the 4.50-metre-high ground floor is suitably utilised to house an archive with 14 kilometres of shelving, a canteen and training rooms. The upper floors with a basic grid unit of 1.35 metres and column spans of 5.40 and 8.10 metres are subdivided into office cells, group offices, open plan offices or combinations thereof according to the tenants' requirements. The underground car park provides spaces for 175 vehicles.

Als Sonderbauteil schiebt sich der Laborbau vor das Ensemble. Die Bürotrakte reagieren durch Form und Gliederung auf die städtebauliche Situation und bilden an der spitzwinkligen Straßeneinmündung einen signifikanten Gebäudekopf aus.

The rectangular projection at the front of the building houses the laboratory. The office wings respond through their form and structure to the urban surroundings and form a pointed head to the building in the acute angle of the road junction.

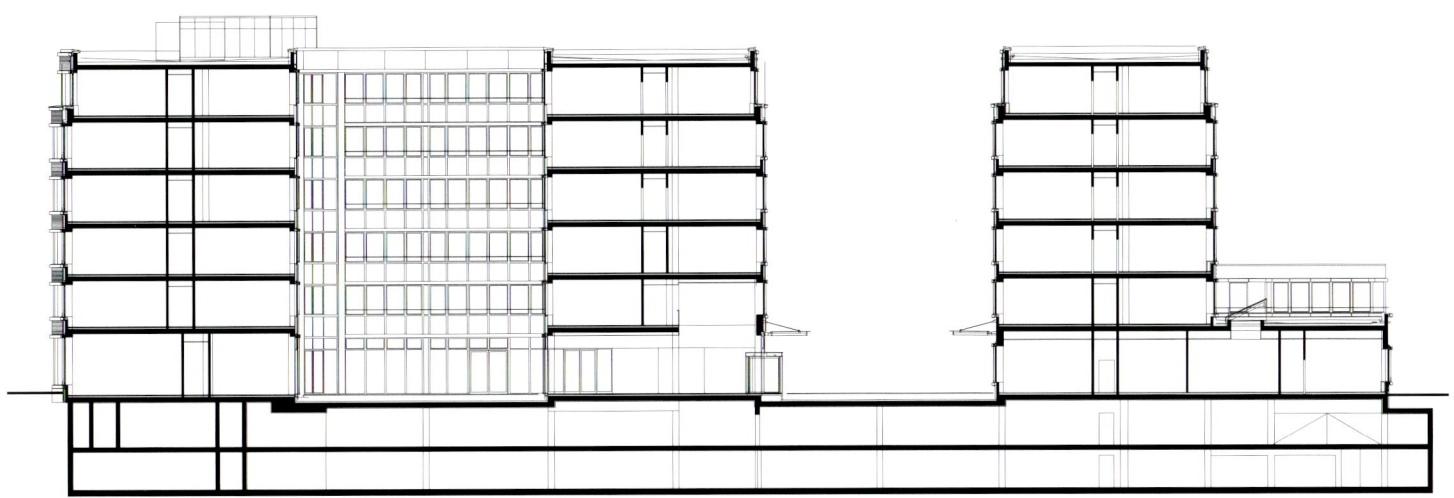

Schnitt | Section

QUARTIER HOFFMANNSTIEG
HOUSING, HOFFMANNSTIEG QUARTER
HAMBURG

Die beiden achtgeschossigen Wohnblöcke auf dem Areal in Hamburg-Rahlstedt am östlichen Stadtrand waren abbruchreif und sollten einer vielfältigeren Bebauung Platz machen. Die neue Anlage besteht aus sechs zweigeschossigen Hausreihen, wobei die Kopfenden jeweils durch drei Geschosse betont sind. Aus Gründen des städtebaulichen Maßstabs sind die Reihenhäuser optisch zu größeren Einheiten zusammengefasst. Durch die roten Abstellräume („Multiboxen"), Hecken und Wegeführungen entstehen feine Differenzierungen zwischen öffentlichem und privatem Freiraum. 52 Wohneinheiten in acht verschiedenen Haus- und Wohnungstypen stehen zur Auswahl. Zentrum und Treffpunkt des Quartiers ist der zentrale „Dorfplatz" um eine alte Ulme mit raumbildenden Pergolen und einem Gemeinschaftshaus.

Two largely vacated eight-storey tower blocks in Hamburg-Rahlstadt on a site on the eastern edge of the city were to be replaced by a more varied development. The new complex consists of six two-storey rows of terraced housing, with a three-storey house marking each end of a row. To increase their urban scale, each row of terraced houses is visually unified to form a single unit. The red storage "multiboxes", hedges and paths are used to create fine differentiations between public and private outdoor space. A total of 52 units offer eight different kinds of house and flat types. The centrepiece and meeting place in the quarter is the "village square" arranged around an old elm tree with a community centre and pergola that frames the space.

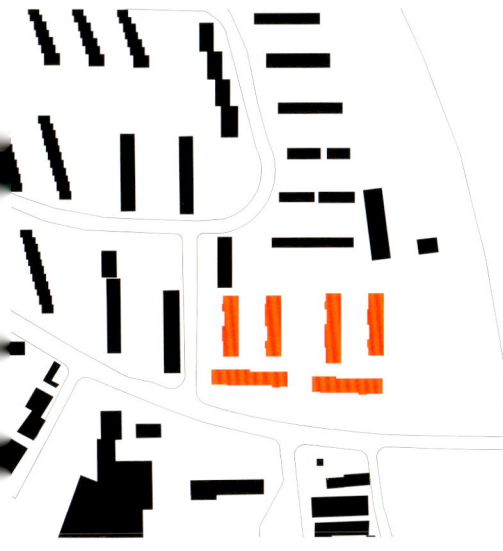

HAUPTVERWALTUNG C&A
C&A HEADQUARTERS
DÜSSELDORF

Gemäß dem städtebaulichen Rahmenplan gliedert sich das Gebäude in zwei Hauptbaukörper, die im Hintergrund der zwischenliegenden Vorfahrt durch ein gläsernes Foyergebäude miteinander verbunden und erschlossen sind. Flachere Anbauten vermitteln zur rückwärtigen Grünfläche, die nach Osten durch einen Parkhausriegel entlang der Bahntrasse abgeschlossen wird.

Die Wandflächen der vier Hauptbaukörper sind mit Glastafeln verkleidet, die durch ein Siebdruckverfahren mit einer Marmorstruktur dekoriert wurden und gemeinsam mit der Metallrahmung wie eine Kassettierung als moderne Art Deco-Übersetzung wirken. Das Art Deco-Motiv ist eine Reminiszenz an den Konzern, der sich besonders auf junge, farbenfrohe Modekleidung eingestellt hat.

Die Baukörper sind durch unterschiedliche Nuancen der Farbfamilien Grün, Blau, Gelb und Rot zu unterscheiden und bieten im Sonnenlicht ein sanftes Farbspiel. Diese Leitfarbe der Außenfassaden findet sich jeweils in der Farbgestaltung der Innenräume wieder und erleichtert dort die interne Orientierung.

Following the stipulations of the master plan, the building is divided into two volumes that are joined at the end of the driveway that runs between the two by a glazed foyer and access wing. Smaller extensions at the rear of the building extend out into the landscaped grounds behind, which are bounded to the east by an elongated parking building alongside the railway lines.

The surfaces of the walls of the four main buildings are clad with glass panels that have been screen-printed with a decorative marbled pattern and together with the metal frame look like a modern interpretation of Art Deco panelling. The Art Deco motif is a reference to the client, a company that focuses on colourful fashionable clothing for young people.

Subtle colour nuances in shades of green, blue, yellow and red help to differentiate between the individual buildings and produce a gentle play of colour when the sun shines. The key colour of the exterior is also reflected in the colour schemes of the respective interiors and helps to provide orientation inside the complex.

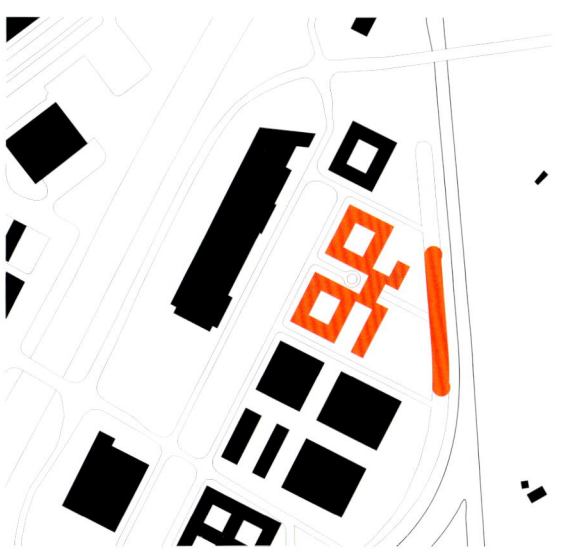

Die Baukörper des Ensembles orientieren sich am städtebaulichen Masterplan. Die gläsernen Brüstungsfelder sind durch ein im Siebdruckverfahren aufgebrachtes Marmordekor geschmückt. Der Aufblick und die Galerieansicht in der Treppenhalle zeigen die blaue Farbstimmung eines Gebäudeteils, der so farblich von den anderen differenziert wird.

The form of the ensemble of buildings follows the arrangement of the master plan. The glazed parapets beneath the windows are decorated with a screen-printed pattern reminiscent of marble. The upward view of the stairwell and view from the gallery show the blue colouring of one of the colour-coded wings of the building.

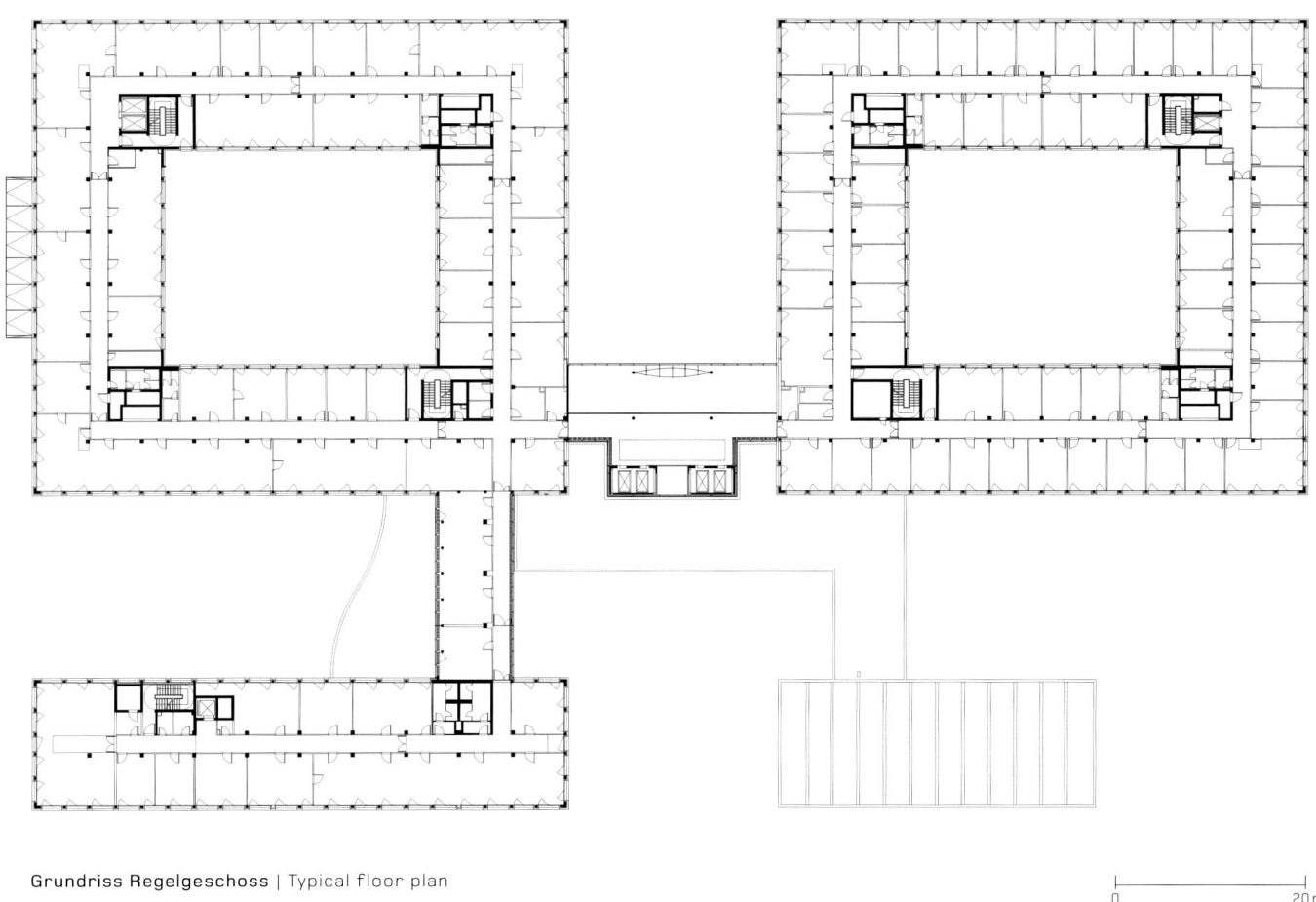

Grundriss Regelgeschoss | Typical floor plan

0   20 m

BEROLINAHAUS
BERLIN

Das von Peter Behrens entworfene bauhistorische Kleinod am Alexanderplatz, eines der wenigen im Umkreis erhaltenen historischen Gebäude, stand naturgemäß unter besonderem Kuratel der Denkmalschützer. Sie interessierten sich vor allem für die Rekonstruktion des äußeren Erscheinungsbildes, den detailgetreuen Nachbau der Fenster etc. Neu gestaltet wurde die Nordfassade, mit horizontal kannelierten Natursteinplatten und einem zweigeschossigen Aussichtserker. Sowohl der Nordeingang an der neuen Fassade als auch der Südeingang am Alexanderplatz wurden neu gestaltet und erhielten eine aufwändige Türanlage in golden hochglänzendem Messing sowie ein repräsentatives Vestibül in poliertem, schwarz-grünem Serpentin. Treppengeländer, Bodenbeläge und Wandverkleidungen wiederholen spielerisch das von Peter Behrens eingesetzte Formenvokabular.

Um in den unteren vier Geschossen (Untergeschoss bis zweites Obergeschoss) die für heutige Einzelhandelsformen geforderten Raumgrößen zu gewinnen und die Stützweiten zu halbieren, wurden die Obergeschosse mit zwei das Gebäude in ganzer Länge durchziehenden Unterzügen abgefangen.

This historic jewel of modern architecture on the Alexanderplatz, designed by Peter Behrens, is one of the few remaining historic buildings in the area and is therefore listed and protected by the conservation authorities. Their primary interest lay in the correct reconstruction of the external appearance, the detailed reconstruction of the windows and so on. The north façade was given a new design and clad in stone with horizontal stone channelling and features a two-storey bay window. Both the entrance on the north in the new façade and the entrance from the Alexanderplatz on the south side were redesigned with elaborate doors made of golden polished brass that open onto imposing vestibules faced with polished green-black serpentine. The banisters, floor surfaces and wall panelling playfully echo Peter Behrens' formal vocabulary.

In order to create sufficiently large retail spaces in the bottom four storeys (lower ground to second floor) and to halve the number of columns required, two new supporting beams were inserted that span the entire length of the building and bear the load of the upper storeys.

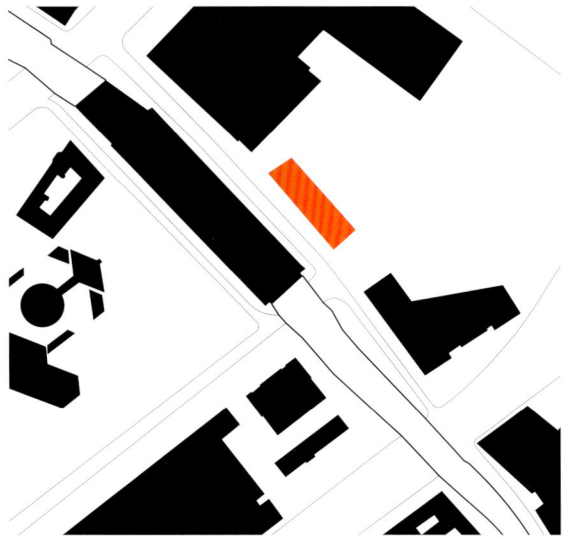

Die Nordfassade erhielt einen neuen Erker und die Eingänge der Nord- und Südfassade wurden neu gestaltet. Im Längsschnitt wird der Wechsel der Stützweiten über dem dritten Stockwerk deutlich.

The north façade was given a bay window and the entrances to the north and south façade were redesigned. The change in the column grid above the third floor is clearly apparent in the longitudinal section.

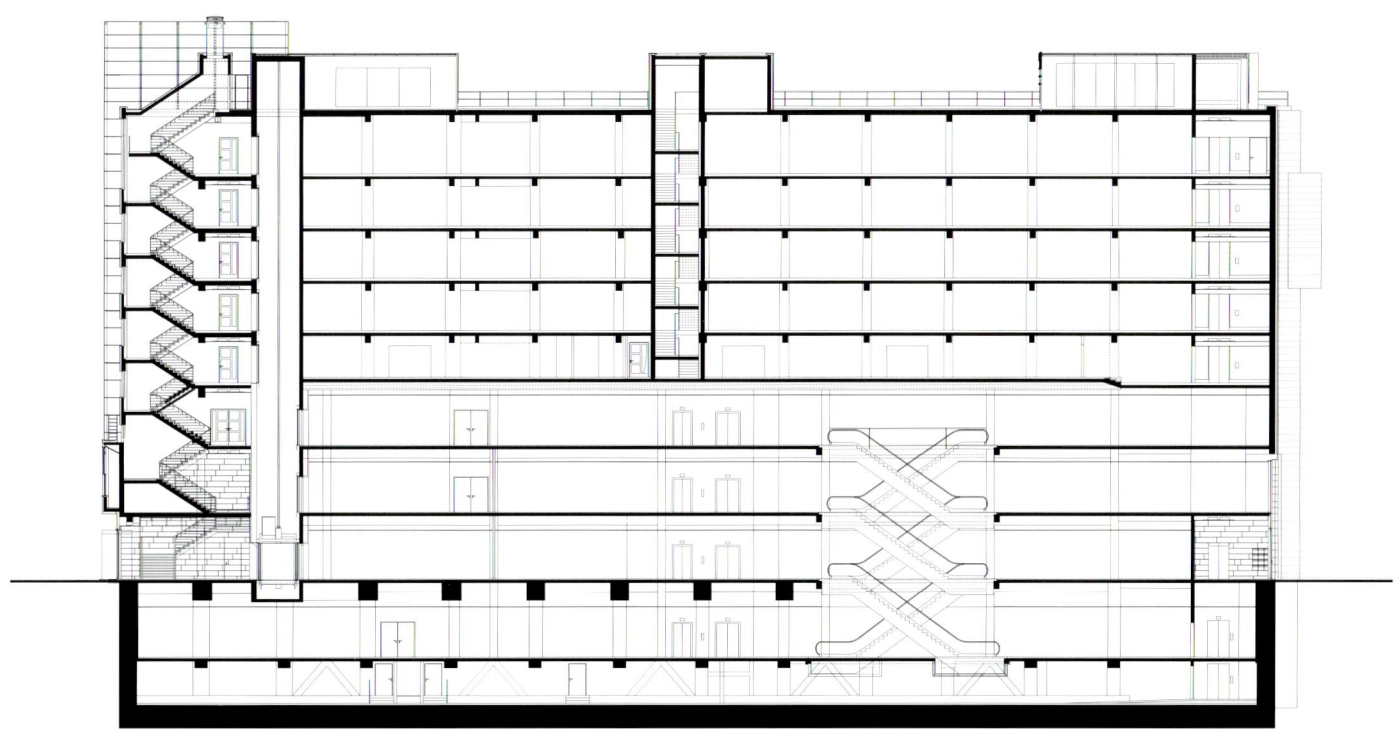

Längsschnitt | Longitudinal section

0   10 m

Polierter schwarz-grüner Serpentin und heller Travertin
sowie hochglänzendes Messing entfalten im Vestibül
und im Treppenhaus eine noble Wirkung. Die architektonischen Motive der grafischen Gestaltung sind den
Außenfassaden abgeschaut.

Polished green-black serpentine and light travertine and
polished brass lend the vestibule and staircase a luxurious character. The architectural motifs of the decorative stone panels are inspired by the external façade of
the building.

WOHNPFLEGEHEIM HAVELGARTEN
HAVELGARTEN NURSING HOME
BERLIN

Die drei gebogenen, viergeschossigen Baukörper in Berlin-Spandau, zum Teil die Spur der frühmittelalterlichen Palisaden des Spandauer Burgwalls verfolgend, fügen sich in einer bergenden Geste zusammen und umfangen einen ruhigen internen Hof. Im Gegensatz dazu schafft ein öffentliches Bistro am Havelufer Gelegenheit zur Kontaktaufnahme zwischen Heimbewohnern und Passanten. Für die weniger mobilen Pflegepatienten unter den 130 Bewohnern sind vielfache Ausblicke in den Hof und über die Havel inszeniert. Zwanzig betreute Altenwohnungen im zurückgestuften Dachgeschoss profitieren ebenfalls von der Aussicht und ergänzen das vielfältige Angebot des Wohnpflegeheims.

The three curved four-storey buildings in Berlin-Spandau, which partly follow the line of the palisade of the Spandau Burgwall from the early Middle Ages, interlock in a protective gesture that enclose a peaceful internal courtyard. By contrast, a public riverside bistro on the banks of the river Havel encourages contact between passers-by and the inhabitants. For the less mobile patients among the 130 residents, the complex provides numerous vantage points that look into the courtyard or out across the Havel. Twenty sheltered flats in the stepped-back top floor on the roof also enjoy expansive views and complement the variety of facilities offered by the nursing home.

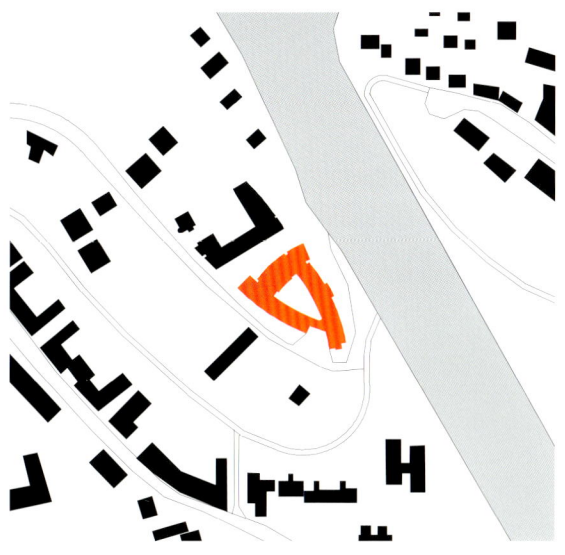

Idyllisch am Havelufer gelegen bildet das Wohnpflegeheim mit seinen drei gebogenen Flügeln einen Innenhof, der als begrünter Freibereich genutzt wird. So entstehen eine außenorientierte und eine introvertierte, zum ruhigen Hof orientierte Seite. Durch die gebogenen Baukörper bekommen die Flure Spannung und Aussagekraft. Auch der Andachtsraum profitiert von dieser Spannung.

Situated idyllically on the banks of the Havel, the three curved wings enclose an interior courtyard which is used as a recreational area. The result is an extroverted façade outside and an introverted peaceful courtyard within. The curved shape of the building lends dynamism and orientation to what would otherwise be long, dull corridors. The chapel is likewise enlivened by the curve of the building.

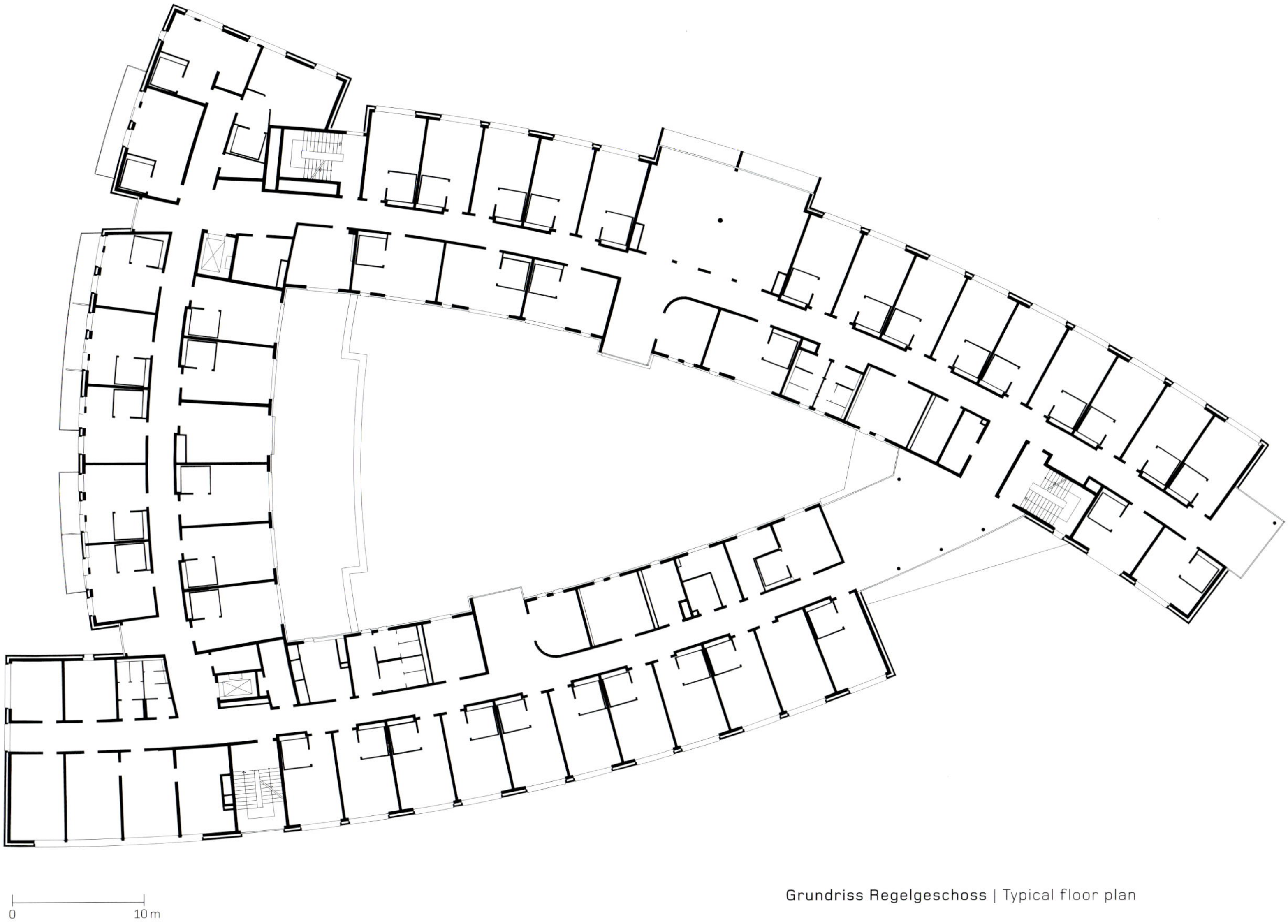

Grundriss Regelgeschoss | Typical floor plan

0 _____ 10 m

SYNAGOGE CHABAD LUBAWITSCH
CHABAD LUBAVITCH SYNAGOGUE
BERLIN

Als das Umspannwerk in Berlin-Wilmersdorf 1922 in Betrieb ging, hatte der Kaiser schon abgedankt, war die wilhelminisch-klassizistische Attitüde eigentlich schon von gestern. Die neue Nutzung verträgt sich mit dem konservativen Äußeren schon eher. Die jüdisch-orthodoxe Gemeinde Chabad Lubawitsch ist in das Haus eingezogen und betreibt darin ein Bildungs- und Gemeindezentrum mit Bibliothek, Restaurant, Festsaal, Seminarräumen und Mikwe. Einrichtungen im Foyer wie Judaika-Laden, Theke und Sitzinsel sind wie eingestellte dynamische Designobjekte geformt. Zentrum des Baus ist die Synagoge in der ehemaligen Transformatorenhalle. Wände, Böden, Podium und Thoraschrein sowie das Gestühl sind aus mittelbraunem Walnussholz gefertigt. Der Raum ist kompromisslos modern gestaltet und hat dennoch eine Atmosphäre, wie man sie in holzvertäfelten, historischen Interieurs erlebt. Ein Okulus in der Decke bringt als spirituelle Quelle Zenitlicht in den Raum, dem nach den Wünschen der Auftraggeber eine intensive Sakralität und eine emotional bewegende Stimmung zu eigen ist.

By the time the transformer substation in Berlin-Wilmersdorf was put into operation in 1922, the Kaiser had already abdicated and the neo-classicist stance of Wilhelminian times was passé. The new use of the building has more to do with its conservative exterior than the original use. The Jewish-orthodox Chabad Lubavitch community has taken up residence in the building and set up a community and education centre with a library, restaurant, assembly hall, seminar rooms and a Mikwe. Additional facilities in the foyer such as a Judaica shop, reception and seating are arranged freely in the form of dynamically designed objects. The centre of the building is the synagogue, located in the former transformer hall. The walls, floor, podium and torah shrine as well as the seating are made of walnut. Although the design of the space is uncompromisingly modern, its atmosphere is more akin to that of a historic wood-panelled interior. An oculus in the ceiling, a spiritual source, allows light from above into the room below lending it both a spiritual intensity as well as an emotionally moving atmosphere, succinctly fulfilling the wishes of the client.

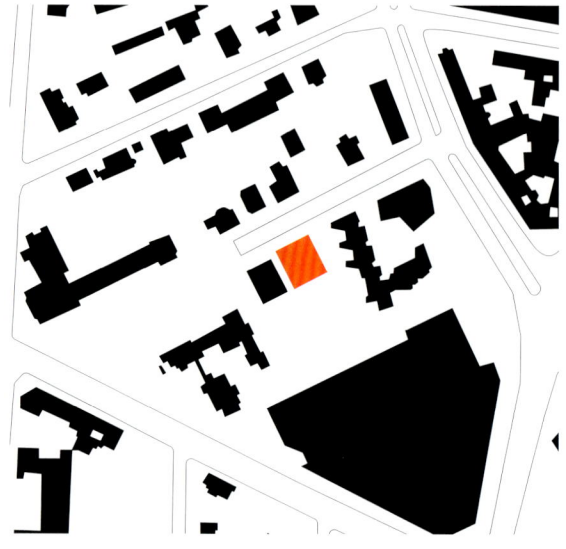

Das neue Treppenhausfenster gibt nach außen hin den einzigen Hinweis auf die veränderte Nutzung des einstigen Umspannwerkes.

The new staircase window is the only outwardly visible hint of the new function of the former transformer substation.

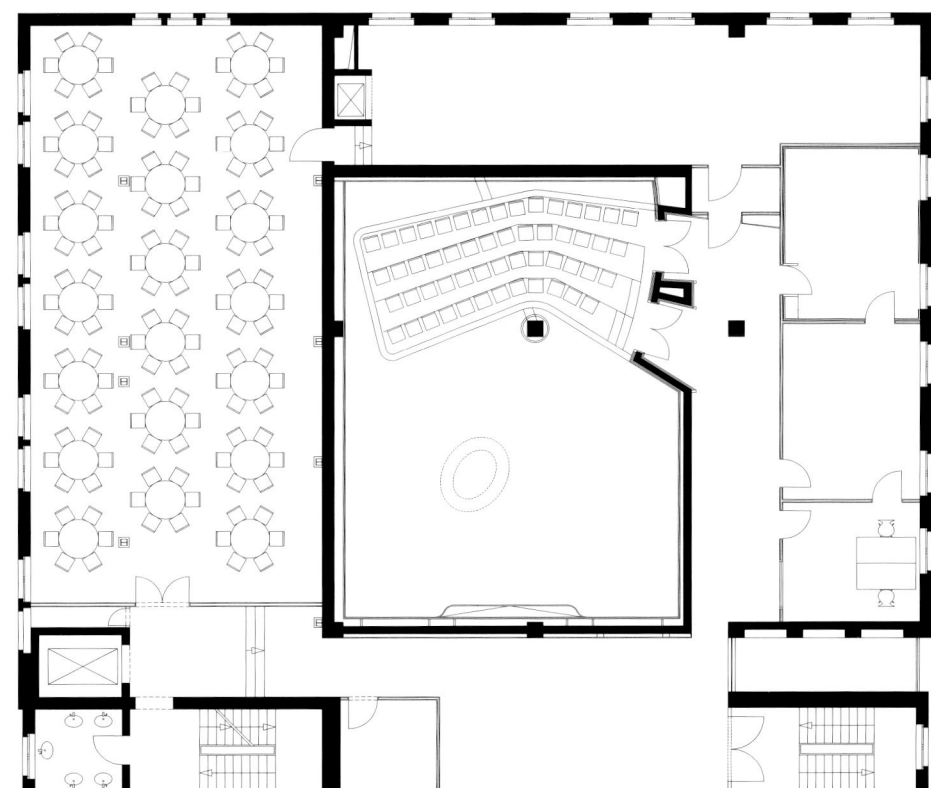

Grundriss 1. Obergeschoss mit Festsaal (links),
Betsaal Frauenempore (Mitte), koschere Küche
(oben) und Verwaltung (rechts) | First floor
plan with assembly hall (in the plan on the left),
women's gallery in the prayer hall (centre),
kosher kitchen (top) and administration (right)

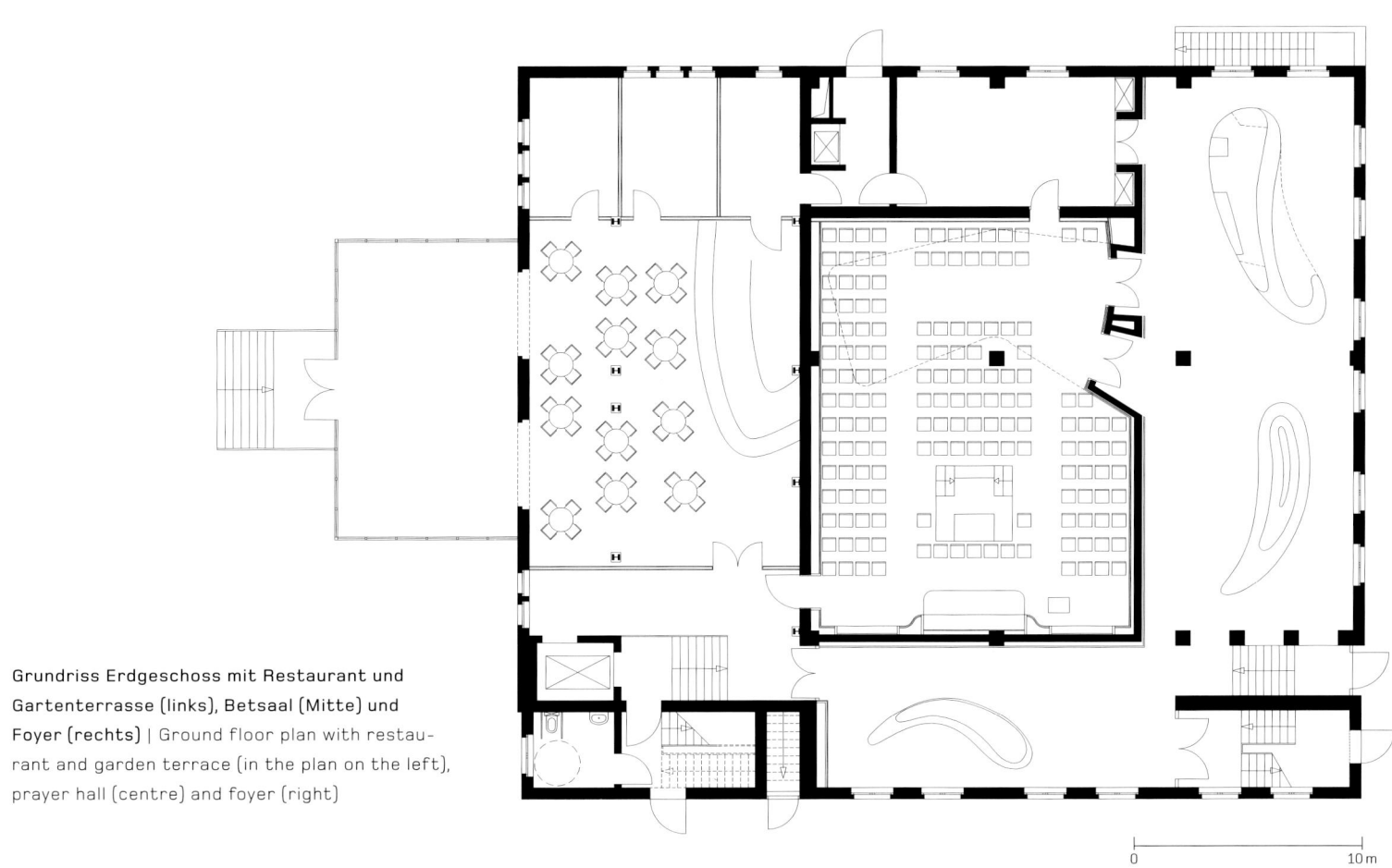

Grundriss Erdgeschoss mit Restaurant und
Gartenterrasse (links), Betsaal (Mitte) und
Foyer (rechts) | Ground floor plan with restau-
rant and garden terrace (in the plan on the left),
prayer hall (centre) and foyer (right)

0   10 m

Die Empore im Betraum ist für die Frauen bestimmt.
Wände, Gestühl und Thoraschrein sind aus Walnussholz
gefertigt.

The gallery in the prayer hall is reserved for women.
The wall panelling, chairs and torah shrine are all made
of walnut.

Eine Wand in der Eingangshalle ist eine Nachbildung der Klagemauer des Tempels in Jerusalem. Die Einbauten, Theken und Vitrinen sind als beschwingte Möbel in den Raum gestellt, deren Form von den Lichtdecken nachgezeichnet wird.

A wall in the entrance hall is a reproduction of the Wailing Wall from the Temple in Jerusalem. The curved forms of the furniture, counters and cabinets are placed like freestanding objects in the hall and are accentuated by lighting panels of a similar shape in the ceiling.

HERRENHAUS WELLINGSBÜTTEL
WELLINGSBÜTTEL MANOR
HAMBURG

Mit dem Umbau dieses historischen Gebäudes zur Seniorenresidenz des gehobenen Standards ist es gelungen, dem um 1750 errichteten und 1888 durch Martin Haller aufgestockten spätbarocken Herrenhaus Wellingsbüttel eine neue, angemessene Nutzung zu geben, insbesondere, da die größeren Repräsentationsräume im Erdgeschoss nicht unterteilt wurden, sondern in ihrem ursprünglichen Zuschnitt erhalten blieben und als Café und Gemeinschaftsräume dienen. Mit großer Sorgfalt wurde die erhaltene Bauzier – der Stuck in allen Räumen, die reich verzierte Holztreppe, die Malereien – restauriert und wurden Fenster originalgetreu nachgebaut. Zwei Erweiterungen sind beiderseits symmetrisch an das Herrenhaus angefügt. Sie ergänzen den Bau sinngemäß, sind jedoch durch Schattenfugen abgesetzt, in modernem Stil gehalten und verleugnen ihre Entstehungszeit nicht.

In Obergeschoss und Dachkörper wurden 14 Appartements eingebaut, im Untergeschoss ein Wellnessbereich und ein medizinisches Pflegebad in stilvollem Ambiente.

Through the conversion of this historic building to a luxurious home for the elderly it was possible to find an appropriate use for the late Baroque manor house, which was built in 1750 and extended in 1888 by Martin Haller. In particular, the large imposing interiors on the ground floor could be retained in their original form without subdivisions and are used as communal rooms and a café. The existing decorative elements – the stucco in all the rooms, the richly decorated wooden staircase and the paintings – were restored with the utmost care and the windows replaced with replicas of the originals. Two symmetrical extensions were added on either side of the manor house. They complement the building accordingly but are slightly offset from the building and given a modern treatment, clearly indicating their contemporary origins.

The upper floor and the attic were converted to contain 14 apartments, with a wellness area and medicinal baths in the cellar, all with a most elegant ambience.

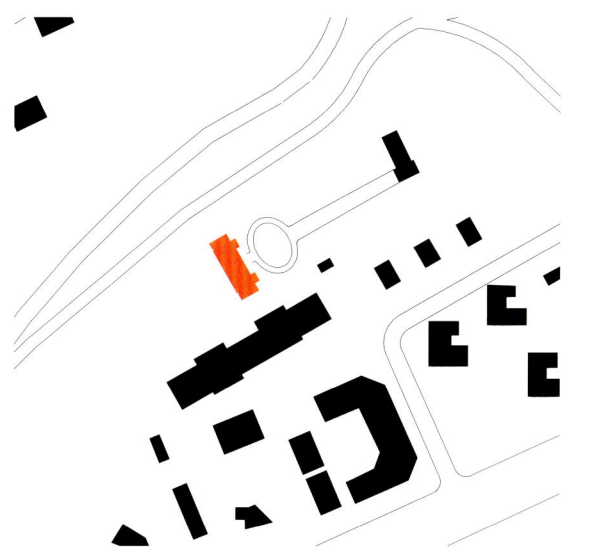

Unauffällig in reduzierter Formensprache, aber deutlich als moderne Zutat ausgewiesen und mit einer verglasten Schattenfuge abgesetzt sind die Erweiterungen an das nach Art eines französischen Palais gestaltete Herrenhaus angefügt.

Unassuming and an exercise in formal reduction, the two unmistakably modern extensions to the manor house, which is modelled after a French Palais, are separated from the main building by a narrow glazed slot.

Ansicht | Elevation

0   5m

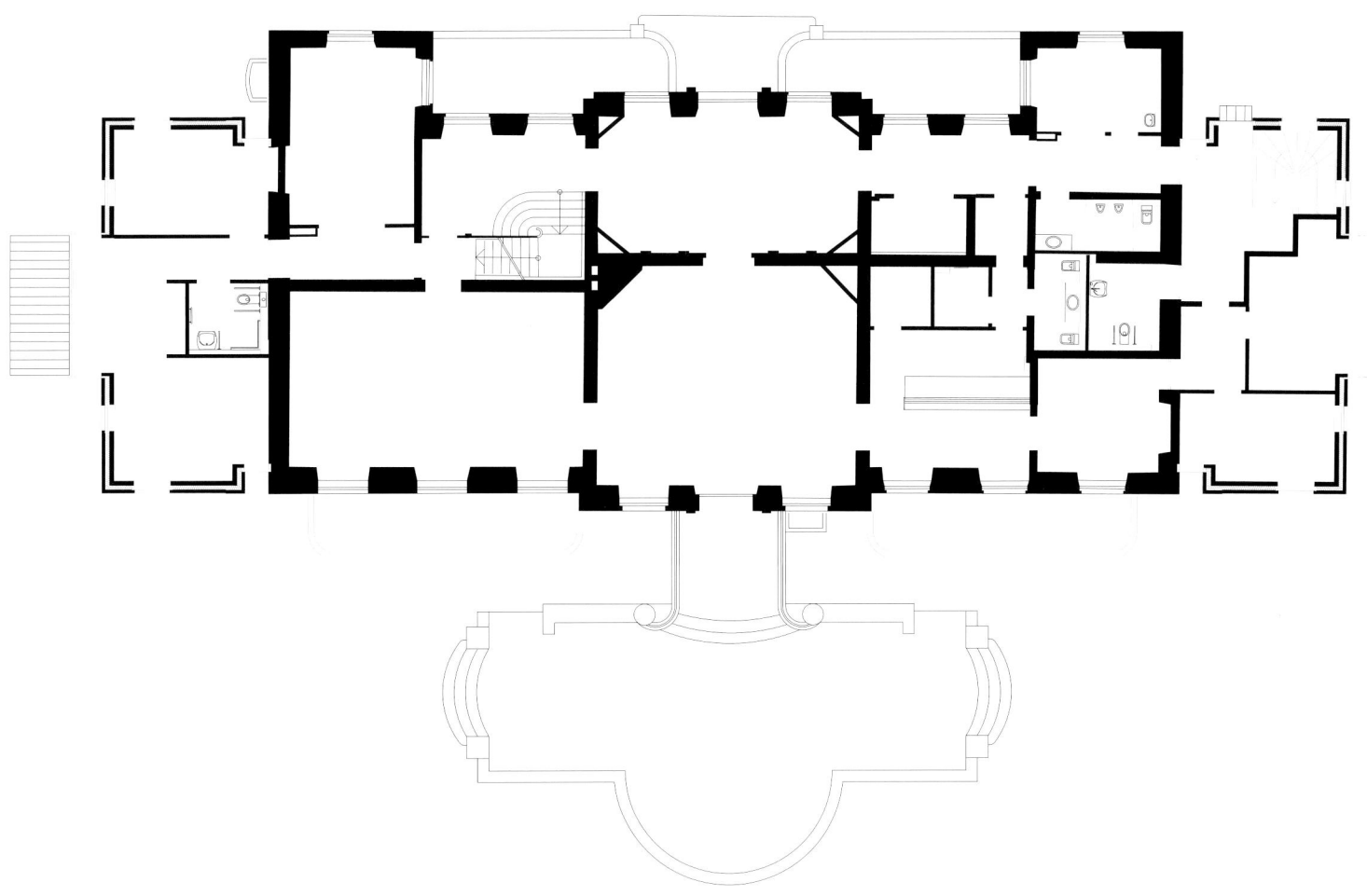

Grundriss Erdgeschoss | Ground floor plan

JAVATURM
JAVATOWER
HAMBURG

Der nüchtern-schmucklose Baukörper des Turms der Kaffeerösterei in Hamburg-Langenhorn, der sich vier Geschosse hoch über der Fabrikhalle erhebt, wurde zu einem Loft- und Atelierhaus umgebaut. Mit seinem neuen Erscheinungsbild bildet er eine Landmarke an der Langenhorner Chaussee. Über einen eigenen Eingangsvorbau aus markanten Sichtbetonschotten gelangt man in den Turm, in dem Büroräume und die höheren Atelierräume im obersten Geschoss durch „Fallreep-Treppen" erschlossen sind. Eine gebogene, skulpturale Stahltreppe führt schließlich vom Atelier durch das Dach in das gläserne Penthouse. Das halbrunde Glashaus und die Dachterrasse profitieren von einer weiten Rundumsicht. Die scheinbar wahllos verteilten Fenster in der Terrakotta-Fassade lassen auf die räumliche Vielfalt im Inneren schließen. Der Turm wurde durch die kontrastreiche Farbgebung und durch die nach grafischen Regeln komponierte Befensterung zu einer Bauskulptur mit formalen Anklängen an holländische De Stijl-Architektur der zwanziger Jahre.

The neutral unadorned construction of the tower of the coffee roasting facility in Hamburg-Langenhorn, which rises four storeys above the factory below, was converted to a loft and atelier. Its new appearance has made it a landmark on the Langenhorner Chaussee. A new entrance porch made of distinctive fair-faced concrete slabs provides access to the tower, the office spaces and the high atelier space in the top storey, which are reached via gangway-like stairs. A sculptural curved steel stair leads from the atelier through the roof into the glazed penthouse. The semicircular glass turret and the roof terrace afford a panoramic view of the surroundings. The seemingly arbitrary placement of the windows in the terracotta façade hint at the variety of spaces within. Through its strongly contrasting colour scheme and the graphic composition of the windows, it has a sculptural appearance reminiscent of the formal experiments of Dutch De Stijl architecture from the twenties.

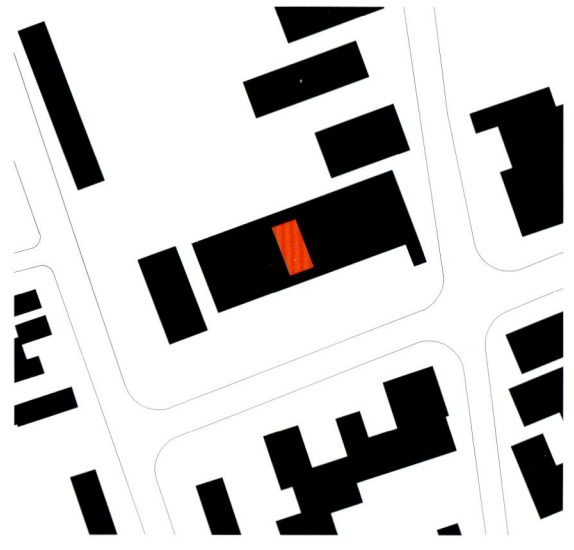

Vorherrschendes architektonisches Thema in den Atelierräumen der Turmgeschosse sind die Treppen, die in Fallreepform, im obersten Geschoss als gebogener, technisch-skulpturaler Lauf nach oben führen.

The dominant architectural elements of the atelier spaces in the tower are the stairs, which, reminiscent of ship gangways, ascend to the next storey, in the upper storey arcing in a sweeping curve.

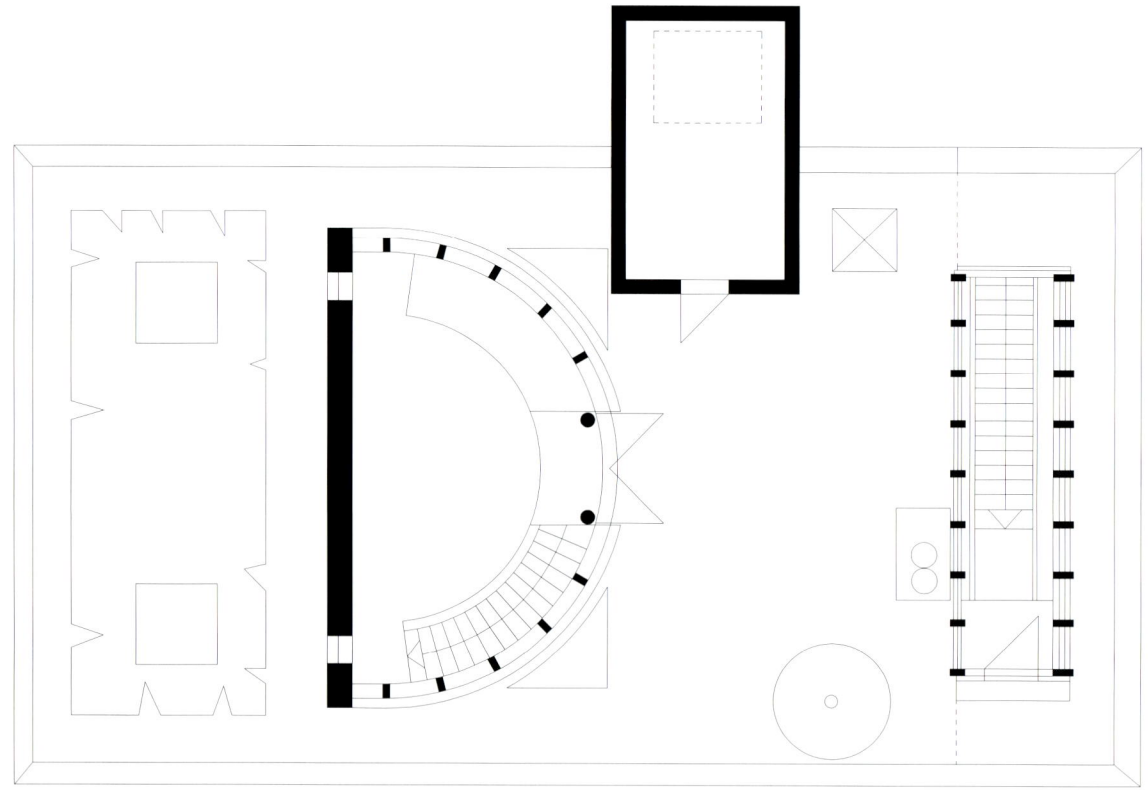

Grundriss Dachgarten mit Pavillon | Roof plan with roof garden and pavilion

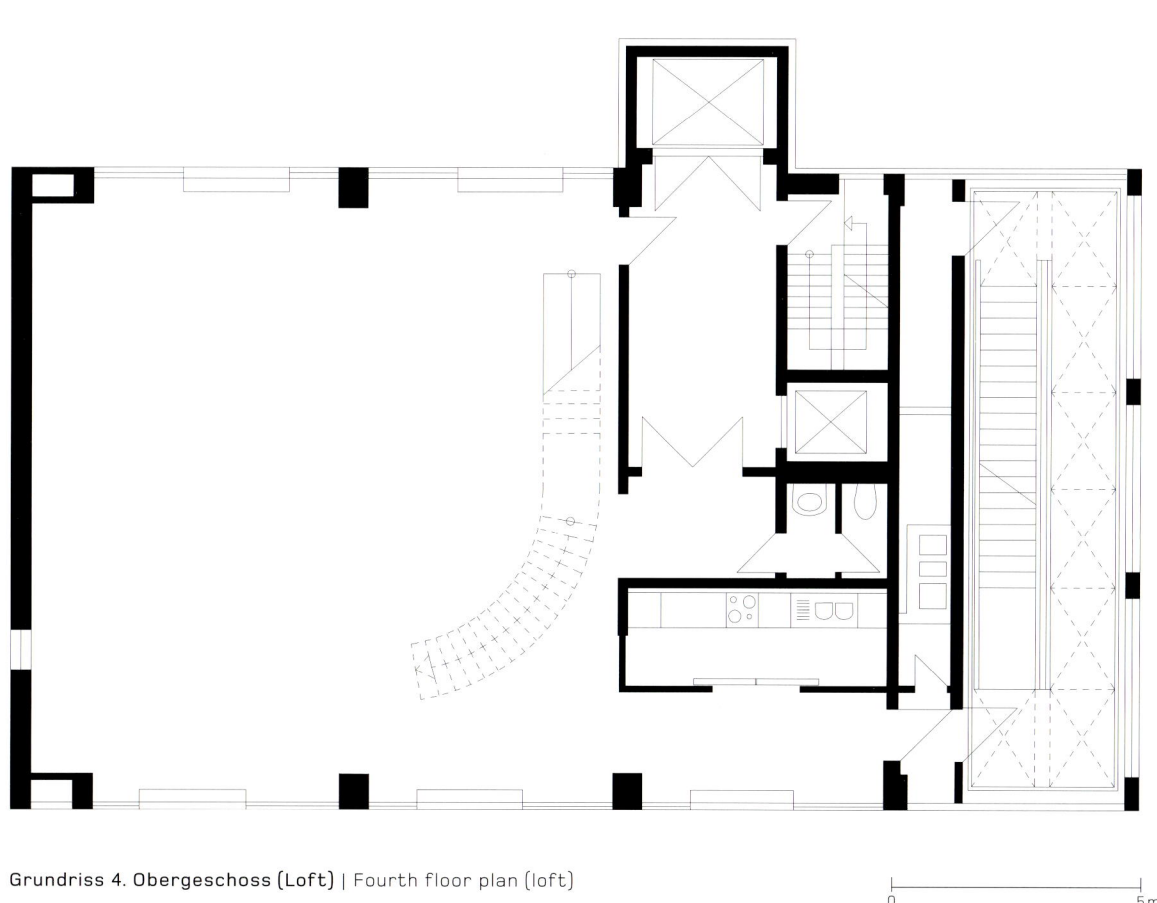

Grundriss 4. Obergeschoss (Loft) | Fourth floor plan (loft)

0   5m

BENOISHAUS
BENOIS BUILDING
ST. PETERSBURG

Eine leer stehende Industrieanlage am Newaufer wird saniert und zu einem Büro- und Geschäftszentrum umgebaut. Das achtgeschossige Gebäude am Piskarewski-Prospekt ist in eine rahmenlose Ganzglasfassade mit einem unregelmäßigen Wechsel aus dunklen und transparenten Scheinen gekleidet. Die neue Fassade ist dem Künstler, Kostümbildner und Theaterförderer Alexander Benois gewidmet, der im 19. Jahrhundert hier eine Datscha gemietet hatte. Hier hatte er miterlebt, wie die Industrie eine wunderschöne Gartenanlage nach und nach verdrängt hatte. Hier ist ihm der eigenständige Wert „der reinen Kunst", Credo des von ihm später gegründeten Vereins „Welt der Kunst" („Mir iskusstwa"), klar geworden. Die Architekten wollen den Rückzug der „reinen Kunst" thematisieren und sie auf den Zweckbau projizieren und damit einem anonymen Investorenobjekt einen eigenständigen künstlerischen Ausdruck verleihen. Die Fassade erinnert an die Vorliebe von Alexander Benois für toskanische Palazzi, aber auch an die Kostümfeste Katharina der Großen. Jedes fünfte der geschosshohen Glasfelder ist mit einem von Benois' Entwürfen für die Theaterkostüme der Djagilew-Aufführungen bedruckt.

A vacant industrial building on the banks of the Newa was renovated and converted for use as offices and a commercial centre. The eight-storey building on Piscarevsky Prospekt is clad entirely with an alternating pattern of tinted and transparent panes of frameless glass. The new façade is dedicated to the artist, costume designer and theatre benefactor Alexander Benois, who in the 19th century rented an allotment garden in the area. This is where he experienced the advance of industry and gradual displacement of the wonderful allotment gardens. This is where he developed his notion of "pure art", a central credo of the "Mir iskusstva" ("World of Art") artistic movement he later co-founded. The architects made the withdrawal advocated by "pure art" a central theme of the design, projecting it onto the functional building in order to give the essentially anonymous investment project an artistic expression of its own. The façade reflects Alexander Benois' love of Tuscan palazzi as well as the costume parties celebrated by Catherine the Great. Every fifth of the storey-high glass panes is printed with one of the theatre costume designs created by Benois for Diaghilev's performances.

Die straßenseitige Fassade des Hauses ist mit Benois'
Theaterkostümentwürfen geschmückt, wobei sich
sieben Motive immer wiederholen. Hofseitig tauchen
die Bilder in extremer Vergrößerung ausschnittweise
als Pixelmuster wieder auf.

The entire street façade of the building is decorated
with Benois' designs for theatre costumes in a repeat-
ing pattern of seven different designs. On the rear
façade, parts of the images are reproduced in an
enlarged form as a pixelated pattern.

BÜROHAUS LANGENZIPEN
LANGENZIPEN OFFICE BUILDING
ST. PETERSBURG

Was zunächst als eine historistisch dekorierte Stuckfassade erscheint, die mit ihrer historischen Nachbarschaft auf der so genannten „Pedrograder Seite" korrespondiert, ist bei genauerem Hinsehen eine moderne Glasfassade. Der Schmuck – spielerisch kombinierte, von Christian Gahl in Rom fotografierte barocke Rustika, Girlanden, Vasen mit floralem Dekor und Hermenpilaster – ist per Tintenstrahldruck auf die Gläser aufgebracht. Das Dekor ist eine moderne Interpretation der französischen und italienischen Motive der Schaufassaden der St. Petersburger Bürgerhäuser des 19. Jahrhunderts in der Nachbarschaft.

Die mit Naturstein verkleidete, nur sparsam mosaikartig mit Fenstern durchbrochene Giebelwand zitiert hingegen die historischen Brandwände der Nachbarhäuser. Sie geht mit einer Rundung in die Dachfläche über und rahmt auf diese Weise mit ihrer Vorderkante die gläsernen Längswände. So wurde aus dem das Stadtbild malträtierenden ehemaligen Fabrikgebäude aus dem Jahr 1965, dessen Stahlskelett in dem Gebäude steckt, ein den kleinen Stadtplatz prägendes, wieder eingegliedertes Mitglied der Häuserfamilie.

An der Südseite ist das Haus durch einen Verbindungsbau mit dem Backsteingebäude einer Fabrik vom Ende des 19. Jahrhunderts verbunden. In diesem kristallinen Zwischenglied zwischen den beiden massiven Häusern verbinden filigrane Brücken und die Aufzugsanlage beide Gebäude funktional miteinander.

What at first looks like a historic decorated stucco frontage that fits in with the period buildings of the neighbourhood in the so-called "Petrograd Side" is in fact on closer inspection a modern glass façade. The decoration – an artful combination of rustic Baroque details, garlands, vases with floral decoration and terminal pilasters based on photographs taken by Christian Gahl in Rome – is printed on the glass surfaces using an inkjet technique. The decoration is a modern interpretation of the French and Italian motifs seen on the sumptuous façades of St. Petersburg's 19th-century town houses in the neighbourhood.

The side gable walls, which by contrast are clad with stone panels punctured only periodically by windows, cite the historical fire walls of the neighbouring buildings. The side walls bend over at the top fusing with the roof plane, their leading edge forming a continuous line that frames the glazed frontages. The former eyesore of a factory building erected in 1965, whose steel frame still serves as the structural core of the building, now assumes a commanding position in the small urban square, standing among its neighbours as if a long-lost member of the family.

To the south, the building is linked to its immediate neighbour, a factory building made of brick from the late 19th century. Between the two solid buildings, a crystalline insertion with delicate bridges, stairs and lifts connects the two buildings functionally with one another.

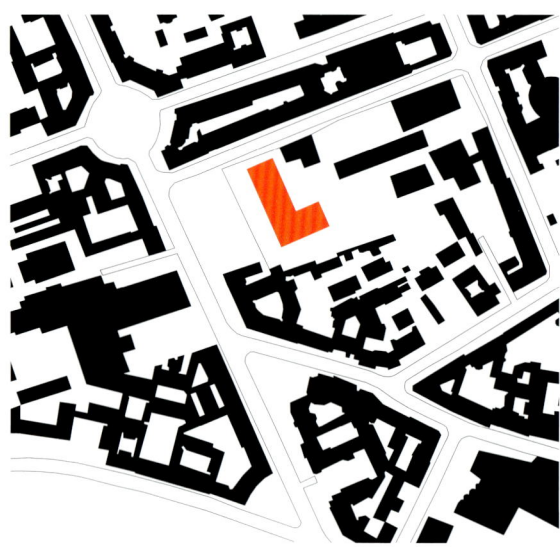

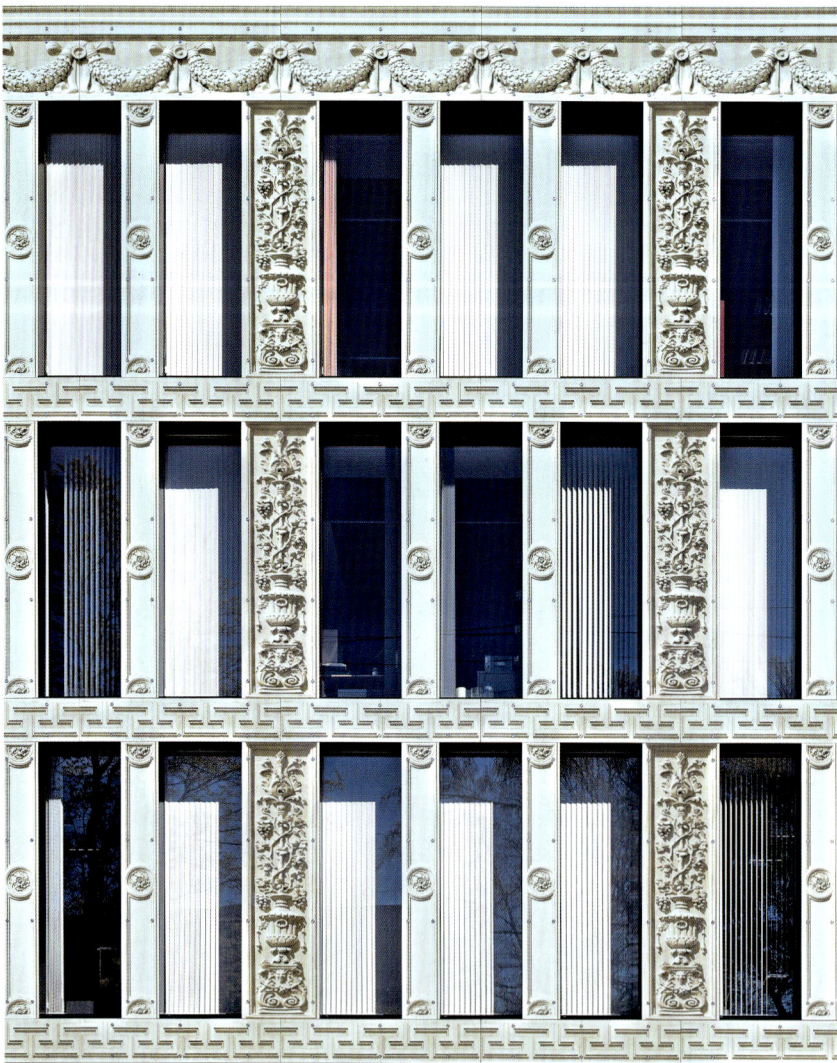

Barockmotive aus Rom, fotografiert und hinter Glas gedruckt, sind hier die moderne Antwort auf das reiche Stuckdekor der Häuser aus Historismus und Jugendstil in der Nachbarschaft.

Baroque motifs from Rome, photographed and printed onto the interior side of the glazing, represent a modern interpretation of the rich stucco decorations of the Historicist and Art Nouveau façades of the neighbouring buildings.

ALTE OBERPOSTDIREKTION
FORMER POST OFFICE HEADQUARTERS
HANNOVER | HANOVER

Bei der Sanierung und Umnutzung wilhelminischer Pracht-bauten sind oft unkonventionelle Wege zu gehen. Für die ehemalige Oberpostdirektion in Hannovers noblem Zooviertel wurde eine neue Bestimmung als Seniorendomizil gefunden. Die herrschaftliche Fassade blieb dabei ebenso erhalten und wurde nach denkmalpflegerischen Gesichtspunkten ergänzt wie die historischen Innenräume und Flure. Naturgemäß er-gaben sich beim Umbau des Verwaltungsgebäudes funktions-bedingte Veränderungen in der Grundrissstruktur, vor allem im Bereich der Zimmer.

Zwei störende eingeschossige Erweiterungsbauten aus den sechziger Jahren im Hof wurden durch neue, im Stil an-gepasste Bauteile ersetzt. Die neuen Anbauten beinhalten einerseits die Räume der Domizilleitung, andererseits Ap-partements und im Obergeschoss zwei großzügige Winter-gärten. Der repräsentative Gestus des Gebäudes wird als Imageträger für die Seniorenresidenz des gehobenen Sek-tors genutzt und schafft ein stilvolles Ambiente.

The renovation and conversion of stately Wilhelminian build-ings such as the former Post Office Headquarters in Hano-ver often leads to unconventional solutions. The magnifi-cent building in the city's prestigious Zoo quarter has been converted for use as a home for the elderly. Not only has the grand façade been restored and augmented in close consultation with the conservation authorities but also the historic interiors and corridors. Naturally, some alterations to the floor plans were necessary to adapt the adminis-trative spaces for residential use, particularly in the rooms themselves.

Two unsightly single-storey extensions in the courtyard from the sixties were replaced with new more fitting build-ings. The new additions contain the director's rooms on the one hand and apartments on the other, with two spacious conservatories on the upper floors. The building's stately appearance serves as a strong image for the up-market residence for the elderly and communicates an ambience of elegance.

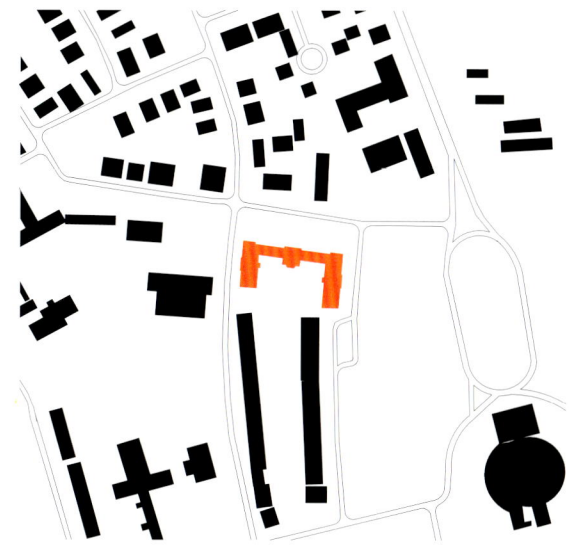

EINRICHTUNGSHAUS IKEA
IKEA FURNITURE STORE
HANNOVER | HANOVER

Ein Grundstück an der Straße der Nationen auf dem ehemaligen EXPO 2000-Gelände hatte sich das schwedische Möbelhaus als Standort gewählt. Ungewöhnlich für einen IKEA-Markt ist die Organisation und Erschließung des Hauses, denn die Parkierungsflächen liegen im Untergeschoss und im Erdgeschoss unter den Verkaufsflächen der beiden oberen Stockwerke. Der Kunde gelangt über Fahrtreppen und Lifts ohne weite Wege zur Eingangshalle und zu den Verkaufs- und Ausstellungsräumen, die in gewohnter Weise als mäandrierender Ausstellungsraum, als Markthalle und als zehn Meter hohes Regallager organisiert sind.

Die äußere Gestalt des mit Trapezblech in den Farben des Hauses verkleideten Baukörpers bildet diese Aufteilung ab und signalisiert deutlich den Haupteingang und den gebäudehoch verglasten Eingangs- und Restaurantbereich.

Die Ostseite an der Straße der Nationen und die Fassade zum Messeschnellweg sind durch die skulptural wirkenden Anlagen der Fluchttreppen akzentuiert. Die dominante Corporate Identity des Markendesigns wird in einen konzeptionell und gestalterisch eigenständigen Bau integriert.

The Swedish furniture retailer had selected a plot on the Strasse der Nationen in the grounds of the former EXPO 2000. The entrance and organisation of the retail outlet is unusual for an IKEA store in that the car parking is arranged on the ground and lower ground floors with the retail spaces on the two upper floors. Escalators and lifts bring the customers directly to the entrance hall and retail and exhibition areas, which follow the usual pattern of a meandering exhibition floor, market hall and a ten-metre-high shelving warehouse.

The external appearance of the corrugated metal building in the house colours reflects the internal organisation, clearly signalling the main entrance and the full-height glazed entrance and restaurant area.

The east side of the Strasse der Nationen and the elevation facing the Messeschnellweg are accentuated by the sculptural repetition of the fire escape stairs. The building represents a specific conceptual and design solution while fully integrating the dominant corporate identity and branding of the retailer.

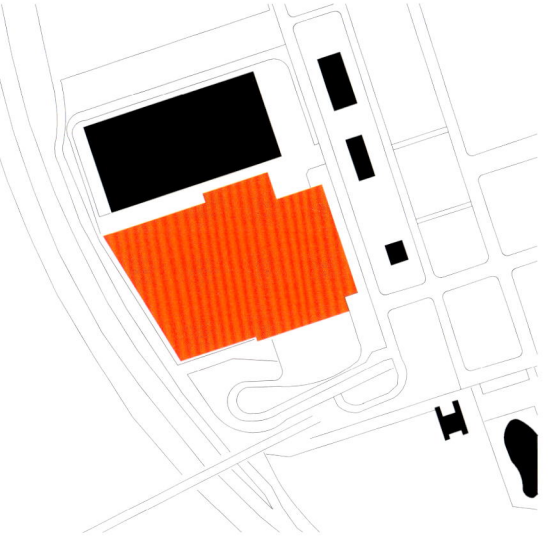

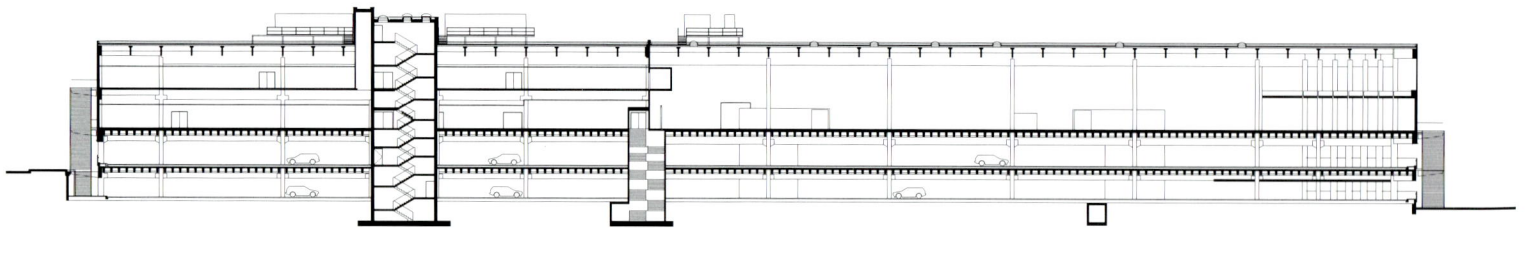

Längsschnitt | Longitudinal section

0   20m

Aus Fluchtwegen werden attraktive Treppenkaskaden, die auf dem voluminösen Baukörper einen Reigen inszenieren. Die Markenfarbe Gelb signalisiert die Publikumsbereiche Eingangshalle und Restaurant.

Fire escape stairs are formed into an attractive cascade of stairways, tumbling rhythmically from the voluminous rectangle of the building. The corporate colour yellow is used to signal the public areas, the entrance and restaurant.

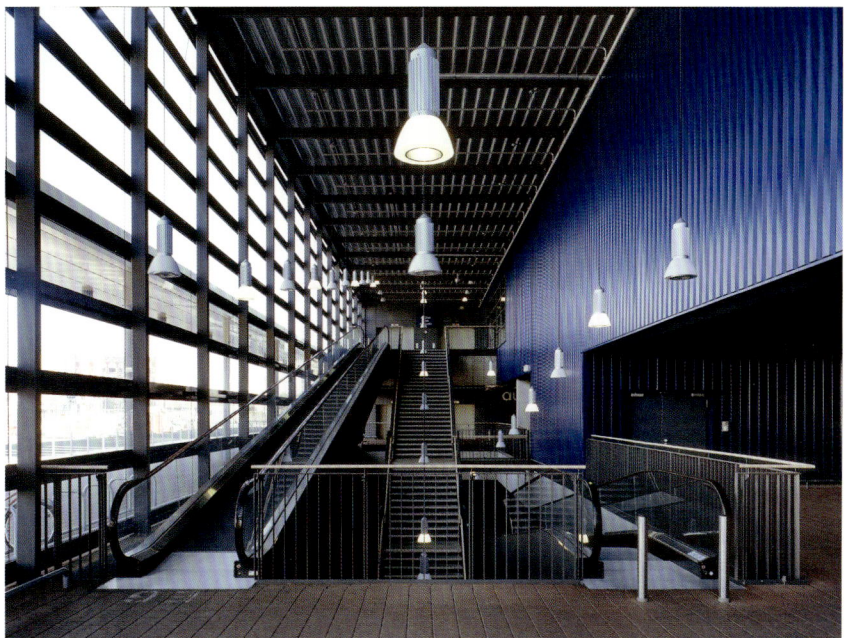

KAISER-WILHELM-KONTOR
HAMBURG

Ein Bürohaus der fünfziger Jahre war zu revitalisieren. Zunächst wurde es um zwei Vollgeschosse aufgestockt. Der Grundriss wurde zum Dreibund mit Nebennutzungsflächen in der Mittelzone. Das Achsmaß erlaubt die Einrichtung unterschiedlichster Bürotypen. Erschlossen sind die in bis zu vier Tranchen zu vermietenden Etagen von dem über sechs Geschosse durchgesteckten Foyer aus, mit zwei gläsernen Lifts an der Rückwand.

Die neue Fassade aus hellem Kalkstein mit tiefem Relief verleiht dem Bau eine solide Statur. Sie ist nach klassischem Vorbild in Erdgeschoss, Mittelteil und Attikageschoss gegliedert. Durch optische Zusammenfassung jeweils zweier Etagen mittels zweigeschossiger Holz-Aluminium-Kastenfenster wird die Monumentalität des Erscheinungsbildes gesteigert. Die großflächigen Fenster der aufgesetzten Geschosse reichen jeweils über drei Achsen.

The task was to renovate an office building from the fifties. Two additional storeys were added and the floor plan reorganised into a tripartite arrangement with ancillary spaces in the central zone. The window spacing allows the interior to be subdivided into a variety of different kinds of offices. Each floor can be let in up to four separate sections and is accessed via a central six-storey-high foyer with two glass lifts on the rear wall.

The new façade is clad in a light-coloured limestone with a pronounced surface profile that lends the building a solid stature. Its proportions follow the classical pattern of plinth, central section and attica. The monumental appearance of the building is heightened by visually combining two storeys into one through the use of two-storey-high timber and aluminium box windows. The large-format windows of the new upper storeys span the width of three normal windows.

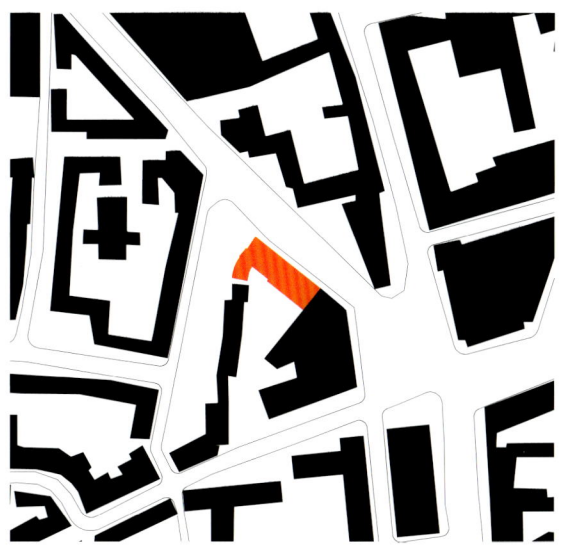

Ein heller Naturstein kleidet das erneuerte und auf-
gestockte Haus, das nun mit einem neuen Maßstab im
Quartier auftritt.

A light-coloured stone has been used to clad the re-
newed and extended building which now asserts itself
with greater stature in the urban neighbourhood.

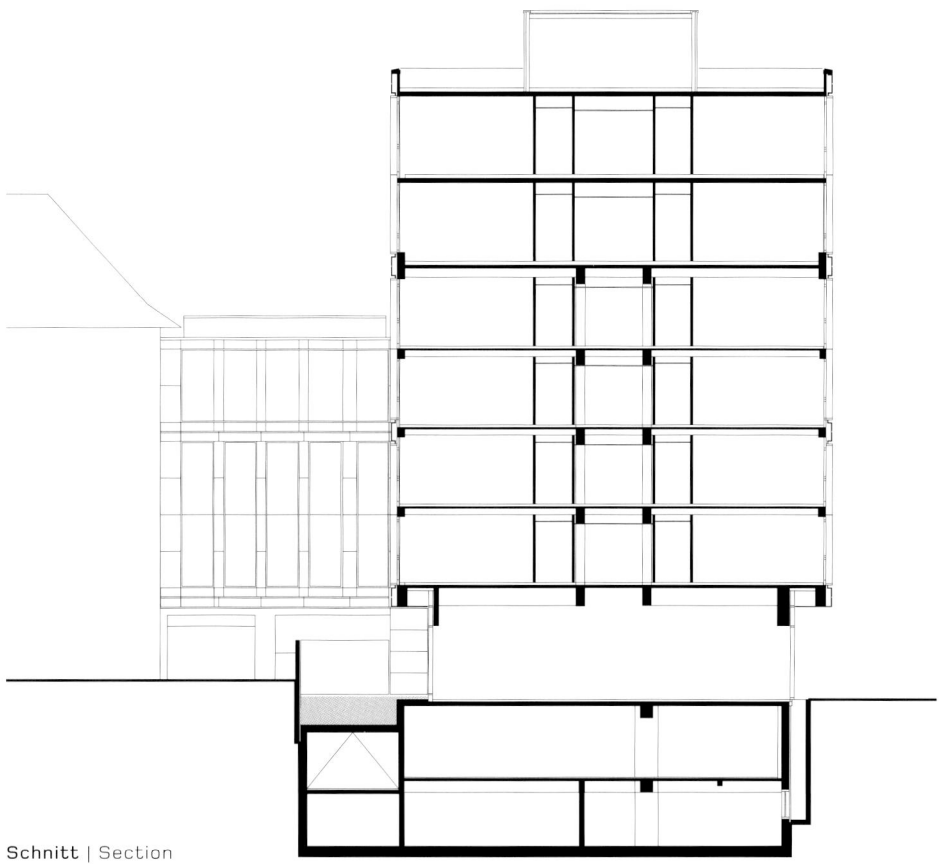

Schnitt | Section

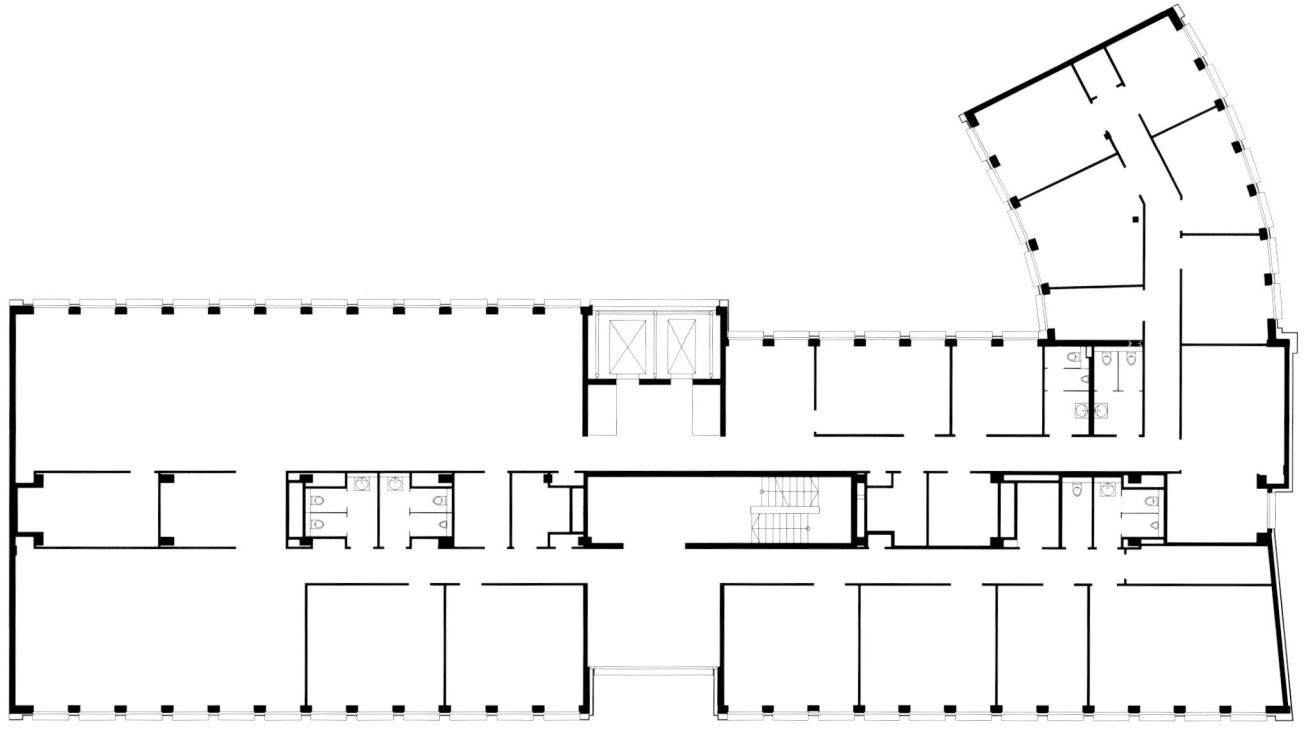

Grundriss Regelgeschoss | Typical floor plan

0   10 m

Jeweils drei Fensterachsen sind in den aufgestockten Geschossen zusammengefasst. Edle Materialien, ein ambitioniertes Beleuchtungskonzept und gläserne Lifts signalisieren schon in der Eingangshalle einen gewissen Repräsentationsanspruch der hier anzutreffenden Klientel.

The windows of the two new upper storeys span the width of three of the lower storey windows. Luxurious materials, an ambitious lighting concept and glazed lifts in the entrance hall create a high-class impression for the arriving clients.

BÜROGEBÄUDE AM KAISERKAI
OFFICE BUILDING KAISERKAI
HAMBURG

Der Bauplatz für das achtgeschossige Bürogebäude liegt in privilegierter zentraler Lage mitten in der HafenCity zwischen Sandtorhafen und Grasbrookhafen - Grund genug, einen signifikanten Bau mit markanter Gestalt an diesen prominenten Ort zu setzen. Eingebunden in den die Baufluchten und Kubaturen vorgebenden Masterplan, bildet er den Kopf der südlichen Bauzeile des Kaiserkais und dessen Entree am Großen Grasbrook.

Die städtebaulichen Bezüge waren wichtige Prämissen für die Baukörpergliederung. Die Flucht der Straße am Dalmannkai mündet in die zweigeschossige Eingangshalle des Hauses. Mit Auskragungen und Erkern antwortet der Bau auf Sichtachsen und das Panorama. Die vielfältigen Blickbeziehungen entlang der Straßen und über den Grasbrookhafen hinweg werden zum Thema gemacht. Durch eine stark gegliederte Kubatur und ein hierarchisches Fassadengliederungssystem mit Primär- und Sekundärteilungen vermeidet der voluminöse Kopfbau am Kaiserkai Monumentalität und gewinnt an spielerischer Leichtigkeit. Gleichzeitig macht er den Mietern mit seinen Vor- und Rücksprüngen, mit Balkons, Loggia und Dachterrasse ein differenziertes Angebot an innen- und außenräumlichen Situationen und bietet dadurch individuelle, identifizierbare Büroadressen.

The site of the eight-storey office building lies in a privileged location in the centre of the HafenCity between the Sandtor Harbour and the Grasbrook Harbour – reason enough to place a significant building with a distinctive form in this most prominent position. Bound by the building lines and volume constraints of the master plan, it forms the end of the southern row of buildings on the Kaiserkai and its entrance from the Große Grasbrook.

References to and from the urban surroundings were important premisses for determining the formal subdivision of the building. The building line of the street on the Dalmannkai leads directly towards the two-storey entrance hall of the building. Cantilevered projections and bays respond to sight lines and the surrounding panorama. The manifold views along the streets and across the Grasbrookhafen and beyond become a central theme of the building. Through its strongly modulated form and a hierarchical formal vocabulary with primary and secondary divisions in the façade, the large building avoids becoming overly monumental and exhibits a certain playful lightness. At the same time, through its projections and recesses, balconies, loggias and roof terraces, it provides a wealth of differentiated indoor and outdoor spaces, offering its future tenants individual and identifiable office addresses.

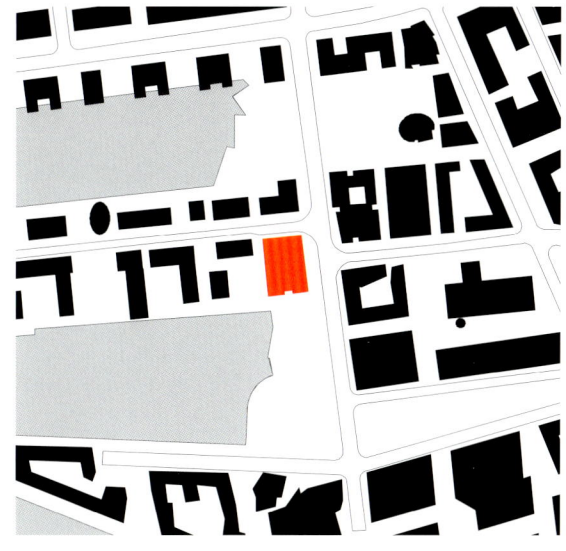

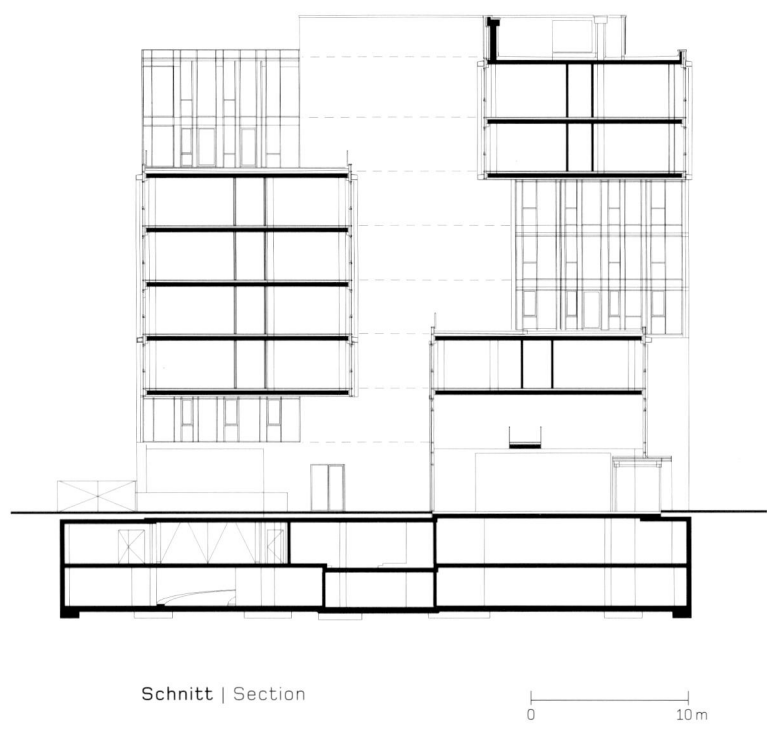

Schnitt | Section

0   10 m

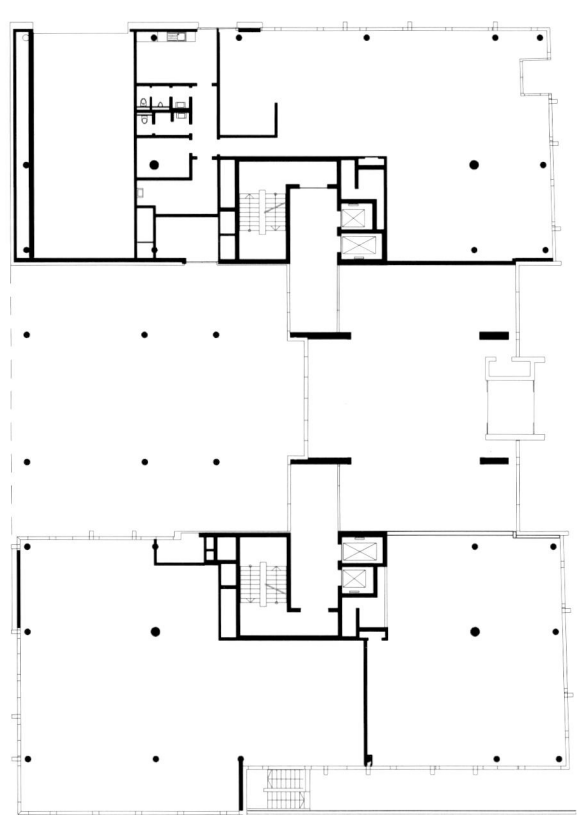

Grundriss Erdgeschoss | Ground floor plan

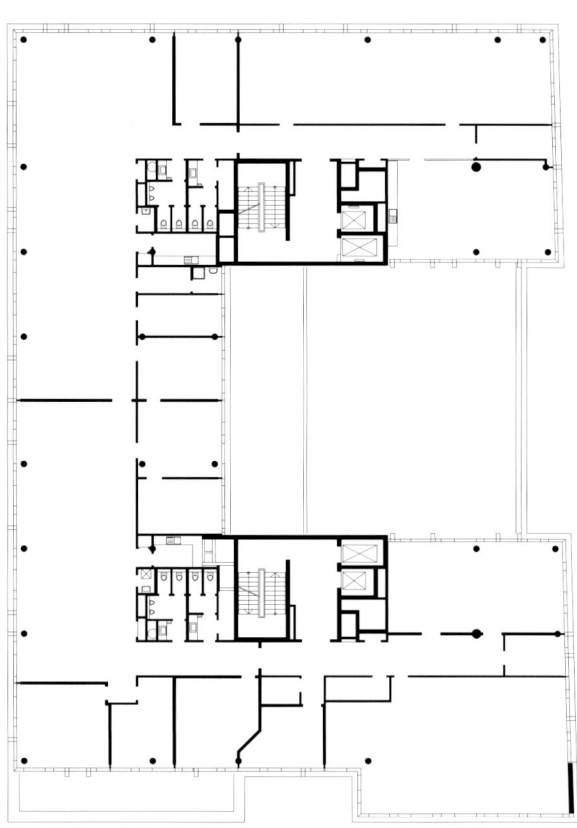

Grundriss Regelgeschosse | Typical floor plan

Gestapelte Baukuben, Vor- und Rücksprünge gliedern den großen Baukörper im Rahmen der Bebauungsplanvorgaben. Gleichzeitig entstehen räumlich differenzierte und vielfältig nutzbare Situationen wie Durchblicke und Terrassen.

Stacked volumes, projections and recesses break down the large size of the building while respecting the building regulations, resulting in a series of different spatial situations, terraces and lookouts that can be used for a variety of purposes.

PROJEKTE | WORK IN PROGRESS

FEDERATION TOWER
MOSKAU | MOSCOW

Nur vier Kilometer vom Kreml entfernt hat sich Moskau moskwaaufwärts ein neues Geschäfts- und Bürozentrum „Moscow City" mit 2,5 Millionen Quadratmetern Nutzfläche gegeben, das im Wesentlichen von westlichen Architekten mit Hochhäusern bebaut wurde und wird.

Der im Kreis einer Hochhausfamilie am Ufer der Moskwa stehende Federation Tower mit 365 Metern Höhe und seiner bis in 509 Meter Höhe in den Himmel ragenden Antennenadel ist der vorerst höchste Wolkenkratzer Europas.

Über einem sechsgeschossigen Sockelbauwerk mit Foyerhalle, Handel, Gastronomie, Konferenzzentrum und einem sich in die Untergeschosse entwickelnden „Lifestyle Center" mit Unterhaltungsangebot erheben sich zwei unterschiedlich hohe Büro- und Wohntürme. Die Turmbauten mit sphärischen Dreiecken als Grundrissform verjüngen sich stetig nach oben und enden in einer Kappe. Ein Aufzugsturm zwischen den beiden ist mit den Türmen über Brücken verbunden und mündet in die Antennenspitze. So entstand eine plastische Konfiguration, die aus allen Richtungen als Wahrzeichen gesehen wird. Während der Sockelbau mit einer aufwändig gestalteten Doppelfassade mit gebogenen Glaselementen verkleidet ist, reflektieren die Türme mit ihrer gläsernen Elementfassade Himmel und Wolken.

Just four kilometres from the Kremlin, a new business district called "Moscow City" with a planned 2.5 million square metres of floor area is being developed further along the Moskwa. Most of the site is destined to be filled with skyscrapers designed by western architects.

The Federation Tower stands among a group of skyscrapers on the banks of the River Moskwa and with a height of 365 metres – the needle of the antenna extends 509 metres into the sky – will for the moment be the tallest skyscraper in Europe.

Above a six-storey plinth with foyer, retail areas, restaurants and conference centre, and a "Lifestyle Center" with entertainment facilities in the floors below, two office and residential towers of differing height extend skywards. The towers have a curved triangular floor plan and become more slender towards the top, each ending in a cap. A lift tower between the two is connected to the towers via bridges and culminates in the antenna. The result is a sculptural configuration that will be a visible landmark from all directions. While the plinth building at the foot of the tower features a complex double-skin façade with curved glazing elements, the glazing of the towers reflects the sky and the clouds.

Im 94-geschossigen Turm Ost finden Büros, darüber das Hotel „Grand Hyatt" und in der 63. bis 86. Etage Appartements Platz. Die Rezeption in aussichtsreicher Lage im 91. Stock fahren die Hotelgäste mit den Expressaufzügen an und begeben sich von dort aus hinab in die Geschosse mit den Gastzimmern. Bars und Restaurants nehmen die Spitze des Turmes über dem Hotelempfang innerhalb des mehrgeschossigen Luftraumes mit Galerieebenen ein. Turm West beinhaltet 34 Bürogeschosse, Appartements und im Kopf des Turmes einen Spa- und Wellnessbereich, der auch vom Hotel und den Appartements des größeren Turmes aus über eine der Brücken zwischen den beiden Türmen zugänglich ist.

In den öffentlichen Panoramaaufzügen des mittleren Aufzugsturmes erreichen die Besucher aus dem 50 Meter hohen Foyer auftauchend die Aussichtsplattform im höheren der beiden Türme. So sind die oberen Geschosse jeweils öffentlich zugänglich, um die fantastischen Aussichten für die Besucher erlebbar zu machen.

Tower East totals 94 storeys and contains predominantly offices with the Grand Hyatt Hotel at the top and apartments in floors 63 to 86. From the hotel reception with an unparalleled panoramic view on the 91st floor, express lifts convey guests up and down to the hotel rooms in the floors below. Bars and restaurants occupy the galleries above the hotel reception in the multi-storey cap of the tower. Tower West contains 34 floors of offices and apartments and a spa and wellness area in its cap, which can also be reached from the hotel and apartments in the higher tower via the bridges that connect the two.

The public panorama lifts in the central lift tower convey visitors from the 50-metre-high foyer to the viewing platform in the higher of the two towers. Accordingly, the upper storeys of both towers are accessible to the general public to enjoy the fantastic views.

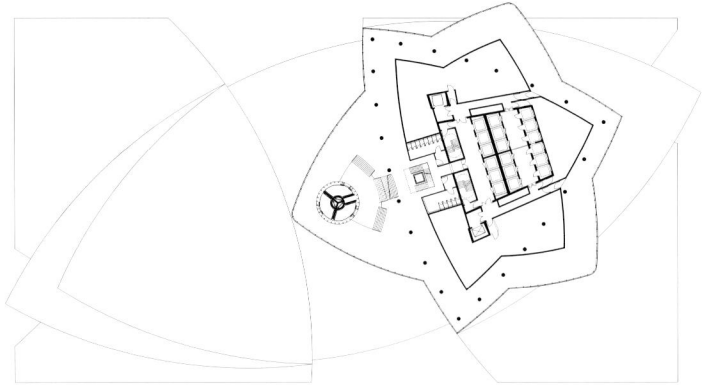

Grundriss 88. Obergeschoss
88th floor plan

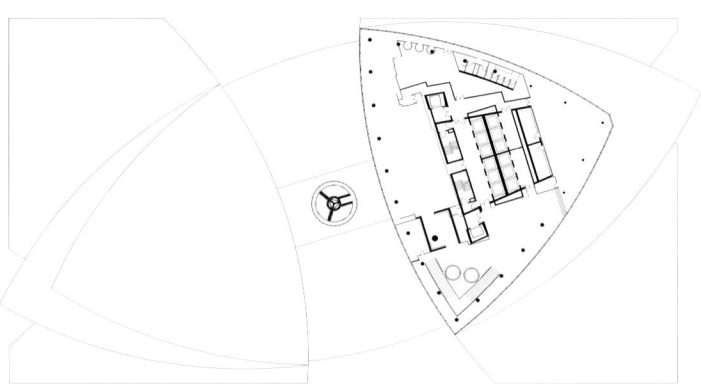

Grundriss 90. Obergeschoss
90th floor plan

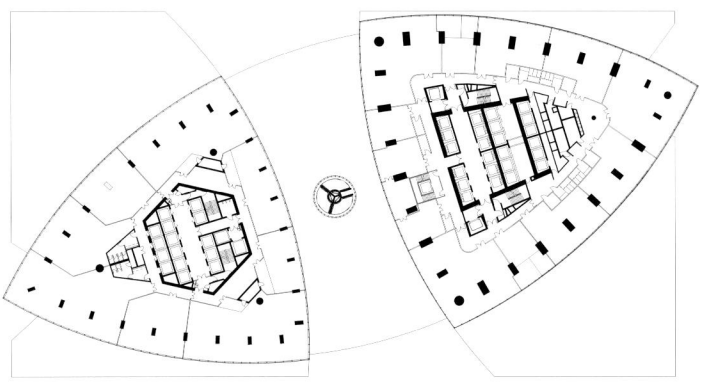

Grundriss 24. Obergeschoss
24th floor plan

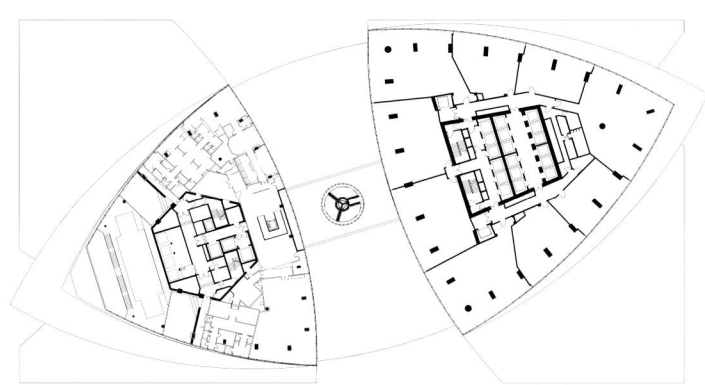

Grundriss 60. Obergeschoss
60th floor plan

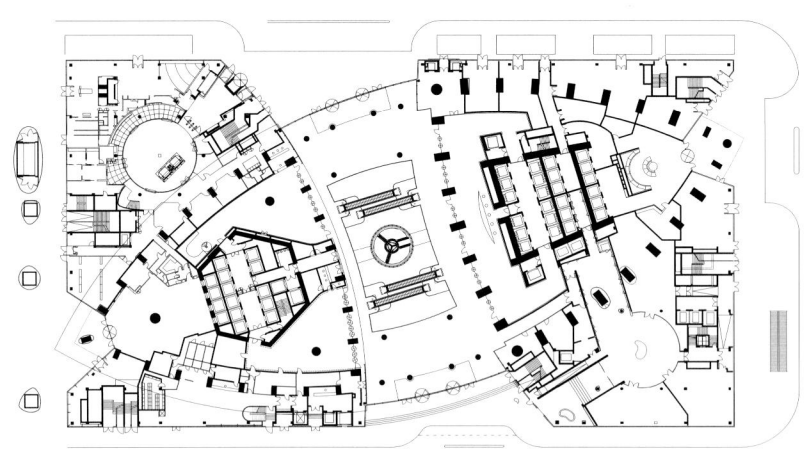

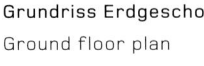

Grundriss Erdgeschoss
Ground floor plan

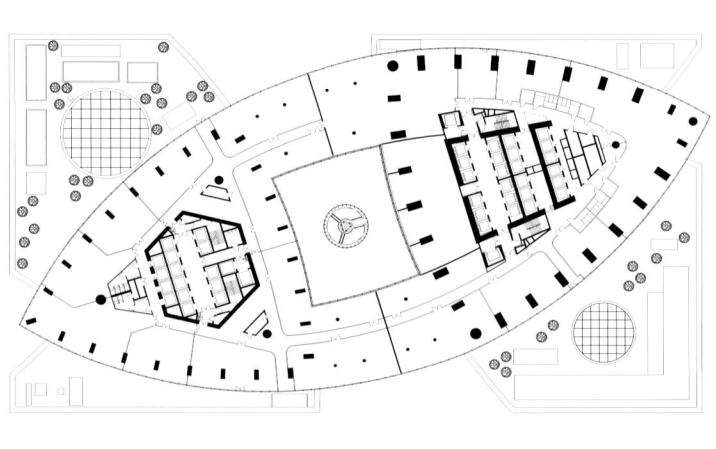

Grundriss 6. Obergeschoss
Sixth floor plan

0   50 m

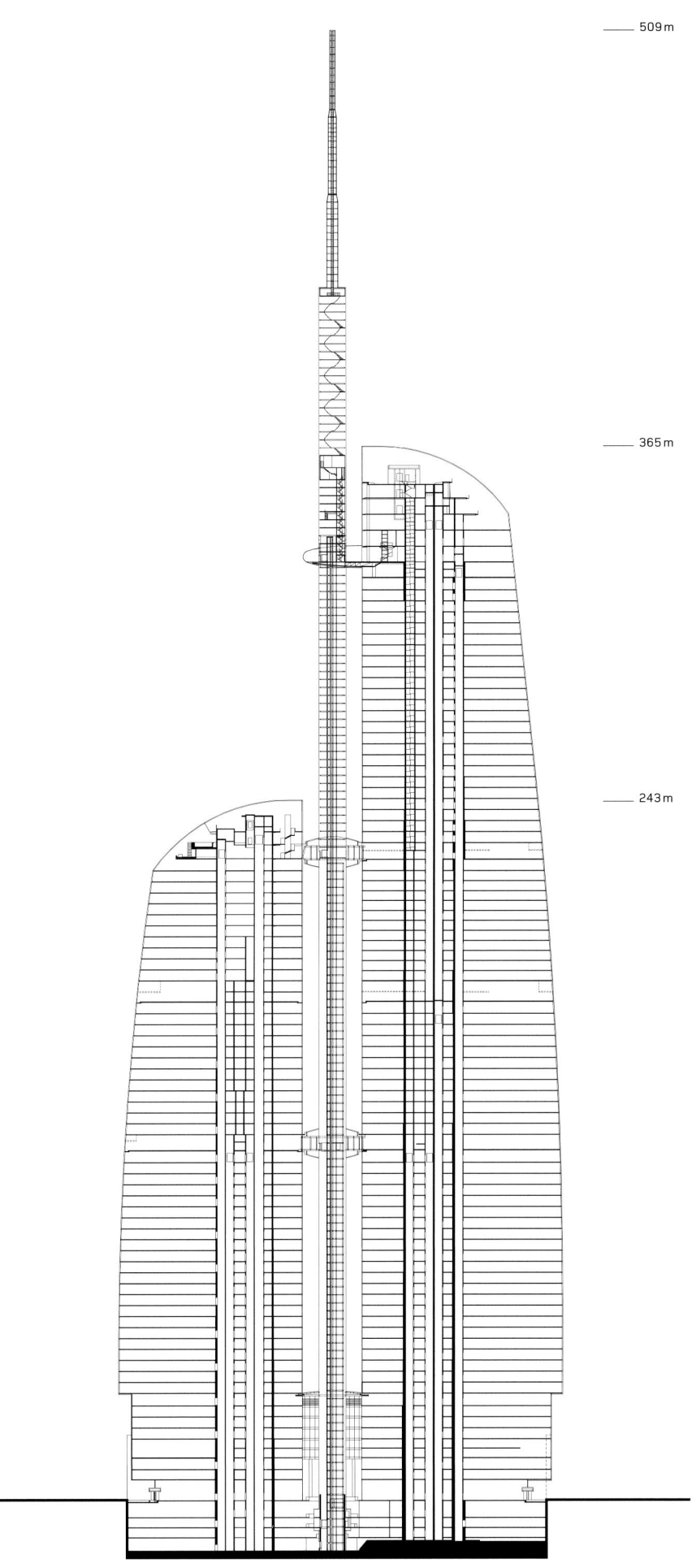

——— 509 m

——— 365 m

——— 243 m

Schnitt | Section

FUSSGÄNGERBRÜCKE ALTER HAFEN
FOOTBRIDGE ALTER HAFEN
BREMERHAVEN

Das „Mediterraneo", das „Klimahaus" und ein Hotelturm an der Weser in der Nachbarschaft des Deutschen Schifffahrtsmuseums werden durch den Alten Hafen von der Verkehrsachse Columbusstraße, einem Ladenzentrum und der Innenstadt getrennt. Der Brückenschlag über das Hafenbecken verbessert die Anbindung und bietet eine bequeme, überdachte Fußwegverbindung zu den neuen Publikumsattraktionen. Auf der Stadtseite beginnt die Brücke in einem an die Columbuspassage angeschlossenen Wintergarten. Auf der Kaiseite mündet sie unmittelbar in das Foyer des Klimahauses. Ein Treppen- und Aufzugturm am Columbusdamm verknüpft die Wegverbindung mit den von einem leichten Stahl-Glas-Dach geschützten Bushaltestellen.

Die Brücke, in Zusammenarbeit mit WTM Engineers als Generalplaner entstanden, gesellt sich als technisches Bauwerk der Bremerhavener Brückenfamilie hinzu und präsentiert sich als attraktive dynamische Form. Die als steife Röhre konstruierte Brücke überwindet eine große Spannweite und kommt mit wenigen Stützen aus. Um die Durchfahrt für Schiffe zu ermöglichen, ist das mittlere Segment über dem Alten Hafen als Drehbrücke ausgebildet. Zum Öffnen dreht sich das auf einem Pylon im Hafenbecken aufgeständerte Rohrbrückenteil um 90 Grad und gibt die Passage zum Museumshafen frei.

The old harbour separates the "Mediterraneo", the "Klimahaus" and a hotel tower on the banks of the Weser near to the German Maritime Museum from the city centre, the Columbusstraße, a key traffic artery, and a shopping arcade. The building of a bridge across the harbour basin improves access to the area and provides a comfortable and covered pedestrian walkway for visitors to reach the new attractions.

On the city-ward side, the bridge is entered from a glazed winter garden attached to the Columbuspassage shopping arcade. On the quayside it opens directly into the foyer of the "Klimahaus". A stair and lift tower on the Columbusdamm links the covered walkway with a lightweight steel and glass bus stop.

The bridge, designed in cooperation with WTM Engineers as general planners, is one of a small family of high-tech bridge constructions in Bremerhaven and presents an attractive and dynamic form. The rigid pipe construction spans a considerable distance with only a few supporting pillars. To allow ships to pass, the central segment directly over the Alter Hafen is built as a swing bridge. An elevated section of the pipe rests on a pylon in the centre of the harbour basin and swivels through 90° to afford free passage to the museum's harbour.

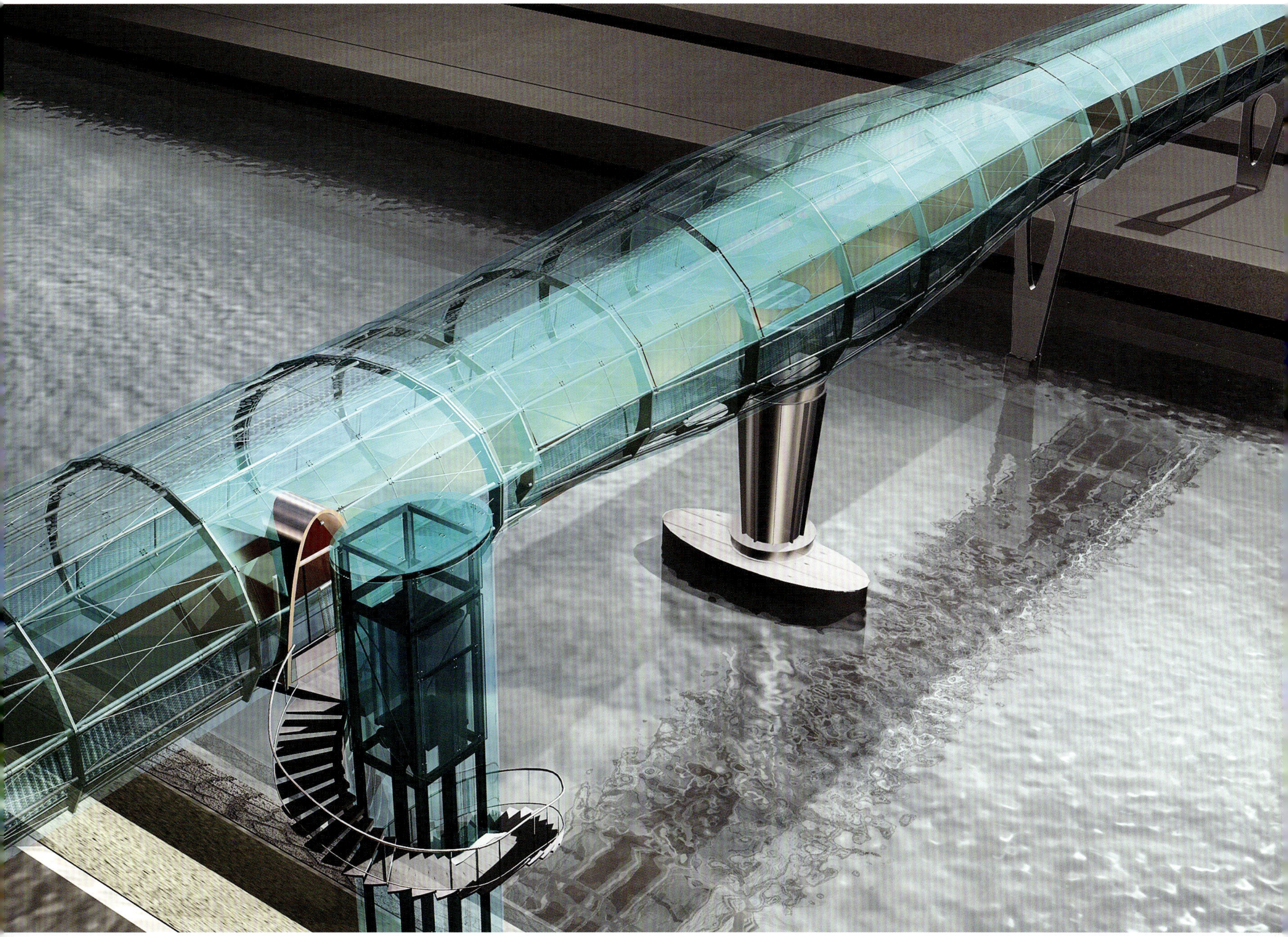

WOHNKOMPLEX MARTINOW-UFER
MARTINOV RIVERSIDE HOUSING COMPLEX
ST. PETERSBURG

Die Wasser-, Sport- und Freizeitlandschaft im Norden des St. Petersburger Stadtzentrums auf der Kreuzinsel (Krestowskij Ostrow) wird mehr und mehr zum exklusiven Wohn- und Erholungsgebiet entwickelt. Der Hotel- und Wohnkomplex am Martinowufer mit seinen drei- bis siebengeschossigen Appartementhäusern ist ein Motor dieser Entwicklung.

Durch die Anordnung der zwölf Einzelhäuser in einer S-förmigen Schlange mit durchlaufendem Sockel ergeben sich zwei lang gestreckte, zum Wasser offene Höfe. Der eine ist als repräsentative „Parade Esplanade" mit Baumreihen und Wasserbecken ausgebildet und nimmt die Achse der Regattastrecke des Grebny-Kanals auf, der andere ist als ruhiger Gartenhof mit Privatparkcharakter gestaltet. Durch diese Anordnung erhält eine größtmögliche Anzahl an Wohnungen den Bezug zum Wasser. Die großzügig geschnittenen Wohnungen des gehobenen Standards sind in der Regel von zusätzlich engagierten Innenarchitekten ausgebaut und ausgestattet worden.

Die Gliederung der Bauten, ihre Typologie und die dekorativen Fassadenmotive erinnern an südländische Bauweisen und verleihen der Wohnanlage eine singuläre Exklusivität. Mit ihren aufwändig gegliederten Natursteinfassaden lässt die Anlage zusätzlich St. Petersburger Bautraditionen anklingen, wenngleich die Einzelformen moderner Architektursprache verpflichtet sind.

The waterside sports and recreational landscape to the north of St. Petersburg's inner city on the Krestovsky Island is becoming an increasingly exclusive residential and recreational area. The hotel and housing complex on Martinov Quay with apartment blocks ranging from three to seven storeys, is a further motor of this development.

The arrangement of the twelve individual buildings on a common plinth with an S-shaped path creates two elongated courtyards that open out onto the water. The first is a representative "Parade Esplanade" with tree-lined pools and fountains and is an extension of the axis of the Grebny Canal regatta course; the second is a quiet garden courtyard with a more private character. This arrangement ensures that a maximum number of flats have a direct relationship to water.

The generously proportioned luxury flats have in most cases been designed and fitted out by interior architects hired by the clients.

The form of the buildings, their typology and the decorative motifs of the façades have a Southern European or Mediterranean flair that adds to the singular exclusiveness of the complex. With their carefully proportioned stone façades, the complex also makes references to the local building tradition in St. Petersburg, even though the individual forms are expressed in a modern architectural language.

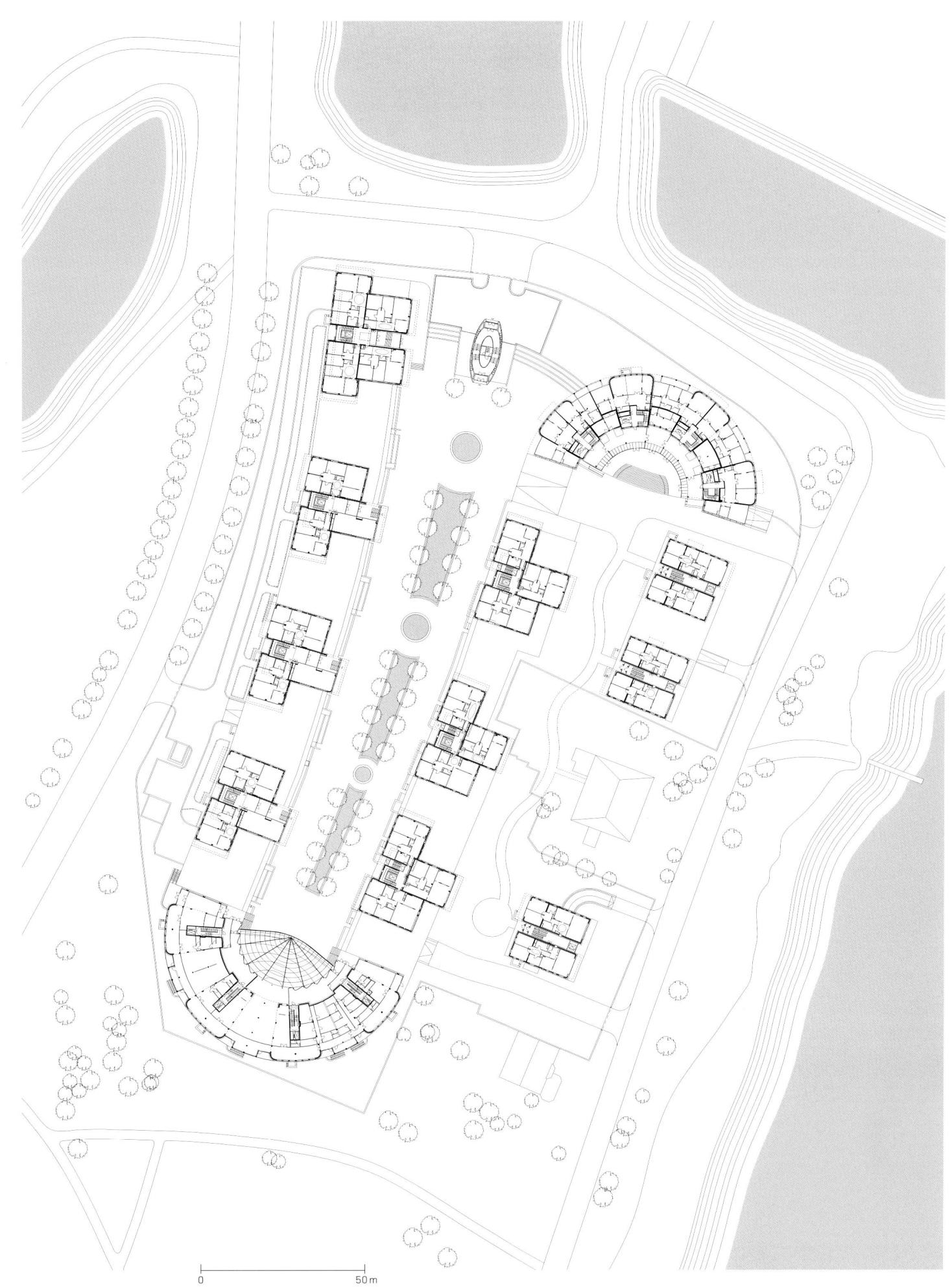

0   50 m

MESSEZENTRUM EXPO-GATE
EXPO-GATE TRADE FAIR
ST. PETERSBURG

Vor den Toren der Stadt unweit des Flughafens entsteht das neue Messegelände im Süden St. Petersburgs. Das Gefälle des Geländes wird für die Eintiefung einer viergeschossigen, das gesamte Grundstück einnehmenden Sockelplatte genutzt, in deren unteren Etagen Stellplätze für 11.000 PKW und 130 Busse untergebracht sind. Das erste Untergeschoss dient als ausgedehntes Foyer der Orientierung und Verteilung der Besucher. Zudem bietet es Platz für Läden, Restaurants und Serviceeinrichtungen.

Das expressive, schlangenförmige Gebäude oberhalb des Sockels ist das Wahrzeichen und das Tor zur Messe und nimmt die Kongressräume und das Messehotel mit 450 Zimmern sowie die Verwaltung der Messegesellschaft auf. Eine Art barockes Gartenparterre mit Wasserspielen und symmetrisch angelegten Baumreihen und Pflanzbeeten leitet über zum mit einer gläsernen Membran überdachten zentralen Bereich vor den eigentlichen Ausstellungsgebäuden. Die Messehallen, drei kleinere, nahezu quadratische, und ein größerer mit insgesamt 90.000 Quadratmeter Ausstellungsfläche, sind in kleinere Einheiten unterteilbar. An der Westseite, wo das Gelände an einen See stößt, bietet eine Bühne Gelegenheit für Open-Air-Veranstaltungen.

The new trade fair centre in St. Petersburg will be built on a site at the gateway to the city not far from the airport. The incline of the site is utilised to bury a four-storey plinth that extends over the entire area of the site and provides parking for 11,000 vehicles and 130 buses. The lower ground level serves as an expansive foyer for visitor orientation and circulation. In addition it provides space for shops, restaurants and service facilities.

The expressive snake-like winding building that rises above the plinth is both emblem and gateway to the trade fair grounds and contains the congress centre, the trade fair hotel with 450 rooms and the trade fair administration.

A kind of Baroque parterre with water features and symmetrically arranged rows of trees and planting leads on towards a central area covered with a glass membrane roof in front of the trade fair halls. The trade fair halls themselves, three smaller and almost square and one larger hall providing a total of 90,000 square metres exhibition area, can be subdivided into smaller sections as required.

On the west side, where the trade fair grounds open onto an inland lake, an outdoor stage provides a location for open-air events with a view across the water.

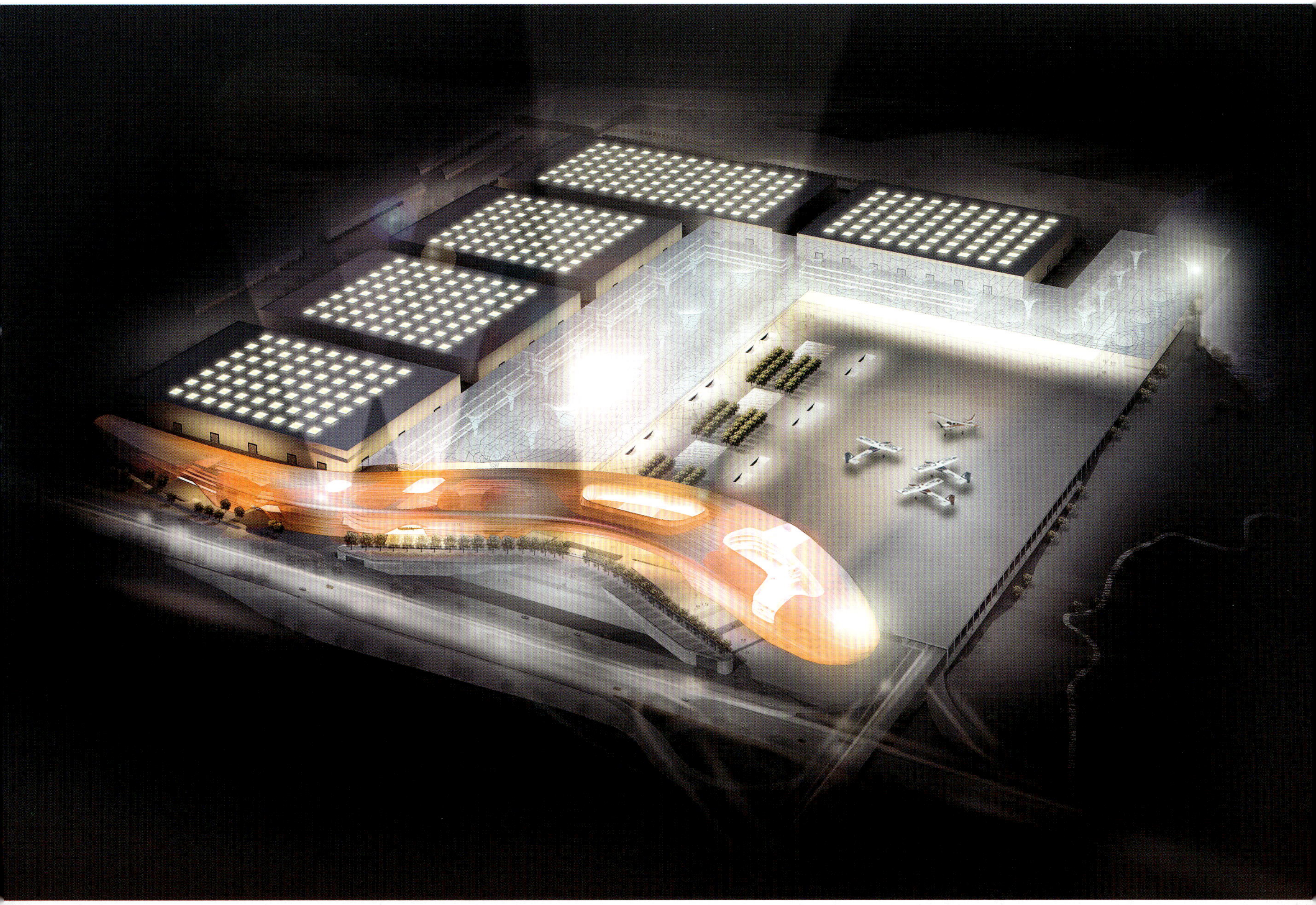

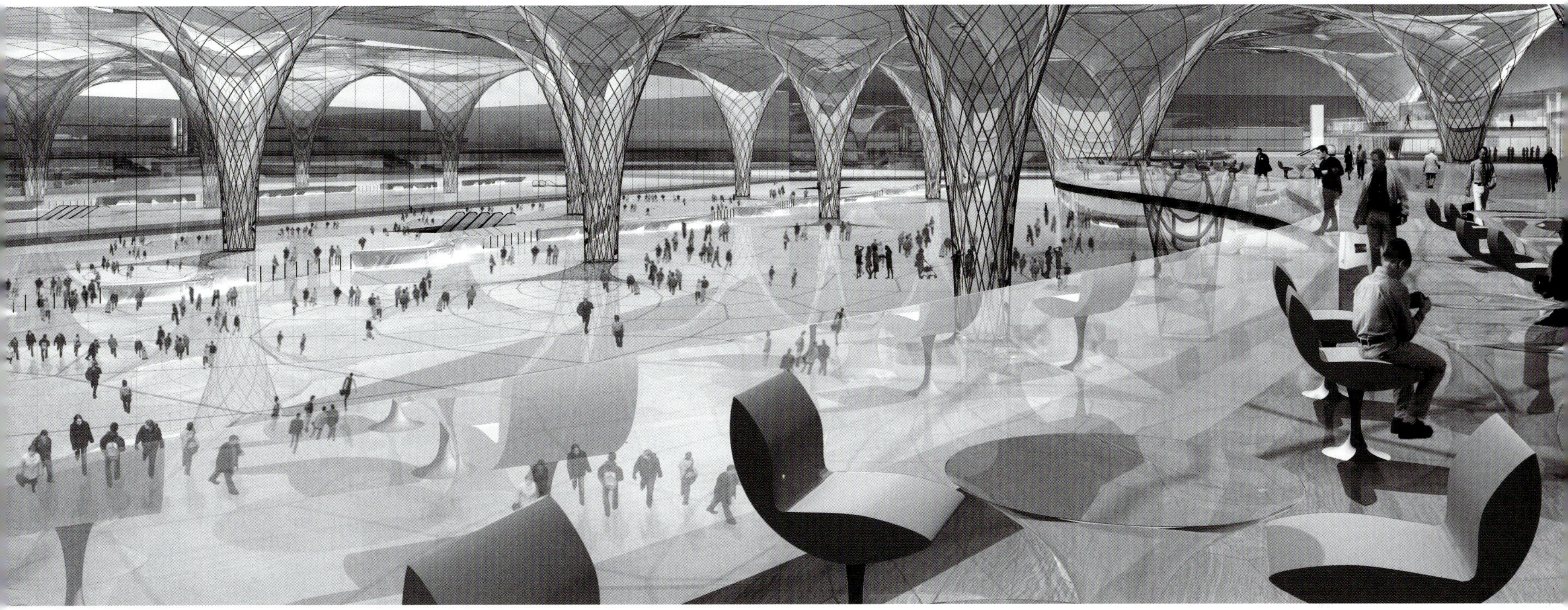

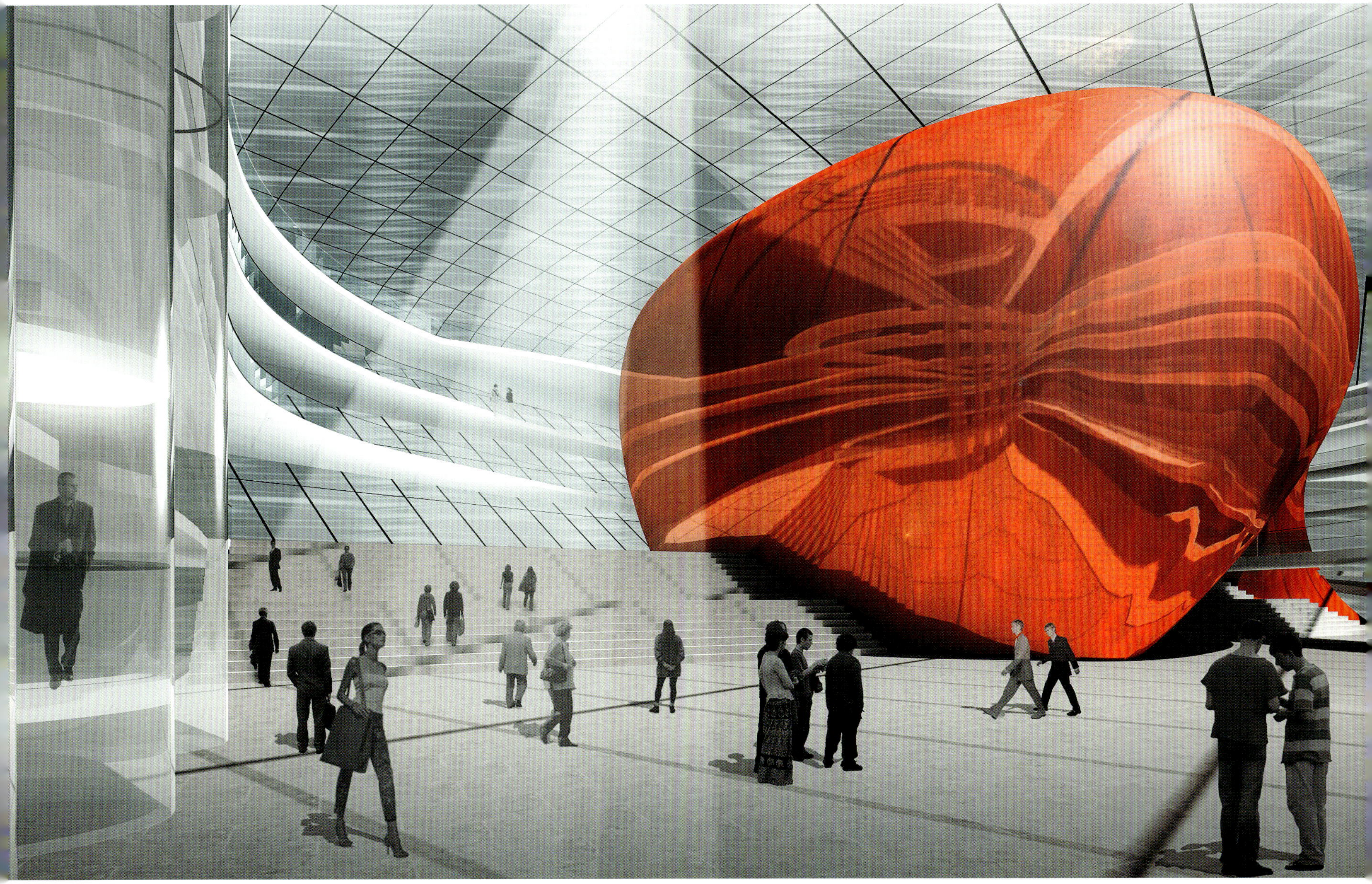

ARCHITEKTUROLYMPIADE
ARCHITECTURAL OLYMPICS
HAMBURG

Die Stadt des 21. Jahrhunderts wächst nach innen, dieser Erkenntnis entspricht die Planung für das „Bahngelände Altona", dessen nps tchoban voss sich im Rahmen der Architekturolympiade 2006 angenommen haben. Die Baubehörde hatte eingeladen, in einem „olympischen Wettstreit" gestalterische Perspektiven für zehn ausgewählte Stadträume der Hansestadt zu entwickeln. 80 Teams aus dem In- und Ausland hatten sich beteiligt.

Die Vision geht von einer Verlegung des Fernbahnhofs Altona Richtung Norden aus. Der Bau des neuen Bahnhofs Diebsteich und die unterirdische Führung der Bahntrasse bis zum S-Bahnhof Altona würden die epochale Chance eröffnen, die trennende Wirkung der Bahnlinie aufzuheben. Die neu entstehenden Freiräume sollen eine Grünachse „Central Park" bilden. Anliegen der Planer sind das Verknüpfen des Straßennetzes in West-Ost-Richtung und das Angebot einer leistungsfähigen Nord-Süd-Verbindung im Einbahnstraßenbetrieb beiderseits der Grünachse. Zwischen den beiden Bahnstationen ist ein großstädtisches Zentrum aus zwölf Hochhäusern mit bis zu 40 Geschossen auf den der Achse benachbarten Bauflächen vorgesehen.

The city of the 21st century grows inwards. This insight informs the plan for the "Altona railway site" which nps tchoban voss chose to examine as part of the Architectural Olympics in 2006. The planning authorities had extended an open invitation to take part in an "Olympic Competition" to produce design ideas for ten selected urban areas in Hamburg. 80 teams from Germany and abroad took part.

The visionary scheme is based on an assumption that the Altona main-line railway station would be relocated further to the north. The building of a new railway station at Diebsteich and the routing of the railway lines underground as far as the S-Bahn station at Altona would present a momentous opportunity to eliminate the dividing line of the railway tracks. The resulting open space should become a green axis, a "Central Park" for Hamburg. The proposal enables the planners to reconnect the road networks in a west-east direction and to introduce a central high-capacity north-south route via one-way streets either side of the green axis. For the site between the two railway stations and alongside the axis, the plan proposes the creation of an urban centre consisting of twelve high-rise buildings with up to 40 storeys.

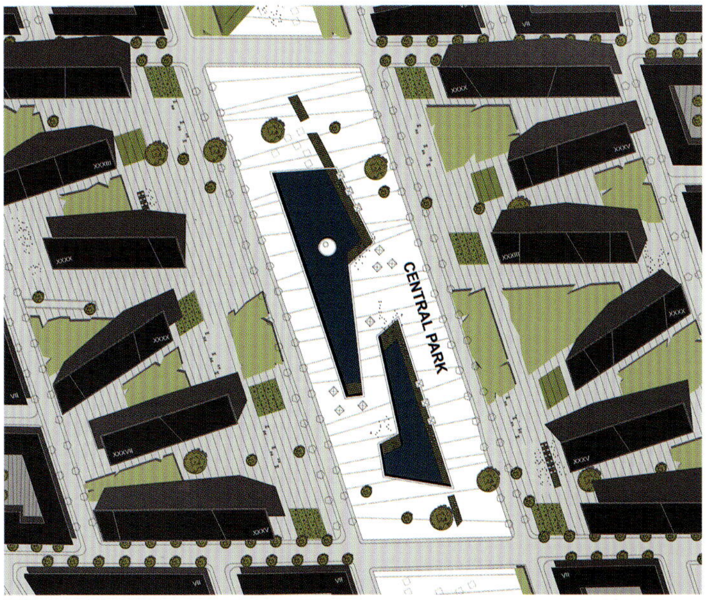

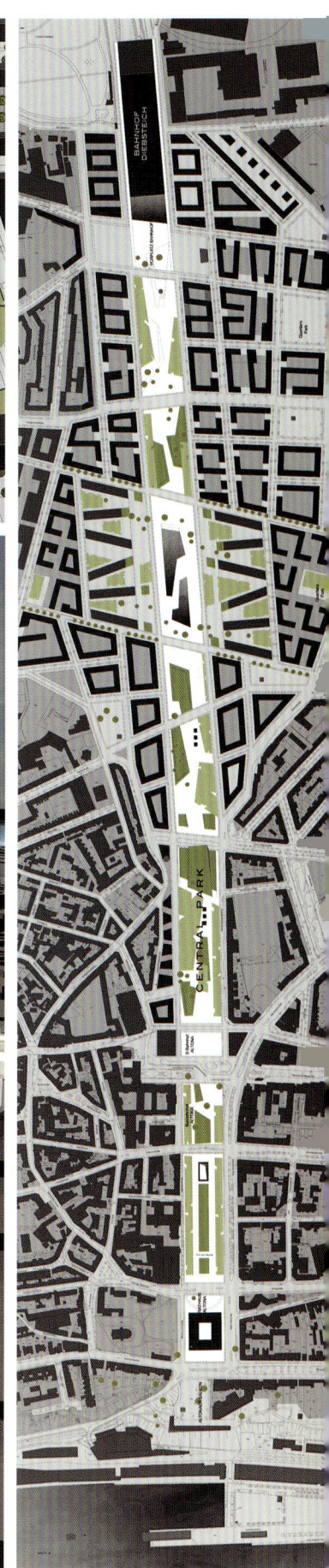

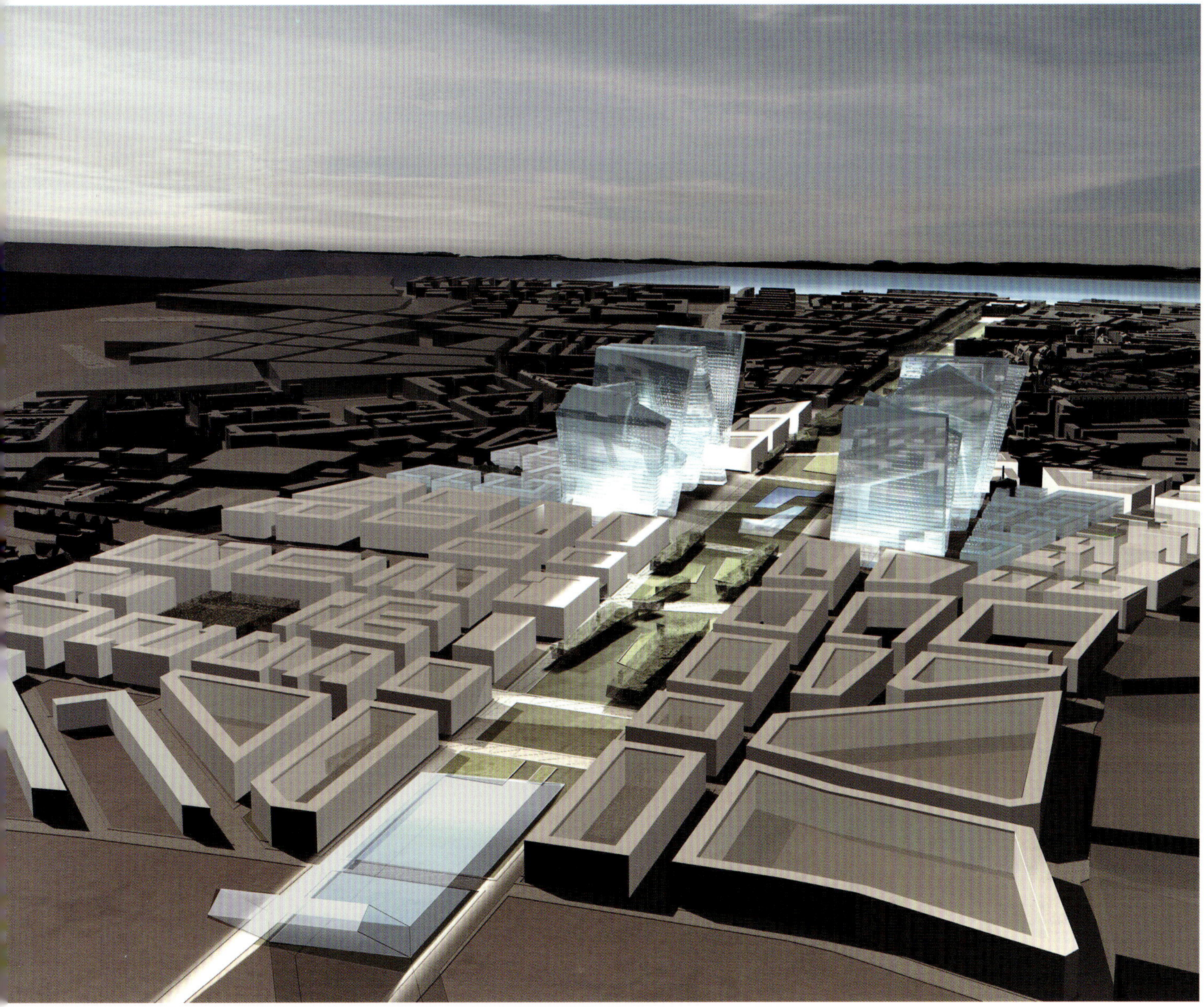

MASTERPLAN ÜBERSEEQUARTIER
ÜBERSEEQUARTIER MASTER PLAN
HAMBURG

Für den mittleren Bereich der neuen HafenCity war ein Geschäftszentrum mit eigenem Fluidum zu planen. Dazu wurde ein Investoren-Auswahlverfahren durchgeführt, das nps tchoban voss in enger Zusammenarbeit mit den Büros Erick van Egeraat, Rotterdam; Rem Koolhaas, Rotterdam; BDP, London und Netzwerk Architekten, Darmstadt, bearbeiteten. Im Nachgang wurden für die einzelnen Blocks Realisierungswettbewerbe ausgelobt.

Das „Überseequartier" im Geviert zwischen Elbe, Magdeburger Hafen und St. Annen-Fleet , in dem lediglich das Alte Hafenamt als existierende Bebauung bestehen bleibt, wird auf dem Masterplan in mehr als ein Dutzend unregelmäßig geschnittene Blocks unterteilt. Sie bieten Raum für Büros, Gewerbe sowie an den ruhigeren Plätzen Wohnungen. Besonderheit ist ein auf der ganzen Länge das Quartier diagonal durchquerender Boulevard, der sich der orthogonalen Ordnung entzieht und einen abwechslungsreichen Flanierweg bildet. Der Platz und die Terrassen um das Alte Hafenamt sind zum Magdeburger Hafen und zur Speicherstadt hin orientiert. Der Boulevard endet an der Elbe am aussichtsreichen Überseeplatz.

A business and shopping district with a particular flair was required for the central area of the new HafenCity. An investor selection procedure was instated in which nps tchoban voss took part in close cooperation with the offices of Erick van Egeraat and Rem Koolhaas in Rotterdam, BDP in London and Netzwerk Architekten in Darmstadt. A second round of realisation competitions then followed for the individual blocks.

The master plan subdivided the "Überseequartier", a rectangular site between the Elbe river, the Magdeburg Harbour and St. Annen-Fleet, in which only the former harbour master's office still stands, into more than a dozen irregularly-shaped blocks. They house offices and shops as well as flats and housing in the quieter areas. A particular feature is a boulevard that winds its way diagonally across the entire site, never adhering to the orthogonal, and provides a varied and interesting path through a series of different spaces. The square and terraces around the former harbour master's office are oriented towards the Magdeburger Hafen and the warehouses of the Speicherstadt. The boulevard leads towards the waterfront of the Elbe culminating at the Überseeplatz.

NEWSKIJ-RATHAUS
NEWSKIJ CITY HALL
ST. PETERSBURG

Das neue Rathaus und städtische Verwaltungszentrum entsteht auf dem Gelände eines ehemaligen Straßenbahndepots im nordöstlichen Bereich der Innenstadt. Mit seinem geschwungenen Vordach in Traufhöhe und der linsenförmigen, gläsernen Kuppel bildet der Rathausbau an der Nowgorodskaja-Magistrale einen städtebaulichen Blickpunkt und eine repräsentative Eingangsfront. Eine Passage führt in die zentrale Rundhalle und zum rückwärtigen, von Ladengalerien gesäumten Innenhof, wo sich Büro- und Geschäftshäuser sowie ein Hotel anschließen. Das elfgeschossige Rathaus und ein 13-geschossiges ovales Business-Zentrum sind mit gläsernen Fassaden gestalterisch hervorgehoben. Die anderen Bauten entsprechen mit ihren steinernen Lochfassaden mehr dem Duktus der historischen Innenstadt und binden das Neubauprojekt in die Umgebung ein. Die Wände des Straßenbahndepots wurden erhalten und integriert. Ein alter Schornstein dient als Schacht für den Aufzug zum Dachrestaurant.

Die vielfältigen publikumsintensiven Nutzungen fördern die Transparenz der öffentlichen und demokratischen Funktionen des Zentrums der Stadtregierung und sind somit gebautes Abbild einer neuen Zeit.

The new city hall and urban administration centre will be built on the site of a former tram depot on the northeast edge of the city centre. With its arcing eaves-level canopy and projecting lens-shaped glazed 'dome', the city hall on the Novgorodskaya ulitsa forms an unmistakable urban landmark and presents a suitably imposing entrance. An arcade leads towards the central circular hall and the rear courtyard, which is surrounded by galleries of shops and is adjoined by offices and shops as well as a hotel. The eleven-storey city hall and the 13-storey oval business centre are given particular prominence through their glazed façades. The other buildings with their stone façades punctuated by windows refer to the typical characteristics of the historical city and help integrate the extensive project into its surroundings. The exterior walls of the tram depot will be conserved and integrated into the new building and an old chimney is to be repurposed as a shaft for the lift to the restaurant.

The many and varied public functions underline the transparency of the public and democratic functions of the seat of urban governance and as such represent a built image of a new age.

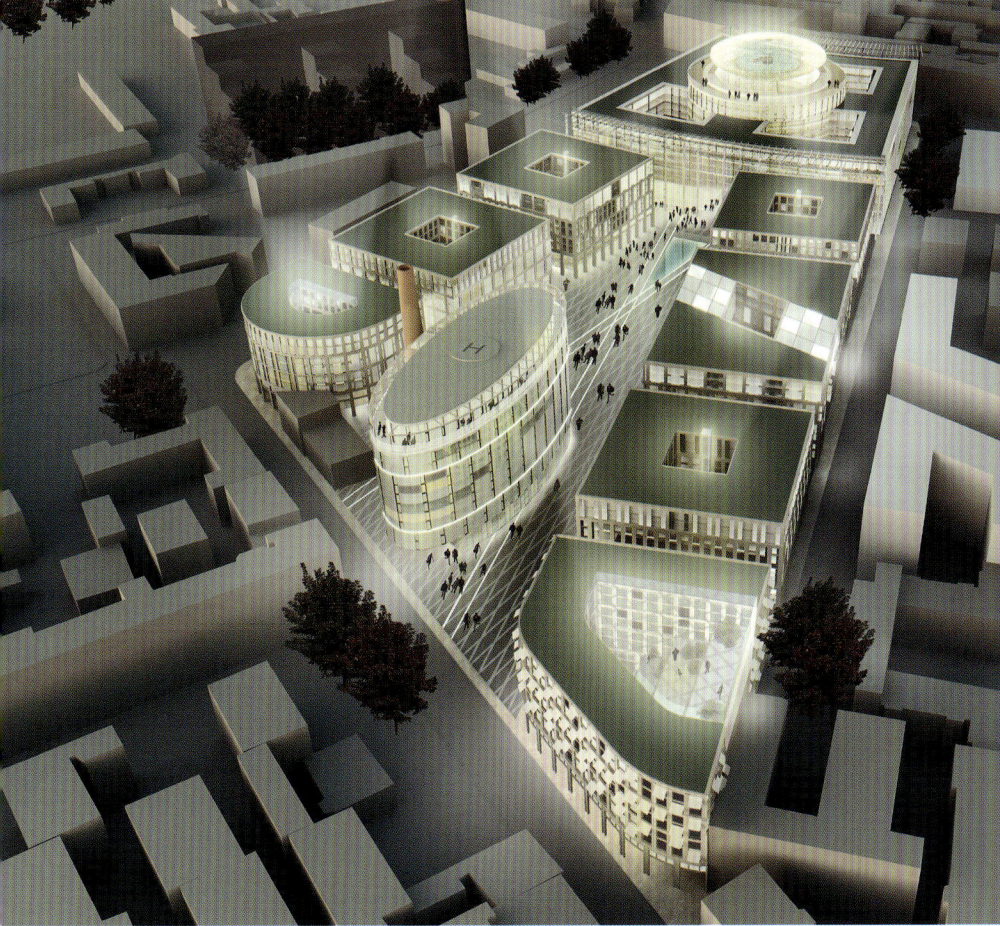

HAUPTVERWALTUNG VOLKSWOHL BUND
VOLKSWOHL BUND HEADQUARTERS
DORTMUND

Das 17-geschossige Hochhaus setzt ein selbstbewusstes Zeichen am Dortmunder Südwall. Die an der Höhe der Nachbarhäuser orientierte Sockelbebauung folgt der Baugrenze des Blockrandes, lässt jedoch an der Blockecke einen Vorplatz frei, an dem sich das Hochhaus wirkungsvoll in Szene setzen kann. Die aus dünnen Pfeilern und Stegen gebildete Fassade zieht sich gleichförmig über alle Oberflächen des gesamten Ensembles hinweg, um die Gleichheit aller Räume zum Ausdruck zu bringen, die im Regelfall im ganzen Haus als Bürozellen organisiert sind. Das Hochhaus ist im Grundriss aus zwei L-Formen zusammengesetzt, deren kurze Schenkel jeweils auskragen und so dem hohen Baukörper etwas an Massivität nehmen. Viel Wert legten die Architekten auf die Öffnung des Gebäudes gegen den öffentlichen Raum. Der Bodenbelag des Vorplatzes fließt in die Lobby und weiter bis in den Innenhof. Patio und Blockinnenbereich wiederum sind als miteinander durch die Gestaltung und durch Wasserspiele verbundene Gartenanlage entworfen. Der zweite Eingang im Garten ist der Zugang für die per PKW anreisenden Mitarbeiter, die ihren Wagen in der Parkpalette im intensiv begrünten Hof parken.

The 17-storey high-rise office building stands self-assured on the Südwall in Dortmund. The height of the lower level building picks up the eaves line of the neighbouring buildings and follows the perimeter of the block, stepping back at the corner to make space for a forecourt that allows the tower to reveal its full extent. The façade consists of a regular pattern of slender pillars and beams that envelope all the surfaces of the entire ensemble, expressing the uniformity of the spaces within, which for the most part consist of office cells throughout.

The plan of the tower is a composite arrangement of two L-shaped forms whose short arms extend on each side, reducing the massive appearance of the high building.

The architects paid great attention to areas that open out onto public spaces. The paving of the floor of the forecourt continues on into the lobby and through to the interior courtyard. The patio and the interior courtyard of the block are likewise designed as interconnecting gardens, united by the water feature and their formal design. The second entrance to the garden is the entrance for staff arriving by car who park their vehicles in the parking decks in the midst of the rich greenery of the courtyard.

ALBATROS PARK
ISTANBUL

Das Grundstück am Uferboulevard von Büyükçekmece liegt an einer malerischen Bucht des Marmarameers westlich von Istanbul. In der Nachbarschaft einer gleichförmigen Bebauung sollten für die exklusive Wohnanlage keine charakterlosen Hochhäuser entstehen. So wurde ein künstlerischer Ansatz verfolgt, indem die fünf 22-geschossigen Hochhäuser in die Form von Skulpturen gebracht wurden. Auf Stiele gestellt und organisch geformt, scheinen sie Pappeln im Wind oder beieinander stehende Reiher zu symbolisieren.

Jeder Turm steht in einem Wasserbecken und ist über einen hölzernen Steg erreichbar. Das Hanggelände, in dem die Stellplätze und Infrastruktureinrichtungen wie Restaurant, Fitness- und Wellnesseinrichtungen eingebettet sind, ist bis hinab zur Promenade terrassiert.

Die großzügig geschnittenen Wohnungen, jeweils drei pro Geschoss, haben Grundrisse mit organischer Linienführung. Im Kopf der Gebäude sind Maisonettewohnungen mit schönstem Blick auf die „türkische Côte d'Azur" untergebracht.

The site on the waterside boulevard of Büyükçekmece lies in a picturesque bay on the Sea of Marmara to the west of Istanbul. Situated in a neighbourhood characterised by uniform buildings, the tower blocks planned for the exclusive housing complex were to have a distinctive quality. An artistic approach was chosen that gives each of the five 22-storey towers a sculptural form. Raised on stalks and with organic forms, they resemble poplars in the wind or herons standing in a group.

Each tower stands in a pool of water and is reached via a wooden walkway. The sloping site, in which the car parking and auxiliary infrastructure such as restaurants, fitness and wellness facilities are embedded, is terraced down to the waterside promenade.

The floor plans of the generously proportioned apartments, three on each storey, feature rooms with organic shapes. Maisonettes in the head of each building enjoy unparalleled views over the Turkish "Côte d'Azur".

MÖVENPICK HOTEL
DÜSSELDORF

Der Hotelbau steht exponiert am nördlichen Rand des Hofgartens. Die örtlichen Gegebenheiten hatten großen Einfluss auf Konzeption und Gestaltung des Hotels. Zu beiden Seiten schließt das Gebäude in seiner Höhe an die Nachbarbebauung an, auf der einen Seite mit fünf Geschossen und auf der anderen mit sieben Geschossen. Zusammen mit dem die Blockecke überhöhenden elfgeschossigen Eckturm ergibt sich eine gestaffelte Bauvolumenkomposition, die besonders in den Hofgarten hinein Wirkung entfaltet. Der Baumbestand des Parks lieferte auch das Motiv für die Gestaltung der Natursteinfassaden, deren eng stehende, schmale Pfeiler und Holzlamellen Assoziationen an Baumstämme wecken. Auch das eigens entwickelte Interieur in Lobby, Restaurant und Zimmern greift in Farbgebung und Gestaltung auf diese Bilderwelt zurück. Nussbaum- und Räuchereichefurnier prägen die Atmosphäre mit ihren warmen Farben. Die mit abstrahierten Waldmotiven bedruckten Wandverkleidungen erinnern ebenfalls an den Stadtpark.

The hotel building stands in a prominent position at the northern edge of the Hofgarten. The immediate environment had a direct influence on the concept and design of the hotel. On both sides, the building picks up the height of the neighbouring buildings, on one side with five storeys, on the other seven storeys. Together with the eleven-storey tower on the corner a composition of stepped building volumes results that is particularly evident from the Hofgarten. The trees in the park provided the motif for the design of the stone façades whose slender, closely spaced pillars and timber lamellae awaken associations with tree trunks. Similarly, the design of the interiors of the lobby, restaurant and rooms, developed especially for the hotel, draw on the colours and forms of this imagery. The interiors are characterised by the warm colours of walnut and smoked oak veneer. Wall panels printed with abstract forest motifs likewise echo the realm of the park outside.

CUBIX–KINO
CUBIX CINEMA

VERANTWORTLICHER PARTNER
RESPONSIBLE PARTNER
Sergei Tchoban

PROJEKTLEITER | PROJECT MANAGER
Philipp Bauer

ANSCHRIFT | ADDRESS
Rathausstraße 1
D-10178 Berlin

BAUHERR | CLIENT
TLG Immobiliengesellschaft mbH,
Niederlassung Berlin Brandenburg

FERTIGSTELLUNG | COMPLETION
2001

BRUTTOGESCHOSSFLÄCHE
GROSS FLOOR AREA
13 450 m^2

NUTZUNG | USE
Multiplexkino mit 9 Sälen und 2400 Sitz-
plätzen, Gastronomie im EG und 1.OG
Multiplex cinema with 9 theatres and
2400 seats, restaurants on ground and
first floor

→ 28

MENSA UND BIBLIOTHEK HOCHSCHULE ZITTAU/ GÖRLITZ
UNIVERSITY REFECTORY AND LIBRARY

VERANTWORTLICHER PARTNER
RESPONSIBLE PARTNER
Alf M. Prasch

PROJEKTLEITER | PROJECT MANAGER
Stefan Wolff

ANSCHRIFT | ADDRESS
Schliebenstraße
D-02763 Zittau

BAUHERR | CLIENT
Freistaat Sachsen, Sächsisches Staats-
ministerium der Finanzen,

FERTIGSTELLUNG | COMPLETION
2004

BRUTTOGESCHOSSFLÄCHE
GROSS FLOOR AREA
4120 m^2
(Bibliothek / Library 2000 m^2)

NUTZUNG | USE
Mensa und Bibliothek
Refectory and library

→ 36

WORLD TRADE CENTER

VERANTWORTLICHER PARTNER
RESPONSIBLE PARTNER
Alf M. Prasch

PROJEKTLEITER | PROJECT MANAGER
Thomas Bienmüller

ANSCHRIFT | ADDRESS
Ammonstraße 74
01067 Dresden

BAUHERR | CLIENT
Bürohaus Elbflorenz GmbH

FERTIGSTELLUNG | COMPLETION
1997

BRUTTOGESCHOSSFLÄCHE
GROSS FLOOR AREA
148 000 m^2

HOTELZIMMER | HOTEL ROOMS
207

NUTZUNG | USE
Büros, Läden, Dienstleistungseinrich-
tungen, Theater, Hotel, Restaurant,
Tiefgarage
Offices, retail, services, theatre, hotel,
restaurant, underground parking

→ 40

ALTE OBERPOSTDIREKTION
FORMER POST OFFICE HEADQUARTERS

VERANTWORTLICHER PARTNER
RESPONSIBLE PARTNER
Alf M. Prasch

PROJEKTLEITER | PROJECT MANAGER
Hanno Hendrich

ANSCHRIFT | ADDRESS
Gorch-Fock-Wall 3-7
D-20354 Hamburg

BAUHERR | CLIENT
GFW Grundstücks GmbH
c/o Quantum Immobilien AG

FERTIGSTELLUNG | COMPLETION
2005

BRUTTOGESCHOSSFLÄCHE
GROSS FLOOR AREA
16 900 m^2

NUTZUNG | USE
Büros / Offices

→ 48

GALERIE ARNDT
ARNDT GALLERY

VERANTWORTLICHER PARTNER
RESPONSIBLE PARTNER
Sergei Tchoban

PROJEKTLEITER | PROJECT MANAGER
Philipp Bauer

ANSCHRIFT | ADDRESS
Rosenthaler Straße 40/41
Hackesche Höfe, Hof 3
D-10178 Berlin

BAUHERR | CLIENT
Matthias Arndt

FERTIGSTELLUNG | COMPLETION
1998

BRUTTOGESCHOSSFLÄCHE
GROSS FLOOR AREA
27 m^2

NUTZUNG | USE
Ausstellungspavillon
Exhibition pavilion

→ 78

GESCHÄFTSHAUS KURFÜRSTENDAMM
SHOPS AND OFFICES, KURFÜRSTENDAMM

VERANTWORTLICHER PARTNER
RESPONSIBLE PARTNER
Sergei Tchoban

PROJEKTLEITER | PROJECT MANAGER
Axel Binder

ANSCHRIFT | ADDRESS
Kurfürstendamm 38-39/Knesebeckstr. 66
D-10719 Berlin

BAUHERR | CLIENT
BLS Objekt Berlin Kurfürstendamm
GmbH & Co. KG
(Unternehmensgruppe Stoffel)

FERTIGSTELLUNG | COMPLETION
2005

BRUTTOGESCHOSSFLÄCHE
GROSS FLOOR AREA
8150 m^2

NUTZUNG | USE
Gewerbe-, Büro-, Wohnnutzung
und Tiefgarage
Retail, offices, apartments and
underground parking

→ 80

KRONPRINZENKARREE

VERANTWORTLICHER PARTNER
RESPONSIBLE PARTNER
Sergei Tchoban

PROJEKTLEITER | PROJECT MANAGER
Philipp Bauer

ANSCHRIFT | ADDRESS
Reinhardtstraße 48–52/
Unterbaumstraße 4-6
D-10117 Berlin

BAUHERR | CLIENT
Cenda Invest AG

FERTIGSTELLUNG | COMPLETION
2003

BRUTTOGESCHOSSFLÄCHE
GROSS FLOOR AREA
6983 m^2

NUTZUNG | USE
Büro- und Geschäftshaus mit Lofts
und Tiefgarage / Commercial building
with loft apartments and underground
parking

→ 84

OVAL OFFICE

VERANTWORTLICHER PARTNER
RESPONSIBLE PARTNER
Alf M. Prasch

PROJEKTLEITER | PROJECT MANAGER
Hanno Hendrich

ANSCHRIFT | ADDRESS
Überseering 10
D-22297 Hamburg

BAUHERR | CLIENT
Oval Office Gesellschaft f.B. mbH

FERTIGSTELLUNG | COMPLETION
2004

BRUTTOGESCHOSSFLÄCHE
GROSS FLOOR AREA
25 850 m^2

NUTZUNG | USE
Büro und Kantine mit 200 Plätzen,
Tiefgarage mit 295 Stellplätzen
Offices and cafeteria catering for 200
persons, underground parking with
295 parking spaces

→ 90

DOMAQUARÉE

VERANTWORTLICHER PARTNER
RESPONSIBLE PARTNER
Sergei Tchoban

PROJEKTLEITER | PROJECT MANAGER
Manfred Treiling, Stephan Lohre,
Axel Binder, Ulrike Graefenhain,
Christian Strauß

ANSCHRIFT | ADDRESS
Karl-Liebknecht-Str. 1-5,
D-10178 Berlin

BAUHERR | CLIENT
DIFA Deutsche Immobilien Fonds AG

FERTIGSTELLUNG | COMPLETION
2004

BRUTTOGESCHOSSFLÄCHE
GROSS FLOOR AREA
123 000 m^2
(31700 m^2 Hotel mit 450 m^2 Wellness-
Bereich und Konferenzräume für 850
Personen; 22000 m^2 Bürofläche; 8500 m^2
Wohnen; 20000 m^2 Gewerbe; 40800 m^2
Tiefgarage / 31700 m^2 hotel with 450 m^2
wellness space and conference facilities
for up to 850 persons; 22000 m^2 offices;
8500 m^2 residential; 20000 m^2 retail;
40800 m^2 underground parking)

HOTELZIMMER | HOTEL ROOMS
427

NUTZUNG | USE
Büros, Wohnen, Hotel
Offices, apartments, hotel

→ 52

INTERCITY HOTEL

VERANTWORTLICHER PARTNER
RESPONSIBLE PARTNER
Alf M. Prasch

PROJEKTLEITER | PROJECT MANAGER
Stefan Niemöller

ANSCHRIFT | ADDRESS
Glockengießerwall 14/15
D-20095 Hamburg

BAUHERR | CLIENT
Hamburger Feuerkasse Vers.-AG

FERTIGSTELLUNG | COMPLETION
2004

BRUTTOGESCHOSSFLÄCHE
GROSS FLOOR AREA
7961 m^2

HOTELZIMMER | HOTEL ROOMS
155

NUTZUNG | USE
Hotel mit Tiefgarage
Hotel with underground parking

→ 66

GRUNDSCHULE HEIDHORST
HEIDHORST
PRIMARY SCHOOL

VERANTWORTLICHER PARTNER
RESPONSIBLE PARTNER
Ekkehard Voss

PROJEKTLEITERIN | PROJECT MANAGER
Karin Folkers

ANSCHRIFT | ADDRESS
Heidhorst 16
D-21031 Hamburg

BAUHERR | CLIENT
Freie und Hansestadt Hamburg,
Behörde für Schule, Jugend und
Berufsbildung

FERTIGSTELLUNG | COMPLETION
2001

BRUTTOGESCHOSSFLÄCHE
GROSS FLOOR AREA
3646 m^2
(Schulgebäude/School 2868 m^2,
Sporthalle/Sports hall 778 m^2)

NUTZUNG | USE
Zweizügige Grundschule mit
Einfeld-Sporthalle
Two-stream primary school
with sports hall

→ 70

ALTE MÄLZEREI
OLD MALTINGS

VERANTWORTLICHER PARTNER
RESPONSIBLE PARTNER
Alf M. Prasch

PROJEKTLEITER | PROJECT MANAGER
Stefan Niemöller

ANSCHRIFT | ADDRESS
Friedenstraße 91
D-10249 Berlin

BAUHERR | CLIENT
Grundstücksgesellschaft
Friedenstraße mbH & Co KG

FERTIGSTELLUNG | COMPLETION
2002

BRUTTOGESCHOSSFLÄCHE
GROSS FLOOR AREA
7437 m^2

NUTZUNG | USE
Büros / Offices

→ 74

GRAFENBERGER HÖFE

VERANTWORTLICHER PARTNER
RESPONSIBLE PARTNER
Alf M. Prasch

PROJEKTLEITER | PROJECT MANAGER
Jörg Rudloff

ANSCHRIFT | ADDRESS
Grafenberger Allee 337 a-c
D-40235 Düsseldorf

BAUHERR | CLIENT
IGH Investitionsgesellschaft
Grafenberger Höfe mbH & Co. KG
Vertreten durch / represented by:
LIP Ludger Inholte Projektentwicklung
GmbH

FERTIGSTELLUNG | COMPLETION
2008

BRUTTOGESCHOSSFLÄCHE
GROSS FLOOR AREA
22060 m^2

NUTZUNG | USE
Büros / Offices

→ 98

BUCHHAUS HABEL
HABEL BOOKSTORE

VERANTWORTLICHER PARTNER
RESPONSIBLE PARTNER
Alf M. Prasch

PROJEKTLEITER | PROJECT MANAGER
Holm Zink

ANSCHRIFT | ADDRESS
Hochstraße 68
D-47792 Krefeld

BAUHERR | CLIENT
Erste Kajen 12 Verwaltungsgesellschaft
mbH vertreten durch die / represented
by B&L Projektentwicklungsgesellschaft
mbH

FERTIGSTELLUNG | COMPLETION
2003

BRUTTOGESCHOSSFLÄCHE
GROSS FLOOR AREA
5539 m^2

NUTZUNG | USE
Buchhandlung und weitere Ladenflächen
Bookstore and additional retail space

→ 102

HAUPTVERWALTUNG
SAGA/GWG
SAGA/GWG
HEADQUARTERS

VERANTWORTLICHER PARTNER
RESPONSIBLE PARTNER
Peter Sigl

PROJEKTLEITER | PROJECT MANAGER
Frank Focke

ANSCHRIFT | ADDRESS
Poppenhusenstraße 2
D-22305 Hamburg

BAUHERR | CLIENT
SAGA, Erste Immobiliengesellschaft
mbH

FERTIGSTELLUNG | COMPLETION
2004

BRUTTOGESCHOSSFLÄCHE
GROSS FLOOR AREA
15400 m^2

NUTZUNG | USE
Büros/Offices

→ 106

WOHNGEBÄUDE
POSSMOORWEG
POSSMOORWEG FLATS

VERANTWORTLICHER PARTNER
RESPONSIBLE PARTNER
Peter Sigl

PROJEKTLEITER | PROJECT MANAGER
Albert Feldkamp

ANSCHRIFT | ADDRESS
Poßmoorweg 40
D-22301 Hamburg

BAUHERR | CLIENT
Hanseatische Baugenossenschaft
Hamburg e.G

FERTIGSTELLUNG | COMPLETION
2005

BRUTTOGESCHOSSFLÄCHE
GROSS FLOOR AREA
3700 m^2

WOHNEINHEITEN | APARTMENTS
23

NUTZUNG | USE
Genossenschaftliche Wohnungen
Cooperative housing

→ 114

HAUPTVERWALTUNG IMTECH
IMTECH HEADQUARTERS

VERANTWORTLICHER PARTNER
RESPONSIBLE PARTNER
Alf M. Prasch

PROJEKTLEITER | PROJECT MANAGER
Bernd Burdinski

ANSCHRIFT | ADDRESS
Hammer Straße 30/34
D-22041 Hamburg

BAUHERR | CLIENT
GIH GmbH & Co. KG

FERTIGSTELLUNG | COMPLETION
2006

BRUTTOGESCHOSSFLÄCHE
GROSS FLOOR AREA
24 330 m^2

NUTZUNG | USE
Firmenzentrale Imtech Nord mit Büros,
Archiv, Konferenzbereich, Kantine mit
180 Plätzen, Tiefgarage mit 213 Stellplätzen
Imtech Nord Headquarters with offices,
archive, conference area, cafeteria
catering for 180 persons, underground
parking with 213 parking spaces

→ 118

QUARTIER HOFFMANNSTIEG
HOUSING, HOFFMANN-
STIEG QUARTER

VERANTWORTLICHER PARTNER
RESPONSIBLE PARTNER
Alf M. Prasch

PROJEKTLEITER | PROJECT MANAGER
Frank Focke

ANSCHRIFT | ADDRESS
Hoffmannstieg 2-12
D-22143 Hamburg

BAUHERR | CLIENT
SAGA Siedlungs Aktiengesellschaft

FERTIGSTELLUNG | COMPLETION
2006

BRUTTOGESCHOSSFLÄCHE
GROSS FLOOR AREA
6270 m^2

WOHNEINHEITEN | APARTMENTS
52

NUTZUNG | USE
Wohnen / Apartments

→ 124

HAUPTVERWALTUNG C&A
C&A HEADQUARTERS

VERANTWORTLICHER PARTNER
RESPONSIBLE PARTNER
Sergei Tchoban

PROJEKTLEITER | PROJECT MANAGER
Stephan Lohre

ANSCHRIFT | ADDRESS
Wanheimer Straße 70
D-40472 Düsseldorf

BAUHERR | CLIENT
Bauwert Portfolio Gamma GmbH

FERTIGSTELLUNG | COMPLETION
2006

BRUTTOGESCHOSSFLÄCHE
GROSS FLOOR AREA
42 150 m^2
(Parkhaus / Parking garage 14 650 m^2)

NUTZUNG | USE
Hauptverwaltung mit Kantine
und Bistro
Headquarters with cafeteria and café

→ 126

BEROLINAHAUS

VERANTWORTLICHER PARTNER
RESPONSIBLE PARTNER
Sergei Tchoban

PROJEKTLEITER | PROJECT MANAGER
Philipp Bauer

ANSCHRIFT | ADDRESS
Alexanderplatz 1
D-10117 Berlin

BAUHERR | CLIENT
Pegasus Grundstücksentwicklung
und Beteiligung GmbH & Co. KG

FERTIGSTELLUNG | COMPLETION
2007

BRUTTOGESCHOSSFLÄCHE
GROSS FLOOR AREA
16 500 m^2

NUTZUNG | USE
Denkmalgerechte Instandsetzung, in
Teilbereichen Umbau für den Einzel-
handel
Refurbishment of listed building,
partial conversion into retail space

→ 130

BENOISHAUS
BENOIS BUILDING

VERANTWORTLICHER PARTNER
RESPONSIBLE PARTNER
Sergei Tchoban

PROJEKTLEITER | PROJECT MANAGER
Paul Olufs, Philipp Gubkin

ANSCHRIFT | ADDRESS
Swerdlowskaja-Naberegnaja 44,
Kalininskij, St. Petersburg, RF

BAUHERR | CLIENT
Teorema

FERTIGSTELLUNG | COMPLETION
2007

BRUTTOGESCHOSSFLÄCHE
GROSS FLOOR AREA
30 400 m^2

NUTZUNG | USE
Bebauung ehemaliges Werksgelände
„Rossija", Fassaden- und Lobbygestal-
tung Benoishaus, Büroflächen und
Einzelhandel
Conversion of former factory site "Ros-
sija", façade and lobby design, Benois
Building, offices and retail space

→ 154

BÜROHAUS LANGENZIPEN
LANGENZIPEN
OFFICE BUILDING

VERANTWORTLICHER PARTNER
RESPONSIBLE PARTNER
Sergei Tchoban

PROJEKTLEITER | PROJECT MANAGER
Frederik-S. Scholz, Dominik Burmeister,
Philipp Gubkin

ANSCHRIFT | ADDRESS
Malaja Monetnaja 2A
St. Petersburg, RF

BAUHERR | CLIENT
Langenzipen & Co

FERTIGSTELLUNG | COMPLETION
2006

BRUTTOGESCHOSSFLÄCHE
GROSS FLOOR AREA
7500 m^2

NUTZUNG | USE
Umbau einer Fabrik zum Büro-
und Wohnhaus
Conversion of a factory into offices
and apartments

→ 160

ALTE OBERPOSTDIREKTION
FORMER POST OFFICE
HEADQUARTERS

VERANTWORTLICHER PARTNER
RESPONSIBLE PARTNER
Ekkehard Voss

PROJEKTLEITER | PROJECT MANAGER
Albert Feldkamp

ANSCHRIFT | ADDRESS
Zeppelinstraße 24
D-30175 Hannover

BAUHERR | CLIENT
Sunrise Hannover Senior Living
GmbH & Co. KG

FERTIGSTELLUNG | COMPLETION
2007

BRUTTOGESCHOSSFLÄCHE
GROSS FLOOR AREA
12 800 m^2

WOHNEINHEITEN | APARTMENTS
89

NUTZUNG | USE
Altenwohnheim mit stationärem
Dementenbereich
Housing for the elderly with
dementia inpatient area

→ 164

EINRICHTUNGSHAUS IKEA
IKEA FURNITURE STORE

VERANTWORTLICHER PARTNER
RESPONSIBLE PARTNER
Ekkehard Voss

PROJEKTLEITER | PROJECT MANAGER
Andreas Hitz

AUSSCHREIBUNG/BAULEITUNG
SPECIFICATION/SITE SUPERVISION
Architekturbüro Olly Bauer

ANSCHRIFT | ADDRESS
Expo-Park Hannover
Straße der Nationen 10
D-30539 Hannover

BAUHERR | CLIENT
IKEA Verwaltungs GmbH

FERTIGSTELLUNG | COMPLETION
2006

BRUTTOGESCHOSSFLÄCHE
GROSS FLOOR AREA
38 000 m^2
(Verkaufsfläche / Retail area 19 000 m^2)

NUTZUNG | USE
Grossflächiger Möbeleinzelhandel
mit 2000 Stellplätzen auf zwei Parkebe-
nen unter den Verkaufsgeschossen
Large-scale furniture store with 2000
parking spaces on two underground
levels underneath the retail space

→ 166

WOHNPFLEGEHEIM HAVELGARTEN
HAVELGARTEN NURSING HOME

VERANTWORTLICHER PARTNER
RESPONSIBLE PARTNER
Ekkehard Voss

PROJEKTLEITERIN | PROJECT MANAGER
Marion Mews

ANSCHRIFT | ADDRESS
Spandauer Burgwall 29
D-13581 Berlin

BAUHERR | CLIENT
Bethanien Diakonissen Stiftung

FERTIGSTELLUNG | COMPLETION
2007

BRUTTOGESCHOSSFLÄCHE
GROSS FLOOR AREA
12 337 m²
(Nutzfläche Pflegeheim / Usable floor
area nursing home 9037 m², Nutzfläche
Wohnungen / Usable floor area flats
1353 m²)

ANZAHL ZIMMER | NUMBER OF ROOMS
126 Pflegezimmer / rooms

WOHNEINHEITEN | APARTMENTS
20

NUTZUNG | USE
Pflegeheim und betreutes Wohnen
Nursing home and shettered houses

→ 136

SYNAGOGE CHABAD LUBAWITSCH
CHABAD LUBAVITCH SYNAGOGUE

VERANTWORTLICHER PARTNER
RESPONSIBLE PARTNER
Sergei Tchoban

PROJEKTLEITER | PROJECT MANAGER
Frederik-S. Scholz

ANSCHRIFT | ADDRESS
Münstersche Str. 6
D-10709 Berlin

BAUHERR | CLIENT
Chabad Lubawitsch, vertreten
durch Rabbiner Yehuda Teichtal /
Represented by Rabbi Yehuda Teichtal

FERTIGSTELLUNG | COMPLETION
2007

BRUTTOGESCHOSSFLÄCHE
GROSS FLOOR AREA
2050 m²

NUTZUNG | USE
Umbau eines ehemaligen Umspannwerkes zur Synagoge und jüdischem
Familien- und Kulturzentrum
Conversion of transformer station into
a synagogue and Jewish family and
cultural centre

→ 140

HERRENHAUS WELLINGSBÜTTEL
WELLINGSBÜTTEL MANOR

VERANTWORTLICHER PARTNER
RESPONSIBLE PARTNER
Ekkehard Voss

PROJEKTLEITERIN | PROJECT MANAGER
Beate Schonlau

ANSCHRIFT | ADDRESS
Wellingsbüttler Weg 71
D-22391 Hamburg

BAUHERR | CLIENT
WBB Wulff
Bauträger und Bauregie GmbH

FERTIGSTELLUNG | COMPLETION
2006

BRUTTOGESCHOSSFLÄCHE
GROSS FLOOR AREA
2000 m²

WOHNEINHEITEN | APARTMENTS
14

NUTZUNG | USE
Appartements für betreutes Wohnen mit
Bewohnerrestaurant und Wellnessbereich / Apartments for sheltered housing
with cafeteria and wellness area

→ 146

JAVATURM
JAVA TOWER

VERANTWORTLICHER PARTNER
RESPONSIBLE PARTNER
Sergei Tchoban

PROJEKTLEITER | PROJECT MANAGER
Bernd Burdinski

ANSCHRIFT | ADDRESS
Langenhorner Chaussee 384/
Oehleckerring
D-22419 Hamburg

BAUHERR | CLIENT
Wilhelm Pabel GmbH & Co. KG

FERTIGSTELLUNG | COMPLETION
1997

BRUTTOGESCHOSSFLÄCHE
GROSS FLOOR AREA
720 m² (Bürofläche / Offices)

NUTZUNG | USE
Umbau des Turms einer Kaffeerösterei
zu einem Büro- und Loftgebäude
Conversion of a coffee roasting tower
into offices and apartments

→ 150

KAISER-WILHELM-KONTOR

VERANTWORTLICHER PARTNER
RESPONSIBLE PARTNER
Ekkehard Voss

PROJEKTLEITER | PROJECT MANAGER
Dierk Schafmeyer

ANSCHRIFT | ADDRESS
Kaiser-Wilhelm-Str. 9
D-20355 Hamburg

BAUHERR | CLIENT
VOLKSWOHL BUND
Lebensversicherung a.G.

FERTIGSTELLUNG | COMPLETION
2008

BRUTTOGESCHOSSFLÄCHE
GROSS FLOOR AREA
8335 m²

NUTZUNG | USE
Büro- und Geschäftshaus
Offices and retail

→ 170

BÜROGEBÄUDE AM KAISERKAI
OFFICE BUILDING, KAISERKAI

VERANTWORTLICHER PARTNER
RESPONSIBLE PARTNER
Alf M. Prasch

PROJEKTLEITER | PROJECT MANAGER
Bernd Burdinski, Martina Clasen

ANSCHRIFT | ADDRESS
Am Kaiserkai 1 / Großer Grasbrook
D-20457 Hamburg

BAUHERR | CLIENT
ABG Allgemeine Beteiligungsgesellschaft
für Gewerbeimmobilien mbH & Co

BRUTTOGESCHOSSFLÄCHE
GROSS FLOOR AREA
15 000 m²

NUTZUNG | USE
Büro- und Geschäftshaus und Tiefgarage
Offices with retail space and under-
ground parking

→ 176

FEDERATION TOWER

VERANTWORTLICHER PARTNER RESPONSIBLE PARTNER
Sergei Tchoban

PROJEKTLEITER | PROJECT MANAGER
Matthias Lassen (Projektleitung Moskau/
Project manager Moscow)

Matthias Dahlmann (Projektleitung
Berlin / Project manager Berlin)

PLANUNGSGEMEINSCHAFT DESIGN TEAM
Planungsgesellschaft „Föderationsturm
Moskau" mbH, Hamburg, Deutschland

ASP Schweger Assoziierte Gesamt-
planung, Hamburg
Und / and
nps tchoban voss Architekten BDA,
Berlin

ANSCHRIFT | ADDRESS
Krasnopresnenskaja-Naberegnaja,
„Moskau-City", Lot 13,
123100 Moskau, RF

BAUHERR | CLIENT
GAO „Mirax City"

FERTIGSTELLUNG | COMPLETION
2008 Turm West / Tower West
2010 Turm Ost / Tower East

BRUTTOGESCHOSSFLÄCHE GROSS FLOOR AREA
430 000 m²
(Büroflächen 259 000 m², Wohnungen
86 000 m², Hotel 61 000 m², Einzelhandel
24 000 m² / Offices 259 000 m², residential
86 000 m², hotel 61 000 m², retail 24 000 m²)

Gemeinsames Podium mit 5 Unter-
geschossen, 6 Obergeschossen und
4 Zwischengeschossen (sog. Linse)

Turm West mit 63 Geschossen, davon
6 Geschosse im Podium, 4 Geschosse in
der Linse, 34 Geschosse Büronutzung,
11 Geschosse Appartements sowie 4 Kappengeschosse mit diversen Nutzungen,
Swimmingpool in Ebene +61, Höhe 243 m

Turm Ost mit 94 Geschossen, davon
6 Geschosse im Podium, 4 Geschosse in
der Linse, 34 Geschosse Büronutzung,
12 Geschosse Hotelnutzung mit 368 Zimmern (Grand Hyatt Moskau), 24 Geschosse
Appartements sowie 5 Kappengeschosse
mit diversen Nutzungen, darunter die
Hotelrezeption in Ebene 91 und die Aussichtsplattform in Ebene +89, Höhe 365 m

Aufzugsnadel mit 3 Panoramaaufzügen
zur Erschließung der Aussichtsplattform;
Höhe mit Antenne 509 m

Tower West with 63 floors, 6 in the plinth,
4 in the 'lens', 34 floors of offices, 11 floors
of apartments and 4 floors in the cap with
various functions, swimming pool on
level +61, height 243 m

Plinth beneath both towers with 5 floors
below ground, 6 floors above ground and
4 floors at the base of the towers (the
so-called lens)

Tower East with 94 floors, 6 in the plinth,
4 in the 'lens', 34 floors of offices, 12 floors
of hotel space (Grand Hyatt Moscow) with
368 rooms, 24 floors of apartments and 5
floors in the cap with various functions
sush as the hotel reception desk on level
91 and viewing platform on level +89,
height 365 m

Lift tower with 3 panorama lifts to the
viewing platform, height with antenna
509 m

NUTZUNG | USE
Hochhauskomplex mit Büros,
Wohnen und Hotel und multifunktio-
nalem elfgeschossigem Podium, ober-
und unterirdisch
High-rise with offices, apartments and
hotel and multi-functional podium with
11 floors above and under ground

→ 182

FUSSGÄNGERBRÜCKE ALTER HAFEN
FOOTBRIDGE ALTER HAFEN

VERANTWORTLICHER PARTNER RESPONSIBLE PARTNER
Ekkehard Voss

PROJEKTLEITER | PROJECT MANAGER
Andreas Hitz

GENERALPLANER | GENERAL PLANNING
WTM Engineers, Hamburg

ANSCHRIFT | ADDRESS
Alter Hafen (Columbusstraße)
27568 Bremerhaven

BAUHERR | CLIENT
BEAN-Bremerhavener Entwicklungsge-
sellschaft Alter/Neuer Hafen mbH&Co. KG

FERTIGSTELLUNG | COMPLETION
2008

LÄNGE | LENGTH
100 m

NUTZUNG | USE
Fußgängerbrücke mit drehbarem Mittel-
segment für die Passage von Schiffen
Pedestrian bridge with swivelling centre
segment to allow passage of ships

→ 190

WOHNKOMPLEX MARTINOW-UFER
MARTINOV RIVERSIDE HOUSING COMPLEX

VERANTWORTLICHER PARTNER RESPONSIBLE PARTNER
Sergei Tchoban

PROJEKTLEITER | PROJECT MANAGER
Paul Olufs, Philipp Gubkin

ANSCHRIFT | ADDRESS
Naberegnaja Martinowa 62, 74
Krestowskij Ostrow
St. Petersburg, RF

BAUHERR | CLIENT
LSR Group/
„Wiedergeburt St. Petersburg"

GENERALPLANER | GENERAL PLANNING
EGP Ewgenij Gerasimow & Partner,
St. Petersburg

FERTIGSTELLUNG | COMPLETION
2008

BRUTTOGESCHOSSFLÄCHE GROSS FLOOR AREA
48 000 m²
(Wohnfläche / Apartments 28 000 m²)

NUTZUNG | USE
Appartementhotel- und Wohnkomplex
mit Wellnessbereich und Tiefgarage
Apartment hotel and luxury housing
with wellness area and underground
parking

→ 192

MESSEZENTRUM EXPO-GATE
EXPO-GATE TRADE FAIR

VERANTWORTLICHER PARTNER
RESPONSIBLE PARTNER
Sergei Tchoban

PROJEKTLEITER | PROJECT MANAGER
Matthias Lassen

ANSCHRIFT | ADDRESS
Komplex „Schuschari"
Peterburgskoje Schosse
St. Petersburg, RF

BAUHERR | CLIENT
Expoforum

GENERALPLANER | GENERAL PLANNING
EGP Ewgenij Gerasimow & Partner,
St. Petersburg

FERTIGSTELLUNG | COMPLETION
2011

BRUTTOGESCHOSSFLÄCHE
GROSS FLOOR AREA
172 500 m²

NUTZUNG | USE
Ausstellungspavillons 89 624 m², davon
drei kleine mit 20 164 m² und ein großer
Pavillon mit 29 132 m²
Hotel 28 514 m²; 450 Zimmer
Multifunktionsgebäude 32 325 m² mit
Kongresszentrum und Verwaltung
mit kleinem und großem Kongresssaal
im 2. und 3. Obergeschoss und einem
Schnellrestaurant für 1500 Personen im
5. Obergeschoss, Verwaltung 22 006 m²,
300 Stellplätze

Exhibition pavilions 89 624 m², three
small: 20 164 m², one large 29 132 m²
Hotel 28 514 m²; 450 rooms
Multi-purpose building 32 325 m² with
conference facilities and administration
with large and small conference hall on
second and third level and a cafeteria
catering for 1500 persons on the fifth
level. Administration 22 006 m², 300
parking spaces

→ 196

ARCHITEKTUROLYMPIADE
ARCHITECTURAL OLYMPICS

VERANTWORTLICHER PARTNER
RESPONSIBLE PARTNER
Alf M. Prasch

PROJEKTLEITER | PROJECT MANAGER
Jan Siemer

ANSCHRIFT | ADDRESS
Bahnflächen Hamburg-Altona

BAUHERR | CLIENT
Stadt Hamburg

FERTIGSTELLUNG | COMPLETION
2006 (Bearbeitung/Design)

BRUTTOGESCHOSSFLÄCHE
GROSS FLOOR AREA
1 620 000 m²

NUTZUNG | USE
Büros / Offices

→ 200

HAUPTVERWALTUNG
VOLKSWOHL BUND
VOLKSWOHL BUND
HEADQUARTERS

VERANTWORTLICHER PARTNER
RESPONSIBLE PARTNER
Ekkehard Voss

PROJEKTLEITER | PROJECT MANAGER
Albert Feldkamp, Christoph Klüsserath,
Stefan Niemöller

ANSCHRIFT | ADDRESS
Südwall 37-41
D-44137 Dortmund

BAUHERR | CLIENT
VOLKSWOHL BUND
Lebensversicherung a. G.

FERTIGSTELLUNG | COMPLETION
2010

BRUTTOGESCHOSSFLÄCHE
GROSS FLOOR AREA
30 644 m²

NUTZUNG | USE
Hauptverwaltungsgebäude mit Tiefgarage und Parkdeck
Headquarters with underground
parking and parking garage

→ 206

MASTERPLAN
ÜBERSEEQUARTIER
ÜBERSEEQUARTIER
MASTER PLAN

VERANTWORTLICHER PARTNER
RESPONSIBLE PARTNER
Alf M. Prasch

PROJEKTLEITER | PROJECT MANAGER
Jan Siemer

ANSCHRIFT | ADDRESS
ÜSQ HafenCity
D-20457 Hamburg

BAUHERR | CLIENT
ÜSQ Beteiligungs-GmbH

FERTIGSTELLUNG | COMPLETION
2011

BRUTTOGESCHOSSFLÄCHE
GROSS FLOOR AREA
275 000 m²

NUTZUNG | USE
Stadtquartier mit Wohnen, Büro, Gastronomie, Einzelhandel, Fußgängerzone,
Verkehr, öffentlichen Außenbereichen
City quarter with apartments, offices,
restaurants, retail, pedestrian zone,
traffic infrastructure, public spaces

→ 202

ALBATROS PARK

VERANTWORTLICHER PARTNER
RESPONSIBLE PARTNER
Alf M. Prasch

PROJEKTLEITER | PROJECT MANAGER
Jens Böttcher

ANSCHRIFT | ADDRESS
Albatros Sokak, TR-34900
Büyükçekmece/Istanbul

BAUHERR | CLIENT
GID Development

WOHNEINHEITEN | APARTMENTS
220

BRUTTOGESCHOSSFLÄCHE
GROSS FLOOR AREA
60 516 m²
Wohnfläche/Residential floor area
43 580 m²
Einzelhandel/Retail
5535 m²

NUTZUNG | USE
Hotel, Wohnen, Läden, Freizeit
Hotel, residential, retail, recreation

→ 208

NEWSKIJ-RATHAUS
NEWSKIJ CITY HALL

VERANTWORTLICHER PARTNER
RESPONSIBLE PARTNER
Sergei Tchoban

PROJEKTLEITER | PROJECT MANAGER
Pavel Zemskov

ANSCHRIFT | ADDRESS
Zentralnyj rajon, Quartal 1034B,
St. Petersburg, RF

BAUHERR | CLIENT
KGA St. Petersburg; Ochta-Group

GENERALPLANER | GENERAL PLANNING
EGP Ewgenij Gerasimow & Partner,
St. Petersburg

FERTIGSTELLUNG | COMPLETION
2010

BRUTTOGESCHOSSFLÄCHE
GROSS FLOOR AREA
300 000 m²

NUTZUNG | USE
Öffentliche Verwaltung, Hotel, Büros
Public administration, hotel, offices

→ 204

MÖVENPICK HOTEL

VERANTWORTLICHER PARTNER
RESPONSIBLE PARTNER
Alf M. Prasch

PROJEKTLEITER | PROJECT MANAGER
Frank Focke

ANSCHRIFT | ADDRESS
Freiligrathstraße 1
D-40479 Düsseldorf

BAUHERR | CLIENT
GII Grundbesitz-Investitionsgesellschaft
Inselstrasse mbH

FERTIGSTELLUNG | COMPLETION
2008

BRUTTOGESCHOSSFLÄCHE
GROSS FLOOR AREA
16 000 m²

HOTELZIMMER | HOTEL ROOMS
201

NUTZUNG | USE
Hotel

→ 210

Alf M. Prasch

1941
Geboren in Görlitz / Schlesien
Abitur in Hamburg

1961
Architekturstudium an der TU Berlin
Mitarbeit bei Hentrich und Petschnigg /
Prof. Eiermann / Prof. Düttmann

1968
Examen Dipl.-Ing. Architekt
Mitarbeiter im Büro Prof. H. Stranz Berlin

1970
Freier Mitarbeiter Büro Neve und
Partner Hamburg

1975
Partnerschaft mit Neve, Nietz und Sigl

1979
NPS Nietz - Prasch - Sigl

1993
Bürogründung in Berlin und Dresden

1995
Nietz - Prasch - Sigl und Partner
Architekten BDA

2003
nps tchoban voss Architekten BDA

1941
Born in Görlitz / Silesia
High-school diploma in Hamburg

1961
Studied architecture at Berlin University
of Technology
Worked in the architectural practices of Hentrich
und Petschnigg, Prof. Eiermann and Prof. Düttmann

1968
Diploma as architect
Employed in the architectural practice of
Prof. H. Stranz, Berlin

1970
Freelancer in the architectural practice of
Neve und Partner, Hamburg

1975
Partner in the office of Neve, Nietz und Sigl

1979
NPS Nietz - Prasch - Sigl

1993
Branch offices in Berlin and Dresden

1995
Nietz - Prasch - Sigl und Partner
Architekten BDA

2003
nps tchoban voss Architekten BDA

Peter Sigl

1934
Geboren in Hamburg

1953
Realschulabschluss in Hamburg

1955
Gesellenbrief als Maurer, parallel Ausbildung
im Stahlbeton

1958
Examen an der Ingenieur-Bauschule Hamburg

1958
Angestellter Architekt im Büro Sprotte und Neve

1970
Partnerschaft mit Neve und Nietz

1975
Erweiterung der Partnerschaft durch
Alf M. Prasch

1979
NPS Nietz - Prasch - Sigl

1993
Bürogründung in Berlin und Dresden

1995
Nietz - Prasch - Sigl und Partner
Architekten BDA

2003
nps tchoban voss Architekten BDA

1934
Born in Hamburg

1953
Secondary school diploma in Hamburg

1955
Certificate of apprenticeship as mason with parallel training in the handling of concrete

1958
Diploma at Academy of Structural Engineering
in Hamburg

1958
Employed as an architect at the office of
Sprotte und Neve

1970
Partner in the office of Neve und Nietz

1975
Alf M. Prasch becomes partner in the office

1979
NPS Nietz - Prasch - Sigl

1993
Branch offices in Berlin and Dresden

1995
Nietz - Prasch - Sigl und Partner
Architekten BDA

2003
nps tchoban voss Architekten BDA

Sergei Tchoban, Wolfgang Nietz, Alf M. Prasch, Peter Sigl, Ekkehard Voss

Sergei Tchoban

1962
Geboren in Leningrad (St. Petersburg) Rußland

1974
Mittelkunstschule in St. Petersburg

1980
Architekturstudium in St. Petersburg

1986
Diplom, Tätigkeit als freischaffender und angestellter Architekt in Rußland

1991
Umsiedlung nach Deutschland

1992
Dipl.-Ing. Architekt bei NPS Nietz - Prasch - Sigl

1995
Partner bei Nietz - Prasch - Sigl und Partner Architekten BDA

Mitglied der American Society of Architectural Illustrators

2003
nps tchoban voss Architekten BDA

1962
Born in Leningrad (St. Petersburg), Russia

1974
Arts School in St. Petersburg

1980
Studies of architecture in St. Petersburg

1986
Diploma, work as freelance and employed architect in Russia

1991
Moved to Germany

1992
Architect in the office of NPS Nietz - Prasch - Sigl

1995
Partner in the office of Nietz - Prasch - Sigl und Partner Architekten BDA

Member of American Society of Architectural Illustrators

2003
nps tchoban voss Architekten BDA

Ekkehard Voss

1963
Geboren in Euskirchen, Abitur in Düren / Rheinland

1982
Architekturstudium an der RWTH Aachen

1989
Diplom bei Prof. Döring

1989
Dipl.-Ing. Architekt bei Beucker - Haider - Langhammer - Maschlanka, Architekten und Stadtplaner in Düsseldorf

1992
Dipl.-Ing. Architekt bei NPS Nietz - Prasch - Sigl

1995
Partner bei Nietz - Prasch - Sigl und Partner Architekten BDA

Mitglied im BDA Hamburg

2003
nps tchoban voss und Partner

1963
Born in Euskirchen, high-school diploma in Düren, Rhineland

1982
Studies of architecture at RWTH Aachen University

1989
Diploma with Prof. Döring

1989
Worked as architect for the office of Beucker - Haider - Langhammer - Maschlanka, architects and urban designers in Düsseldorf

1992
Architect in the office of NPS Nietz - Prasch - Sigl

1995
Partner in the office of Nietz - Prasch - Sigl und Partner Architekten BDA

Member of BDA Hamburg

2003
nps tchoban voss Architekten BDA

Wolfgang Nietz

1941
Geboren in Hamburg

1965
Examen Ingenieur-Bauschule Hamburg

1966
Dipl.-Ing. Architekt in St. Louis/USA

1970
Partnerschaft mit Neve und Sigl

1979
NPS Nietz - Prasch - Sigl

1995
Nietz - Prasch - Sigl und Partner Architekten BDA

07.04.2002
Verstorben

1941
Born in Hamburg

1965
Diploma at Academy for Structural Engineering in Hamburg

1966
Architect in St. Louis/USA

1970
Partner in the office of Neve und Sigl

1979
NPS Nietz - Prasch - Sigl

1995
Nietz - Prasch - Sigl und Partner Architekten BDA

07.04.2002
Deceased

Elena Antjufeeva
Simon Bange
Stefan Barme
Nicholas Barsan
Nadejda Bartels
André Bartlewski
Philipp Bauer
Marcel D. Bender
Catrin Berg
Nel Bertram
Clemens Beyer
Axel Binder
Oliver Boersch
Bernd Borgolte
Susanne Born
Michael Both
Jens Böttcher
Dmitri Boykov
Tatiana Brikner
Irina Chipova
Martina Clasen
Anja Dähne
Matthias Dahlmann

Holm Dietrich
Stephan Egert
Anette Engelhardt
Birgit Entzeroth
Nadejda Fedorova
Albert Feldkamp
Lars Fischer
Frank Focke
Karin Folkers
Jörn Frenzel
Katja Fuks
Harald Gatter
Cornelia Giesecke
Manuel González Cardero
Ulrike Graefenhain
Ralf Grigoleit
Silvia Grischkat
Matthias Groth
Sven Grützmann
Jan Hagen
Christoph Heimermann
Katja Heitmann
Frank Helms

Andreas Henße
Maria Herbst
Stephanie Herholz
Felix Hildebrand
Andreas Hitz
Nils Höpken
Marina Hoffmann
Anna Hoffmeister
Achim Hofmann
Ilana Hofmann
Peter Huck
Hubert Jäger
Ulf Jensen
Daniel Jessen
Stefan Kahn
Valeria Kashirina
Ole Kelting
Daniela Klappoth
Janina Klein
Jan Klömich
Christoph Klüsserath
Anja Koch
Birgit Köder

Dirk Kollendt
Tomasz Kozaczek
Norbert Krenz
Anissa Landgraf
Matthias Lassen
Volker Lavid
Simone Liesenberg
Vladimir Litus
Moritz Löer
Stephan Lohre
Natalia Mantler
Igor Markov
Hajo Massel
Holger Mehnen
Svetlana Meshkova
Marion Mews
Jens Mittendorf
Philipp Mogwitz
Andrea Moritz
Stephan Müller
Thomas Muncke
Axel Neubauer
Hoa Nguyen

Stephan Niemöller
Christoph Niethammer
Andreas Oehme
Alexander Off
Paul Olufs
Kenan Ozan
Fabiana Pedretti
Eugen Pfeil
Helge Reichmann
Lidia Rtiseva
Jörg Rudloff
Dierk Schafmeyer
Anja Schmidt
Frederik-S. Scholz
Beate Schonlau
Christoph Schröter
Anja Schroth
Jörg Schulte
Ingo Schwarzweller
Ramona Schwarzweller
Stefanie Seegerer
Sonja Skuin-Dinic
Iris Steinhorst
Katharina Stranz
Christian Strauß
Martine Straßburg
Annika Suck
Elena Tepliakova
Andreas Tschirner
Karsten Waldschmidt-Kaposty
Markus Wehlke
Kay Wenzel
Liss Werner
Silke Wischer
Stefan Wolff
Pavel Zemskov
Holm Zink

Stand Juni / June 2008

STANDORTE | OFFICES

nps tchoban voss
Architekten BDA
Ulmenstraße 40
D-22299 Hamburg
Tel. +49 40–480618–0
hamburg@npstv.de

nps tchoban voss
Architekten BDA
Rosenthaler Straße 40-41
D-10178 Berlin-Mitte
Tel. +49 30–283920–0
berlin@npstv.de

nps tchoban voss
Architekten BDA
Leipziger Straße 51a
D-01127 Dresden
Tel. +49 351-8945730
dresden@npstv.de

www.npstv.de

AUTOR | AUTHOR

Prof. Dr.-Ing. (arch.) Falk Jaeger, geboren 1950, lebt als freier Kritiker, Publizist und Ausstellungskurator in Berlin und lehrt an verschiedenen Hochschulen Architekturkritik. Er studierte Architektur und Kunstgeschichte in Braunschweig, Stuttgart und Tübingen. Er war 1993-2000 Hochschuldozent auf dem Lehrstuhl für Architekturtheorie der TU Dresden und 2001-2002 Chefredakteur der Fachzeitschrift *Bauzeitung*.

Seit 1976 arbeitet er als Architekturkritiker für Tagespresse und Fachzeitschriften, Hörfunk und Fernsehen und verfasst Ausstellungs-, Buch- und Lexikonbeiträge zu Themen der Gegenwartsarchitektur, Baugeschichte und Denkmalpflege. Von ihm sind zahlreiche Fachbücher erschienen, darunter 1985 der Führer zur modernen Architektur *Bauen in Deutschland*, 1991 *Zurück zu den Stilen – Baukunst der achtziger Jahre in Berlin* und 2001 *Baukunst für das neue Jahrtausend*.

Prof. Dr.-Ing. (arch.) Falk Jaeger, born in 1950, is an architectural critic, journalist and curator. He lives in Berlin and teaches architectural criticism at various universities. He studied architecture and art history in Braunschweig, Stuttgart and Tübingen. From 1993 until 2000 he was a lecturer at the chair for architectural theory at Dresden University of Technology. From 2001-2002 he was editor-in-chief of the architectural magazine *Bauzeitung*.

Architectural critic for newspapers and architectural journals, radio and television. He contributes to exhibition catalogues, encyclopedias and other publications on contemporary architecture, the history of architecture and building conservation. He is the author of numerous books, among them a guide to modern architecture, *Bauen in Deutschland* (1985), *Zurück zu den Stilen – Baukunst der achtziger Jahre in Berlin* (1991) und *Baukunst für das neue Jahrtausend* (2001).

BILDNACHWEIS | ILLUSTRATION CREDITS

FOTOGRAFEN | PHOTOGRAPHERS
Blickpunkt Studio 2 / 37, 38, 39
Florian Bolk / 29, 30, 33, 35
Brackrock Studio GmbH / 49
Peter Carmichael / 9 ol tl
Dorfmüller + Kröger / 67, 68, 69
Stephan Eims / 115, 116, 167, 168, 169
Bina Engel / 19, 23
Christian Gahl / 53, 54, 63, 65 o t, 81, 82, 83, 134, 135, 141, 145 u b, 158, 159, 161, 162, 163
Christoph Gebler / 9 m c 71, 73, 107, 108, 109, 110, 112, 113 ur br, 121, 199
Barclay A. Goeppner / 41, 151, 153
Claus Graubner / 10 m c, 62 r, 79, 85, 87, 88, 89, 127, 128
Bernadette Grimmenstein / 95, 97
René Hoch / 130
HOCHTIEF / 12 m c
Julia Jungfer / 13 l, 75, 76, 77, 131, 142, 144, 145 o t
Bernhard Kroll / 188 ul bl
Sergei Kudrjaschow / 64 u b, 65 u b
Heiner Leiska / 9 or tr
Dieter Leistner / 15 l, 16 l, 32
Olaf Mahlstedt / 99, 100, 101

Philipp Meuser / 61 ur br
Anke Müllerklein / 59, 60, 61 l, 61 or tr, 62 l, 64 o t, 91, 92, 93, 96, 119, 122, 123, 177, 179
Aleksej Narodizkij / 155, 156, 157, 188 o t, 188 ur br, 189, 194
Klemens Ortmeyer / 12 l, 111, 113, 125, 137, 138, 139, 165
Thomas Spier / 132, 133
Christian Stelling / 50, 51
Daniel Sumesgutner / 12 r, 103, 104, 147, 148, 171, 173, 174, 175
Rainer Viertlböck / 169 ur br
Michael Wortmann / 41, 42, 43, 46, 47

VISUALISIERUNGEN | RENDERINGS
Denis André / 191, 198, 199, 201, 209
Dorothee Dietz / Hannes Töpper (npstv) / 197
Valeria Kashirina (npstv) / Min Pai+ / 183, 184, 185, 197, 198, 199
Tomasz Kozaczek (npstv) / 207, 209, 211
MinPai+ / 13, 183, 184, 185, 195
SP-Project / 189, 193
Hannes Töpper, Valeria Kashirina, Ramona Schwarzweller (npstv) / pure rendering / 17, 203, 205

MODELLBAU | MODEL MAKING
Stefan Kahn (npstv) / 203

Oben top: o t
Unten bottom: u b
Links left: l
Rechts right: r
Mitte centre: m c

Sofern nicht anders vermerkt, entstammen alle Abbildungen dem Bildarchiv von nps tchoban voss Architekten.

All illustrations were provided by nps tchoban voss Architekten, unless noted otherwise.

NACHWORT UND DANK | AFTERWORD AND ACKNOWLEDGEMENTS

Über 30 Jahre lang wirkte und gestaltete **Wolfgang Nietz** (gestorben 2002) aktiv mit in der Architektenpartnerschaft. Mit dem vorliegenden Buch über uns als Architekten nps tchoban voss verstehen wir sein Werk gleichermaßen als Bestandteil unserer architektonischen Arbeit. Ihm gebührt unser Dank für viele erfolgreiche gemeinsame Schaffensjahre.

Falk Jaeger hat mit Einfühlungsvermögen und kritischem Auge die Entwicklung des Büros herausgearbeitet. Wir danken ihm ganz herzlich für das geduldige Zuhören und seinen unbestechlichen Blick auf qualitätsvolle Architektur, der uns leitete, die eigene Position zum Bauen mit diesem Buch darzustellen.

Auch dem Birkhäuser Verlag mit **Ria Stein** als Lektorin möchten wir besonders danken. Die professionelle Führung und fachkundige Begleitung in allen Fragen dieses Buches hat in ihren Händen gelegen und maßgeblich dazu beigetragen, dass auch der Schaffensprozess Freude bereitet hat.

Oliver Kleinschmidt, der verantwortlich für die grafische Gestaltung war, hat unsere Vorstellungen, Architektur zu präsentieren, in eine klare, präzise Konzeption übersetzt. Seinem kreativen Geschick verdanken wir eine verständliche, visuelle Vermittlung der vorgestellten Bauten und Projekte.

Das Schaffen und Wirken der vergangenen Jahre verdanken wir einem hochmotivierten und engagierten Team von Mitarbeitern in unseren Büros in Hamburg, Berlin und Dresden. Mit der Verschmelzung von professioneller Erfahrung und kreativem Anspruch sichern wir somit uns und unseren Auftraggebern das gewünschte Ergebnis.

Die hausinterne Koordination und Leitung dieses Buchprojektes lag in den Händen von **Axel Neubauer** (Büro Hamburg) mit Unterstützung durch **Silvia Grischkat** (Büro Berlin). Ihnen möchten wir ebenso besonderen Dank sagen wie **Valeria Kashirina, Anette Engelhardt, Maria Herbst, Markus Wehlke und Philipp Bauer**, die mit Rat und Tat sowie Layoutplänen zum Gelingen des Buches beigetragen haben.

For over 30 years **Wolfgang Nietz** (deceased in 2002) actively contributed to and shaped the architectural partnership. Although this monograph is about our work as nps tchoban voss, we regard his contribution to be an equal part of our architectural work. We would like to extend our thanks to him for the many successful years working together.

With sensitivity and a critical eye, **Falk Jaeger** has succeeded in portraying the development of the office. We thank him warmly for listening so patiently and his unerring eye for high-quality architecture, which has helped us to elaborate our own view of architecture in this book.

We are also indebted to Birkhäuser Publishers and our editor **Ria Stein**. Her professional management and expert guidance in all aspects of this book contributed decisively to making the process of creating this publication a productive and joyful experience.

Oliver Kleinschmidt, who was responsible for the graphic design of this book, has successfully translated our ideas on the presentation of architecture into a clear and precise concept. His creative talents are to thank for the clear, visual communication of the buildings and projects.

The work and achievements of the office over the past years is largely due to our highly motivated and committed team of colleagues in our offices in Hamburg, Berlin and Dresden. It is through their combination of professional experience and creative versatility that we are able to achieve the desired results for ourselves as well as for our clients.

The in-house coordination and running of this book project lay in the hands of **Axel Neubauer** (Hamburg office) with assistance from **Silvia Grischkat** in our Berlin office. Particular thanks also go to **Valeria Kashirina, Anette Engelhardt, Maria Herbst, Markus Wehlke and Philipp Bauer**, who with help and advice and the drawing of layout plans contributed to the realisation of this book.

Alf M. Prasch / Peter Sigl / Sergei Tchoban / Ekkehard Voss

GESTALTUNG | GRAPHIC DESIGN
Oliver Kleinschmidt, Berlin

ÜBERSETZUNG INS ENGLISCHE | TRANSLATION INTO ENGLISH
Julian Reisenberger, Weimar

LITHOGRAPHIE | LITHOGRAPHY
Licht & Tiefe, Berlin

DRUCK | PRINTING
Medialis, Berlin

Library of Congress Control Number: 2008930705

Bibliographic information published by Die Deutsche Bibliothek
Die Deutsche Bibliothek lists this publication in the Deutsche
Nationalbibliografie; detailed bibliographic data is available in the
Internet at <http://dnb.ddb.de>.

© 2008 Birkhäuser Verlag AG
Basel · Boston · Berlin
P.O.Box 133, CH-4010 Basel, Switzerland
Part of Springer Science+Business Media

Printed on acid-free paper produced from chlorine-free pulp. TCF ↑
Printed in Germany

ISBN 978-3-7643-8768-6

9 8 7 6 5 4 3 2 1
www.birkhauser.ch